THE HISTORY OF AL-ṬABARĪ

AN ANNOTATED TRANSLATION

VOLUME XVIII

Between Civil Wars:

The Caliphate of Muʿāwiyah

A.D. 661–680/A.H. 40–60

The History of al-Ṭabarī

Editorial Board

Ihsan Abbas, American University of Beirut

C. E. Bosworth, The University of Manchester

Jacob Lassner, Wayne State University, Detroit

Franz Rosenthal, Yale University

Ehsan Yar-Shater, Columbia University (*General Editor*)

SUNY

SERIES IN NEAR EASTERN STUDIES

Said Amir Arjomand, Editor

Bibliotheca Persica
Edited by Ehsan Yar-Shater

The History of al-Ṭabarī

(Ta'rīkh al-rusul wa'l-mulūk)

VOLUME XVIII

Between Civil Wars:
The Caliphate of
Muʿāwiyah

translated and annotated
by
Michael G. Morony
University of California, Los Angeles

State University of New York Press

The preparation of this volume was made possible by a grant from the Translation Program of the National Endowment for the Humanities, an independent federal agency; and by the Persian Heritage Foundation.

Published by
State University of New York Press, Albany

Printed in the United States of America

For information, address State University of New York
Press, State University Plaza, Albany, N.Y., 12246

Library of Congress Cataloging in Publication Data

Ṭabarī, 838?—923.
Between civil wars.

(The history of al-Ṭabarī; v. 18) (Bibliotheca Persica)
(SUNY series in Near Eastern studies)
Translation of excerpts from: Ta'rīkh al-rusul wa-al-mulūk.
Bibliography: p.
Includes index.
1. Islamic Empire—661-750. 2. Mu'āwiyah ibn Abī Sufyān, Caliph, d. 680. I. Morony, Michael G., 1939- .II. Title. III. Series: Ṭabarī, 838?—923. Ta'rīkh al-rusul wa-al-mulūk. English; v. 18. IV. Series: Bibliotheca Persica (Albany, N.Y.) V. Series: SUNY series in Near Eastern studies.

DS38.5.T321325 1987 090'.097671 85-2823
ISBN 0-87395-933-7
ISBN 0-88706-314-4 (pbk.)

10 9 8 7 6 5 4 3 2 1

Acknowledgements

In 1971 the General Editor proposed to the UNESCO to include a translation of al-Ṭabarī's *History* in its Collection of Representative Works. UNESCO agreed, but the Commission in charge of Arabic works favored other priorities. Deeming the project worthy, the Iranian Institute of Translation and Publication, which collaborated with UNESCO, agreed to undertake the task. After the upheavals of 1979, assistance was sought from the National Endowment for the Humanities. The invaluable encouragement and support of the Endowment is here gratefully acknowledged.

The General Editor wishes to thank sincerely also the participating scholars, who have made the realization of this project possible; the Board of Editors for their selfless assistance; Professor Franz Rosenthal for his many helpful suggestions in the formulation and application of the editorial policy; Professor Jacob Lassner for his painstaking and meticulous editing; and Dr. Susan Mango of the National Endowment for the Humanities for her genuine interest in the project and her advocacy of it.

Preface

The History of Prophets and Kings (*Ta'rīkh al-rusul wa'l-mulūk*) by Abū Ja^c^far Muḥammad b. Jarīr al-Ṭabarī (839–923), here rendered as the *History of al-Ṭabarī*, is by common consent the most important universal history produced in the world of Islam. It has been translated here in its entirety for the first time for the benefit of non-Arabists, with historical and philological notes for those interested in the particulars of the text.

Ṭabarī's monumental work explores the history of the ancient nations, with special emphasis on biblical peoples and prophets, the legendary and factual history of ancient Iran, and, in great detail, the rise of Islam, the life of the Prophet Muḥammad, and the history of the Islamic world down to the year 915. The first volume of this translation will contain a biography of al-Ṭabarī and a discussion of the method, scope, and value of his work. It will also provide information on some of the technical considerations that have guided the work of the translators.

The *History* has been divided here into 38 volumes, each of which covers about two hundred pages of the original Arabic text in the Leiden edition. An attempt has been made to draw the dividing lines between the individual volumes in such a way that each is to some degree independent and can be read as such. The page numbers of the original in the Leiden edition appear on the margins of the translated volumes.

Al-Ṭabarī very often quotes his sources verbatim and traces the chain of transmission (*isnād*) to an original source. The chains of transmitters are, for the sake of brevity, rendered by only a dash (—) between the individual links in the chain.

Thus, According to Ibn Ḥumayd—Salamah—Ibn Isḥāq means that al-Ṭabarī received the report from Ibn Ḥumayd who said that he was told by Salamah, who said that he was told by Ibn Isḥāq, and so on. The numerous subtle and important differences in the original Arabic wording have been disregarded.

The table of contents at the beginning of each volume gives a brief survey of the topics dealt with in that particular volume. It also includes the headings and subheadings as they appear in al-Ṭabarī's text, as well as those occasionally introduced by the translator.

Well-known place-names, such as, for instance, Mecca, Baghdad, Jerusalem, Damascus, and the Yemen, are given in their English spellings. Less common place-names, which are the vast majority, are transliterated. Biblical figures appear in the accepted English spelling. Iranian names are usually transcribed according to their Arabic forms, and the presumed Iranian forms are often discussed in the footnotes.

Technical terms have been translated wherever possible, but some, such as qāḍī and imām, have been retained in Arabic forms. Others that cannot be translated with sufficient precision have been retained and italicized as well as footnoted.

The annotation aims chiefly at clarifying difficult passages, identifying individuals and place-names, and discussing textual difficulties. Much leeway has been left to the translators to include in the footnotes whatever they consider necessary and helpful.

The bibliographies list all the sources mentioned in the annotation.

The index in each volume contains all the names of persons and places referred to in the text, as well as those mentioned in the notes as far as they refer to the medieval period. It does not include the names of modern scholars. A general index, it is hoped, will appear after all the volumes have been translated.

Ehsan Yar-Shater

Contents

Translator's Foreword / 1

Between Civil Wars: The Caliphate of, Muʿāwiyah

The Events of the Year 40 (660/661) / 2

The Rendering of Allegiance to al-Ḥasan b. Alī / 2

The Events of the Year 41 (661/662) / 7

Al-Ḥasan's surrender of al-Kūfah to Muʿāwiyah / 9
The departure of al-Ḥasan and al-Ḥusayn for al-Madīnah / 11
The Khārijites at Shahrazūr / 12
Muʿāwiyah's order to kill the sons of Ziyād / 14
Why ʿAbdallāh b. ʿĀmir was put in charge of al-Baṣrah and some events during his Activity there / 18

The Events of the Year 42 (662/663) / 20

What happened to the Khārijites / 21

The Events of the Year 43 (663/664) / 32

The killing of al-Mustawrid b. ʿUllifah / 33

The Events of the Year 44 (664/665) / 71

The Events of the Year 45 (665/666) / 76

Ziyād's governorship over al-Baṣrah / 76

The Events of the Year 46 (666/667) / 88

The death of ʿAbd al-Raḥmān b. Khālid b. al-Walīd / 88

The Events of the Year 47 (667/668) / 91

The Events of the Year 48 (668/669) / 93

The Events of the Year 49 (669/670) / 94

The Events of the Year 50 (670/671) / 96

Al-Faradzaq's flight from Ziyād / 104
Al-Ḥakam b. ʿAmr raids al-Ashall / 119

The Events of the Year 51 (671/672) / 122

Ḥujr b. ʿAdī's execution / 122
Those whom Ziyād sent to Muʿāwiyah / 144
Ḥujr's companions who were killed / 151
Ḥujr's companions who were saved / 152

The Events of the Year 52 (672) / 165

The Events of the Year 53 (672/673) / 166

How Ziyād b. Sumayyah perished / 167
How al-Rabīʿ b. Ziyād al-Ḥārithī died / 170

The Events of the Year 54 (673/674) / 172

Why Muʿāwiyah dismissed Saʿīd and appointed Marwān as governor over al-Madīnah / 173
How ʿUbaydallāh b. Ziyād became governor over Khurāsān / 175

The Events of the Year 55 (674/675) / 180

Why Muʿāwiyah dismissed ʿAbdallāh b. ʿAmr b. Ghaylān and appointed ʿUbaydallāh over al-Baṣrah / 180

The Events of the Year 56 (675/676) / 183

Why Muʿāwiyah made his Son, Yazīd, heir apparent / 183

The Events of the Year 57 (676/677) / 191

The Events of the Year 58 (677/678) / 192

Why ʿUbaydallāh b. Ziyād killed the Kharijites / 196

The Events of the Year 59 (678/679) / 199

Why Muʿāwiyah appointed ʿAbd al-Raḥmān b. Ziyād as governor of Khurāsān / 199
How Muʿāwiyah dismissed and re-appointed ʿUbaydallāh as governor of al-Baṣrah / 201
Why Yasīd b. Mufarrigh ridiculed the sons of Ziyād / 202

The Events of the Year 60 (679/680) / 208

The length of Muʿāwiyah's reign / 210
Muʿāwiyah's last illness / 211
Who led the prayer over Muʿāwiyah when he died / 213
Muʿāwiyah's lineage and his Agnomen / 215
Muʿāwiyah's wives and children / 215
Some of Muʿāwiyah's Affairs and Conduct / 216

Bibliography / 227

Index / 233

Contents

Translator's Foreword

The reign of Muʿāwiyah b. Abī Sufyān as Caliph occupied the two decades between the first and second civil wars among Muslims in the seventh century. Ṭabarī's account of this period is comparatively thin. He covers it in half the space he devoted to the first civil war and in the same amount of space that he gave to the three-year reign of Muʿāwiyah's son and successor, Yazīd. In addition, Ṭabarī's selection of events overwhelmingly concentrates on Iraq and Khurāsān during these years, and his information is drawn mainly from Iraqi sources.

Over sixty percent of this section comes from the earlier works of Abū Mikhnaf and ʿUmar b. Shabbah. The works of Abū Mikhnaf are quoted mainly via Hishām b. Muḥammad al-Kalbī and are used especially for the events at al-Kūfah, the Khārijites, and the affair of Ḥujr b. ʿAdī. ʿUmar b. Shabbah's *Book of Information About the People of al-Baṣrah* (*Kitāb akhbār ahl al-Baṣrah*) is quoted directly by Ṭabarī not only for events at al-Baṣrah, but also for events in Syria and the Ḥijāz.

Except for Ziyād's inaugural speech at al-Baṣrah in 665 and parallel passages in C. E. J. Whitting's translation of Ibn Ṭabāṭabā's *Kitāb al-Fakhrī* (London, 1974), the material in this volume has not been available in English before. However, the section on Muʿāwiyah in Balādhurī's *Ansāb al-Ashrāf* was translated into Italian by Giorgio Levi della Vida and Olga Pinto as *Il Califfo Muʿâwiya I, secondo il "Kitāb Ansāb al-Ašrâf"* (Rome, 1938). Special thanks go to Abdullah al-Askar who helped to check this translation.

Michael Morony
University of California, Los Angeles

The Events of the Year

[1]

40 (cont'd)

(May 17, 660-May 6, 661)

The Rendering of Allegiance to al-Ḥasan b. ʿAlī

In the year 40 (May 17, 660–May 6, 661), allegiance was rendered to al-Ḥasan b. ʿAlī for the Caliphate. The first to render allegiance to him is said to have been Qays b. Saʿd who said to him, "Hold out your hand, and I will pledge allegiance to you on condition [that you follow] the Book of God, Almighty and Great, and the example (*sunnah*) of His Prophet, and fight the violators."[1] Al-Ḥasan answered him, ". . . on condition [that I follow] the Book of God and the example of His Prophet, for that includes every stipulation." So Qays rendered allegiance to him and was silent, and the people (also) pledged their allegiance to him.

(According to) ʿAbdallāh b. Aḥmad b. Mattawayhi[2] al-Marrūdhī[3]—his father—Sulaymān—ʿAbdallāh—Yūnus al-Zuhrī:[4]

---

1. *Al-muhillūn* were originally a group of pre-Islamic tribes west of al-Madīnah whose members attacked caravans during the sacred truce months. See *Jāḥiẓ*, *Ḥayawān*, VII, 216–17; Yaʿqūbī, *Taʾrīkh*, I, 314–15; and Bukhārī, *Ṣaḥīḥ*, VI, 12. This became a term for those who permitted shedding blood, especially the blood of members of Muḥammad's family.

2. Cairo reads: "Shabbawayhi." ʿAbdallāh b. Aḥmad b. Shabbawayh al-Marwazī was a well-known authority on ḥadīth. There is no manuscript authority for the reading, Mattawayhi, at least in this passage.

3. Al-Marrūdh was the popular pronunciation of Marw al-Rūdh, "Marw of the River," a city in eastern Khurāsān on the Murghāb River approximately 160 miles upstream from Marw. See Le Strange, *Lands*, 404–5.

4. Muḥammad b. Muslim b. ʿUbaydallāh b. ʿAbdallāh b. Shihāb al-Zuhrī (ca.

ʿAlī put Qays b. Saʿd in charge of his Iraqi advance forces (marching) toward Adharbayjān,[5] and in charge of Adharbayjān's territory.[6] He also put him in charge of the Shurṭat al-Khamīs[7] which the Arabs instituted. This was a force of forty thousand men who pledged allegiance to ʿAlī until death. Qays continued to postpone that expedition until ʿAlī was killed and the people of Iraq chose al-Ḥasan b. ʿAlī as Caliph. Al-Ḥasan did not favor[8] fighting, but intended to take for himself what he could from Muʿāwiyah and then join the community. He knew that Qays b. Saʿd did not agree with his point of view, so he dis- [2] missed him and appointed ʿAbdallāh b. ʿAbbās[9] as commander. When ʿAbdallāh b. ʿAbbās learned what al-Ḥasan intended to take for himself, he wrote to Muʿāwiyah asking him for a guarantee of safe-conduct with the added condition that he be allowed to keep the wealth which he had acquired. So Muʿāwiyah stipulated that for him.

(According to) Mūsā b. ʿAbd al-Raḥmān al-Masrūqī[10]—ʿUthmān b. ʿAbd al-Ḥamīd (or Ibn ʿAbd al-Raḥmān) al-Majāzī al-Khuzāʿī[11] Abū ʿAbd al-Raḥmān—Ismāʿīl b..Rāshid: The people pledged their allegiance to al-Ḥasan b. ʿAlī as Caliph. Al-Ḥasan then left with them and stayed at al-Madāʾin.[12] He sent Qays b. Saʿd (forward) in charge of his vanguard with twelve

---

50–124 [670–742]) lived at al-Madīnah until about 700, then settled in Damascus about 720. See A. A. Duri, "Al-Zuhri," 1–12. Al-Zuhrī's account tends to be unfavorable towards al-Ḥasan. For a more favorable account see Balādhurī, *Ansāb*, IVA, 138.

5. Adharbayjān is the province in northwestern Iran. See Le Strange, *Lands*, 159–71.

6. C reads: "Of Iṣbahān," a city in western Iran. See Le Strange, *Lands*, 202–7.

7. C reads: "shurṭah of the army." This "Thursday shurṭah" was an elite force or bodyguard. *Shurṭah* (pl. *shuraṭ*) was also the term for the police force in Muslim Arab garrison cities. See *EI*[1], s.v. Shurṭa.

8. C reads: "intend."

9. ʿAbdallāh b. ʿAbbās (d. 68[697/8]) was a cousin of Muḥammad and had been governor of al-Baṣrah from 36(656/7) until 38 (658/9) when he had broken with ʿAlī. See *EI*[2], s.v. ʿAbd Allāh b. al-ʿAbbās.

10. O reads: al-Khuzāʿī.

11. C reads: "al-Ḥarrānī," from Ḥarrān, a town in upper Mesopotamia. See *EI*[2], s.v. Ḥarrān, and Le Strange, *Lands*, 103.

12. Al-Madāʾin, "the cities", was the former Sasanian metropolis and winter capital on both sides of the Tigris River below Baghdād. See *EI*[1], s.v. al-Madāʾin.

thousand men. Muʿāwiyah also advanced with the Syrians and camped at Maskin.[13] While al-Ḥasan was at al-Madā'in someone in the army announced, "Qays b. Saʿd has surely been killed, so flee!" So they fled, having plundered the pavilion of al-Ḥasan, even fighting him for a carpet that was under him. Al-Ḥasan left and stayed at the White Palace[14] in al-Madā'in. At that time the paternal uncle of al-Mukhtār b. Abī ʿUbayd,[15] Saʿd b. Masʿūd, was the governor of al-Madā'in. Al-Mukhtār, who was a young boy, asked him, "Would you have wealth and honor?" When Saʿd asked him what he meant, al-Mukhtār said, "Put al-Ḥasan in fetters and use him to ask Muʿāwiyah for a guarantee of safe-conduct."[16] Saʿd responded, "God's curse upon you! Shall I fall upon the son of the daughter of God's Messenger and put him in fetters! What an evil man you are."[17]

[3] When al-Ḥasan saw that rule was beyond his grasp, he sent to Muʿāwiyah seeking peace, and Muʿāwiyah sent ʿAbdallāh b. ʿĀmir[18] and ʿAbd al-Raḥmān b. Samurah b. Ḥabīb b. ʿAbd Shams[19] to him. When they came to al-Ḥasan at al-Madā'in, they granted him what he wished and arranged peace with him on condition that, among other things, he be allowed to take five million (dirhams) from the treasury of al-Kufāh.[20] Al-Ḥasan

---

13. Maskin was the district along the Dujayl Canal west of the Tigris River above Baghdād. See Le Strange, *Lands*, 51.

14. The White Palace was the former Sasanian royal residence in that part of al-Madā'in called al-Madīnah al-ʿAtīqah, "the Old City," (i.e., Ctesiphon) by the Arabs. It remained in use until its demolition was begun by the Caliph al-Manṣūr (136–58/754–75]), and then it remained in ruins until it was completely demolished by Caliph al-Muktafī (289–92]902–8]) in about 290(903). Al-Muktafī had the materials used to build the Tāj Palace in Baghdād. See *EI*[1], s.v. al-Madā'in.

15. Al-Mukhtār b. Abī ʿUbayd (d. 67[687]) was to lead a Shīʿī rising in al-Kūfah, 66–67(685–87). See Kharbūtlī, *Al-Mukhtār al-Thaqafī*, and ʿA. A. ʿAbd Dixon, *Umayyad Caliphate*, 25–76.

16. O reads: "bring him to Muʿāwiyah."

17. C reads: "what an evil man that would make me."

18. ʿAbdallāh b. ʿAmir (5–59]626–80]) was a native of Mecca who had conquered Fārs and Khurāsān as governor of al-Baṣrah, 29–35(649–55) See *EI*[2], s.v. ʿAbd Allāh b. ʿĀmir.

19. ʿAbd al-Raḥmān b. Samurah (d. 50[670]) was a native of Mecca, conquered Sijistān under ʿAbdallāh b. ʿĀmir, 31–35(651–55) and joined Muʿāwiyah in Syria after the Battle of the Camel in 36(657) See C. E. Bosworth, *Sīstān under the Arabs*, 17–22; and *EI*[2], s.v. ʿAbd al-Raḥmān b. Samura.

20. Al-Kūfah was the Muslim Arab garrison city (*miṣr*) and provincial capital on the Euphrates River near modern Najaf. See *EI*[2], s.v. al-Kūfah.

then rose among the people of Iraq saying, "O people of Iraq, three things make me glad to be rid of you: your killing of my father, your stabbing of me, and your plundering of my possessions." The people submitted to Muʿāwiyah, and, when Muʿāwiyah entered al-Kūfah, the people rendered allegiance to him.

(According to) Ziyād b. ʿAbdallāh—ʿAwānah[21] gave an account similar to that of al-Masrūqī—ʿUthmān b. ʿAbd al-Raḥmān. He added to it: Al-Ḥasan wrote to Mu'āwiyah concerning peace and asked for a guarantee of safe-conduct. When he told al-Ḥusayn[22] and ʿAbdallāh b. Jaʿfar[23] about it, al-Ḥusayn said to him, "I implore you, by God, not to believe the story of Muʿāwiyah but to believe the story of ʿAlī." Al-Ḥasan retorted, "Shut up! I know more about the matter than you do." Now when the letter of al-Ḥasan b. ʿAlī reached Muʿāwiyah, the latter sent ʿAbdallāh b. ʿĀmir and ʿAbd al-Raḥmān b. Samurah, who came to al-Madā'in, and granted al-Ḥasan what he wanted. Al-Ḥasan then wrote to Qays b. Saʿd, who was in charge of his vanguard with twelve thousand men, ordering him to submit to Muʿāwiyah. At that, Qays b. Saʿd rose among the people saying, "O people, choose [between] submitting to a [4]
leader of error or fighting without a leader." They replied, "No, we choose instead to submit to a leader of error." So they rendered allegiance to Muʿāwiyah and Qays b. Saʿd left them. Al-Ḥasan had already made peace with Muʿāwiyah on condition that he concede to him what was in his treasury plus the revenue (*kharāj*)[24] of Dārābjird[25] and that ʿAlī not be reviled in his hearing. So he took what was in his treasury at al-Kūfah which amounted to five million dirhams.

---

21. ʿAwānah b. al-Ḥakam al-Kalbī (d. 147[764] or 153[770]) was a blind Kūfan narrator who composed two historical works on the life of Muʿāwiyah and the Banū Umayyah. See *EI*², s.v. ʿAwāna b. al-Ḥakam al-Kalbī.

22. Al-Ḥusayn b. ʿAli (4–61[626–80]) was al-Ḥasan's younger brother. See *EI*², s.v. Al-Ḥusayn b. ʿAlī.

23. ʿAbdallāh b. Jaʿfar b. Abī Ṭālib (d. 80[699] or 85[704]) was a nephew of ʿAlī. See *EI*², s.v. ʿAbd Allāh b. Djaʿfar.

24. *Kharāj* was a form of tax or tribute. See D. Dennett, *Conversion and the Poll Tax*, 12–13; and F. Løkkegaard, *Islamic Taxation*, index.

25. Dārābjird is a city and district in eastern Fārs. See Le Strange, *Lands*, 288–9.

In this year al-Mughīrah b. Shuʿbah[26] led the people in the pilgrimage. (According to) Mūsā b. ʿAbd al-Raḥmān—ʿUthmān b. ʿAbd al-Raḥmān al-Khuzāʿī[27] Abū ʿAbd al-Raḥmān—Ismāʿīl b. Rāshid: When it was time for the pilgrimage—that is, in the year in which ʿAlī was killed—al-Mughīrah b. Shuʿbah wrote a letter which he forged according to Muʿāwiyah's style,[28] and led the people in the pilgrimage in this year. It is said that he stood at ʿArafat on the Day of Moistening and slaughtered on the Day of ʿArafat,[29] fearing lest his position be noticed. It was also said that al-Mughīrah did so because he learned that ʿUtbah b. Abī Sufyān would replace him the following morning as the official in charge of the (pilgrimage) season, and he therefore rushed the pilgrimage.

In this year Muʿāwiyah was rendered allegiance as Caliph in Jerusalem (Īliyā).[30] (According to) Mūsā b. ʿAbd al-Raḥmān—ʿUthmān b. ʿAbd al-Raḥmān—Ismāʿīl b. Rāshid: He was previously called Commander[31] in Syria. I was told according to Abū Mushīr—Saʿīd b. ʿAbd al-ʿAzīz: ʿAlī was called Commander of the Faithful (*Amīr al-Muʾminīn*) in Iraq, while Muʿā- [5]
wiyah was called Commander in Syria. But when ʿAlī was killed,[32] Muʿāwiyah was called Commander of the Faithful.

---

26. Al-Mughīrah b. Shuʿbah was a native of Ṭāʾif, a member of the Banū Thaqīf, and had been governor of al-Baṣrah, 15–17(636–38).

27. C reads: al-Ḥarrānī.

28. According to Ibn Khayyāt, *Taʾrīkh*, I, 234, al-Mughīrah forged a document in the style of al-Ḥasan.

29. The Day of Moistening (*yawm al-tarwiyah*) is the eighth of Dhū al-Ḥijjah when the pilgrims provide their animals and themselves with water for standing at ʿArafat on the following day. See *EI*², s.v. Ḥadjdj.

30. Īliyā in Arabic comes from Aelia Capitolina, the Roman name for Jerusalem. See *EI*², s.v. al-Ḳuds.

31. "Commander" (amīr) was used of generals and military governors. See *EI*², s.v. Amīr.

32. O reads: "when ʿAlī died."

The Events of the Year 41

(May 7, 661–April 25, 662)

Among the events of this year was al-Ḥasan b. ʿAlī's surrender of power to Muʿāwiyah, the latter's entry into al-Kūfah, and the rendering of allegiance to Muʿāwiyah as Caliph by the people of al-Kūfah.

I was told by ʿAbdallāh b. Aḥmad al-Marrūdhī—his father—Sulaymān—ʿAbdallāh—Yūnus—al-Zuhrī: When the people of Iraq acknowledged al-Ḥasan b. ʿAlī as Caliph, he began to impose conditions on them, (saying), "You must be totally obedient, make peace with whom I make peace, and fight whom I fight." The people of Iraq had misgivings about their situation when he imposed these conditions upon them, and they said, "This is no master for us since he does not want to fight." So shortly after they acknowledged him, al-Ḥasan was stabbed (and wounded, but) not fatally. His dislike for them increased, and he grew more afraid of them. He corresponded with Muʿāwiyah and sent conditions to him saying, "Grant me this and I shall be totally obedient, provided that you fulfill [these conditions] for me." Al-Ḥasan's scroll came into Muʿāwiyah's hand. Muʿāwiyah, however, had previously sent al-Ḥasan a blank

scroll sealed at the bottom and had written to him, "Put whatever condition you wish [to make] on this scroll which I have
[6] sealed at the bottom[33] and it will be yours." When (the scroll) reached al-Ḥasan, he doubled the conditions which he had asked of Muʿāwiyah previously and kept it with him. Muʿāwiyah meanwhile kept the scroll of al-Ḥasan which contained the requests the latter had sent him.

When Muʿāwiyah and al-Ḥasan met, al-Ḥasan asked him to grant him the conditions made by him in the document which Muʿāwiyah had sealed at the bottom. But Muʿāwiyah refused and said, I grant you the requests you made originally in your letter to me, for I had done so already when I received your letter." Al-Ḥasan replied, "[But] I had conditions when I received your letter, and you agreed to fulfill them." Since they argued over them, none of al-Ḥasan's conditions were met.[34]

When they assembled at al-Kūfah, ʿAmr b. al-ʿĀṣ[35] had been talking with Muʿāwiyah, and urged him to bid al-Ḥasan rise and address the people. But Muʿāwiyah disliked that and asked, "Don't you want me to address the people?"[36] ʿAmr replied, "I intend to show the people his incompetence," and he kept it up until Muʿāwiyah gave in to him and went out and addressed the people. Then he ordered someone to call upon al-Ḥasan b. ʿAlī, "Rise, O Ḥasan, and speak to the people." So (al-Ḥasan) began a spontaneous impromptu speech with the *shahādah*[37] and then continued, "O people, God has guided you with the first of us, and spared your blood with the last of us. This regime has a certain duration, and the world is subject to change. God, Almighty and Great, said to His Prophet, "If I knew, per-

33. For examples of first (seventh) century Arabic protocols and documents sealed at the bottom, see A. Grohmann, *From the World of Arabic Papyri*.

34. According to Balādhurī. *Futūḥ*, 299, Muʿāwiyah assigned ʿAyn al-Ṣayd to al-Ḥasan in return for the Caliphate.

35. ʿAmr b. al-ʿAṣ (d. ca. 42[663]), the Muslim conqueror of Egypt (19–21 [640–42]), had joined Muʿāwiyah after the Battle of the Camel during the first civil war. He was Muʿāwiyah's representative at the arbitration at Adhruḥ, 38(658), and his governor of Egypt. See *EI*², s. v. ʿAmr ibn al-ʿĀṣ.

36. C reads: "Why do you want me to have him speak to the people?"

37. The *shahādah* is the Muslim declaration that there is only one God and Muḥammad is His Messenger. For an example of the form of the *shahādah* that may have been used during the reign of Muʿāwiyah, see below, p. 171 (Ṭabarī, II, 163). See also *EI*¹, s.v. Shahāda.

haps it is a temptation for you and a delight for a while.' "[38] When he said that, Mu'āwiyah told him to sit down, and remained furious with 'Amr saying, "This was your idea!" Al-Ḥasan stayed at al-Madīnah.

I was told by 'Umar—'Alī b. Muḥammad:[39] Al-Ḥasan surrendered al-Kūfah to Mu'āwiyah, and Mu'āwiyah entered it five (days) before the end of Rabī' I (before July 30, 661)—or, alternatively, before the end of Jumādā I 41 (before September 27, 661). [7]

Al-Ḥasan's Surrender of al-Kūfah to Mu'āwiyah

I was told by 'Abdallāh b. Aḥmad—his father—Sulaymān b. al-Faḍl—'Abdallāh—Yūnus[40]—al-Zuhrī: When 'Abdallāh b. 'Abbās learned that al-Ḥasan intended to ask Mu'āwiyah for a guarantee of safe-conduct for himself, he (also) wrote to Mu'āwiyah asking him for security on condition that he be allowed to keep the wealth that he had acquired. So Mu'āwiyah stipulated that for him. And when Mu'āwiyah sent Ibn 'Āmir to him with a large force of cavalry, 'Abdallāh went out to them at night and joined them, leaving the army of which he was in charge, including Qays b. Sa'd, without a commander. (When) al-Ḥasan made terms for himself (and) acknowledged Mu'āwiyah, the shurṭat al-khamīs made Qays b. Sa'd their commander. He and they pledged to fight Mu'āwiyah until terms should be made to allow the supporters and followers of 'Alī to keep their wealth and their lives and what(ever) they had acquired during the civil war.

When Mu'āwiyah was finished with 'Abdallāh b. 'Abbās and al-Ḥasan, he was free to employ stratagems against (the) man whom he considered to be the most important person in this

38. Qur'ān 21: 111. That is, God had guided them by means of 'Alī, and al-Ḥasan's abdication had prevented further bloodshed. Mu'āwiyah's power would not last forever, and at some future date others might have the opportunity to take power.

39. 'Alī b. Muḥammad b. 'Abdallāh b. Abī Sayf, Abū al-Ḥasan al-Madā'inī (135–231 [752–845]) belonged to the 'Abd Shams clan of Quraysh. He was born at al-Baṣrah, lived at al-Madā'in, and died in Baghdād. He is credited with over two hundred works on history and literature. See *EI*¹, s. v. al-Madā'inī.

40. O reads: Yūnus b. Mūsā.

respect[41] and who had forty thousand (men) with him. Muʿā-
[8] wiyah, ʿAmr, and the Syrians had camped with them. Muʿāwiyah (now) sent (a message) to Qays b. Saʿd to remind him of God, saying, "For whom are you fighting, since he to whom you gave your obedience has acknowledged me?" But Qays refused to yield to him until Muʿāwiyah sent him a document which he had sealed at the bottom and told (him), "Write what you want on this document and it will be yours." When ʿAmr told Muʿāwiyah not to give him that but to fight him, Muʿāwiyah replied, "Calm down! We would not be able to kill them until they had killed an equal number of Syrians, and what good would life be after that? By God, I will never fight him until I have no other alternative." When Muʿāwiyah sent that document to him, Qays asked in it that he and the supporters of ʿAlī be exempt from punishment for the lives and wealth they took. He did not ask Muʿāwiyah for wealth in that document of his.[42] When Muʿāwiyah granted his request, Qays and those who were with him submitted to him.

When the civil war broke out, five persons were regarded as the most cunning. The Arabs who had (useful) opinions and stratagems were said to be Muʿāwiyah b. Abī Sufyān, ʿAmr b. al-ʿĀṣ, al-Mughīrah b. Shuʿbah, and Qays b. Saʿd, as well as ʿAbdallāh b. Budayl al-Khuzāʿī among the Muhājirūn. Qays and Ibn Budayl sided with ʿAlī, while al-Mughīrah b. Shuʿbah and ʿAmr sided with Muʿāwiyah, although al-Mughīrah remained neutral[43] at Ṭā'if[44] until both arbiters were chosen and met at Adhruḥ.[45]

According to another report, peace was concluded between al-Ḥasan and Muʿāwiyah in Rabīʿ II 41 (August 4–September 1,

---

41. I.e., with respect to strategems.

42. C reads: "Muʿāwiyah granted him whatever wealth he requested in that document of his."

43. *Muʿtazilan*, used of Muslim neutralists beginning in the first civil war.

44. Al-Ṭā'if is a town in western Arabia, southeast of Mecca. See EI^1, s.v. al-Ṭā'if.

45. Adhruḥ is an oasis in southern Jordan where the arbitration between ʿAlī and Muʿāwiyah took place in Shaʿbān 38 (January 2–30, 659). The arbiters condemned the murderers of ʿUthmān and recognized Muʿāwiyah's right to vengeance, but they were unable to agree on a Caliph. See E. L. Petersen, *ʿAlī and Muʿāwiya*, 186–95.

661) and Muʿāwiyah entered al-Kūfah at the beginning of Jumādā I (September 2, 661). Yet another account claims that he entered it in the month of Rabīʿ II. This is what al-Wāqidī[46] says.[47] [9]

In this year ʿAlī's sons, al-Ḥasan and al-Ḥusayn, left al-Kūfah for al-Madīnah.

The Departure of al-Ḥasan and al-Ḥusayn for al-Madīnah

When peace was made between al-Ḥasan and Muʿāwiyah at Maskin, (al-Ḥasan) rose—as I have been told on the authority of Ziyād al-Bakkāʾī—ʿAwānah—to speak to the people, saying, "O people of Iraq, I am glad to be rid of you for three reasons: your killing of my father, your stabbing of me, and your plundering of my possessions." Then al-Ḥasan, al-Ḥusayn, and ʿAbdallāh b. Jaʿfar left with their servants[48] and baggage and went to al-Kūfah. When al-Ḥasan arrived there, having recovered from his wounds, he went out to the mosque (*masjid*) of al-Kūfah and said, "O people of al-Kūfah, be God-fearing toward your neighbors and guests and toward the members of the family of your Prophet, from whom[49] God removed sinfulness and whom He purified completely." And the people began to weep. Then they departed for al-Madīnah. ʿAwānah continued: The people of al-Baṣrah[50] refused him the revenue (*kharāj*) of Dārābjird, saying, "It is our booty [*fay*ʾ]."[51] And when al-Ḥasan left

---

46. Abū ʿAbdallāh Muḥammad b. ʿUmar al-Wāqidī (130–207[747/8–822/3]) was a native of al-Madīnah who moved to Baghdād and authored works on historical and religious subjects. See *EI*¹, s.v. al-Wāḳidī.

47. According to Ilyās of Naṣībīn, al-Ḥasan made peace with Muʿāwiyah on Sunday, twenty-one Rabīʿ (July 25, 661). See F. Baethgen, *Fragmente*, 25; Ibn Khayyāṭ, *Taʾrīkh*, I, 234, reports that peace was concluded either in Rabīʿ II (August) or in Jumādā I (September).

48. C reads: "army."

49. *ʿanhum*, that is, the family.

50. Al-Baṣrah was the Muslim Arab garrison city (*miṣr*) and provincial capital near the Tigris-Euphrates estuary in lower Iraq, just to the south of the modern city. See *EI*², s.v. al-Baṣra.

51. *Fay*ʾ, "permanent booty," was the income from tribute or taxes from which the stipends of Muslim soldiers were paid.

for al-Madīnah, people confronted him at al-Qādisiyyah[52] and accused him of having demeaned the Arabs.

During this year the Khārijites[53] who stood aside at Shahrazūr[54] in the days of ʿAlī rebelled against Muʿāwiyah.

The Khārijites at Shahrazūr

[10] I was told on the authority of Ziyād—ʿAwānah: Before al-Ḥasan left al-Kūfah, Muʿāwiyah came and halted at al-Nukhaylah.[55] At that, the five hundred Ḥarūriyyah[56] who had been standing aside at Shahrazūr with Farwah b. Nawfal al-Ashjaʿī said, "Since someone about whom there is no doubt has come, [let us] march against Muʿāwiyah and wage *jihād*[57] against him." They approached, with Farwah b. Nawfal in charge of them, and entered al-Kūfah. When Muʿāwiyah dispatched some of the Syrian cavalry against them, they routed the Syrians. So Muʿāwiyah said to the Kūfans, "By God, you will have no guarantee of safe-conduct where I am concerned until you deal with your own misfortunes." When the Kūfans went forth against the Khārijites and fought them,[58] the latter said to them, "Woe unto you! What do you want from us? Is not Muʿāwiyah both our enemy and yours? Leave us alone so that we may fight him. If we should defeat him, we will have protected

52. Al-Qādisiyyah was a town south of modern Najaf, nineteen miles from al-Kūfah, where the Muslims had defeated the Persians in 16(637) and marked the border of Iraq. See *EI*², s.v. al-Ḳādisiyya.

53. The Khārijites (Khawārij, sg. Khārijī) were "seceders" who had rebelled against ʿAlī after he agreed to arbitration at Ṣiffīn. See *EI*², s.v. al-Khawāridj.

54. Shahrazūr was a town north of Ḥulwān on the border between Iraq and Iran. See Le Strange, *Lands*, 190.

55. Al-Nukhaylah was the mustering and demobilization point for Kūfan soldiers just outside the city. See Dīnawarī, *Akhbār*, 176; Mubarrad, *Kāmil*, 665; and Yāqūt, *Muʿjam*, IV, 771. S. El-ʿAlī, "Minṭaqat al-Kūfa," 238, has identified its location near the modern Jisr al-ʿAbbāsiyyāt.

56. The Ḥarūriyyah were those opponents of ʿAlī's agreement to arbitration who had seceded to the village of Ḥarūrā' near al-Kūfah in 37(658) This continued to be a common designation for the Khārijites. See *EI*² s.v. Ḥarūrā'.

57. *Jihād* is making an effort on God's behalf, including warfare against unbelievers. Its use implies that they considered their enemies to be unbelievers. See *EI*² s. v. Djihād.

58. For a Khārijite account of al-Ḥasan's part in pursuading the Kūfans to fight them, see Sirhān b. ʿUmar b. Saʿīd, *Kashf al-ghummah*, f. 211a.

you from your enemy; and if he should defeat us, you will have been protected from us." They replied, "No, by God [not] until we fight you." Then they said, "May God have mercy on our brothers among the people [who fought at] al-Nahr.[59] They knew you better, O people of al-Kūfah." (The clan of) Ashjaʿ took their commander, Farwah b. Nawfal—who was the chief of the folk—and they put ʿAbdallāh b. Abī al-Ḥurr—a man of the Ṭayyi'—at their head. (The Kūfans) fought them, and (the Khārijites) were killed.

When Muʿāwiyah put ʿAbdallāh b. ʿAmr b. al-ʿĀṣ in charge of al-Kūfah, al-Mughīrah b. Shūʿbah came to Muʿāwiyah, saying, "You put ʿAbdallāh b. ʿAmr in charge of al-Kūfah while ʿAmr is in charge of Egypt. You are between the jawbones of the lion." So (Muʿāwiyah) dismissed (ʿAbdallāh) from al-Kūfah, and put al-Mughīrah in charge there. When ʿAmr learned what al-Mughīrah had said to Muʿāwiyah, he went to Muʿāwiyah and asked, "Did you put him in charage of the revenues?" (When) he replied that he had, (ʿAmr) said, "If you put al-Mughīrah in charge of the revenues, he will seize the wealth and vanish, and you won't get anything from him. Put someone who fears and respects you in charge of the revenues." So (Muʿāwiyah) dis- [11]
missed al-Mughīrah from (control of) the revenues and put him in charge of worship. When al-Mughīrah confronted ʿAmr, he asked, "Did you give the Commander of the Faithful the same advice that I gave him concerning ʿAbdallāh?" ʿAmr replied that he had. Then al-Mughīrah told him, "This for that." But from what I've heard, ʿAbdallāh b. ʿAmr b. al-ʿĀṣ never left for al-Kūfah nor arrived there.

When Ḥumrān b. Abān[60] took possession of al-Baṣrah in this

---

59. Al-Nahr, "the canal," refers to Nahrawān, a town and canal with the same name east of al-Madā'in where the Khārijites were defeated by ʿAlī on the ninth of Ṣafar 38 (July 17, 658). Their exit from al-Kūfah prior to this battle is the probable origin of the Khārijite name. See *EI*², s.v. al-Khawāridj; Le Strange, *Lands*, 57–61.

60. Ḥumrān b. Abān, as a Jewish child called Ṭuwayd, had been taken captive by the Muslims at ʿAyn Tamr during the conquest of Iraq. He became a mawlā of ʿUthmān, but was deprived of his protection when he gave a false report about the governor of al-Kūfah. He had then settled at al-Baṣrah where he was given ʿAbbādān as a land grant. See Balādhurī, *Futūḥ*, 247, 368; Ibn Qutaybah, *Maʿārif*, 435–6; Ibn Saʿd, *Ṭabaqāt*, VII(1), 108; and Ṭabarī, I, 2122.

year, Muʿāwiyah sent Busr[61] to him, having ordered (Busr) to kill the sons of Ziyād.[62]

Muʿāwiyah's Order to Kill the Sons of Ziyād

I was told by ʿUmar b. Shabbah—ʿAlī b. Muḥammad: When al-Ḥasan b. ʿAlī made peace with Muʿāwiyah at the beginning of this year, Ḥumrān b. Abān seized al-Baṣrah and took control there. Muʿāwiyah wanted to send a member of the Banū al-Qayn[63] there, but ʿAbdallāh b. ʿAbbās persuaded him not to do so and to send someone else. So he sent Busr b. Abī Arṭāt who claimed that (Muʿāwiyah) had ordered him to kill the sons of Ziyād.

I was told by Maslamah b. Muḥārib:[64] He seized one of Ziyād's sons and imprisoned him. At that time Ziyād was in Fārs[65] where ʿAlī had sent him against the Kurds who had rebelled there. Ziyād defeated them and stayed at Iṣṭakhr.[66] He continued: Abū Bakrah[67] asked Busr for a postponement while he rode to Muʿāwiyah, who was at al-Kūfah. So (Busr) gave him a week's delay, going and coming. He travelled seven days and wore out two mounts beneath him, and when he spoke to Muʿāwiyah the latter wrote (to Busr) to leave (Ziyād's sons) alone.

---

61. Busr b. Abī Arṭāt was an Arab general belonging to the Banū ʿĀmir clan of Quraysh. He lived until the time of ʿAbd al-Malik or his son al-Walīd. See *EI*², s.v. Busr b. Abī Arṭāt.

62. Ziyād b. Abīhi was an Arabized mawlā of the Thaqīf from al-Ṭāʾif. During the conquest he had migrated to al-Baṣrah where he became a protégé of al-Mughīrah b. Shūʿbah and served in the finance administration for twenty years before he became governor of Fārs for ʿAlī during the first civil war. See H. Lammens, "Ziād ibn Abihi;" K. A. Fariq, "Ziyād ibn Abih."

63. The Banū al-Qayn were a branch of the Qudāʿah living in Syria. See *EI*¹, s.v. al-Ḳain.

64. C reads: Makhlad.

65. Fārs is a province in southwestern Iran. See Le Strange, *Lands*, 248–98.

66. Iṣṭakhr was a district and city, near Persepolis, in northern Fārs. The city was a Magian religious center and the capital of Fārs under the Sasanians and in the early Islamic period until the foundation of Shīrāz in 64(684). See *EI*², s.v. Iṣṭakhr.

67. Abū Bakrah, Nufayʿ b. Masrūḥ (d. 51 or 52[671–72]) was a former slave of Thaqīf from Ṭāʾif, and Ziyād's half-brother on his mother's side. See *EI*², s.v. Abū Bakra.

He continued: One of our learned people told me that Abū Bakrah approached al-Baṣrah on the seventh day, when the sun had risen. Meanwhile Busr brought out the sons of Ziyād, awaiting sunset in order to kill them if necessary. The people assembled for that, while their leaders were eagerly anticipating Abū Bakrah. Suddenly he came into view on a camel or steed [12] with he urged on, exhausted and strained. He rose upon it, dismounted, waved his cloak, and exclaimed, "God is great!." And the people said likewise. He then approached quickly on foot[68] in order to reach Busr before he killed them. When he handed (Busr) Muʿāwiyah's letter, he released them.

I was told by ʿUmar—ʿAlī b. Muḥammad: When Busr spoke on the pulpit (*minbar*)[69] of al-Baṣrah, he reviled ʿAlī. Then he said, "I implore God, that anyone who knows that I am truthful should say so, or likewise if I am a liar." When Abū Bakrah said, "By God! We know you only as a liar," (Busr) ordered him to be strangled. But Abū Lu'lu' al-Dabbī jumped up, threw himself at (the man who was carrying out the order) and restrained him. Afterwards Abū Bakrah assigned (Abū Lu'lu') one hundred *jarībs*.[70] Abū Bakrah was asked, "What did you wish to do?" He replied, "When he adjures us by God, should we not tell him the truth?" Busr remained in al-Baṣrah for six months; then he left. We don't know whether he put anyone in charge of his police force (*shurṭah*).[71]

I was told by Aḥmad b. Zuhayr—ʿAlī b. Muḥammad—Sulaymān b. Bilāl—al-Jārūd b. Abī Sabrah: When al-Ḥasan made peace with Muʿāwiyah and left for al-Madīnah, Muʿāwiyah sent Busr b. Abī Arṭat to al-Baṣrah in Rajab 41 (October 31–November 29, 661), while Ziyād was fortified in Fārs. Muʿāwiyah wrote to Ziyād, "Since you have some of God's wealth, having been put in charge of administration, bring the money you have." Ziyād wrote (back) to him, "I don't have any money left, having spent what I had properly, deposited some of it

68. C reads: "he rode his female camel."

69. A *minbar* is the pulpit in the *masjid*.

70. A *jarīb* is sixty sq. *dhirāʿah*, between 1,592 and 5,837 1/3 sq. meters depending on the length of the *dhirāʿah*. See W. Hinz, *Islamische Masse und Gewichte*, 65–6.

71. See above, n. 7.

with folk in case of misfortune, and delivered the rest to the Commander of the Faithful." Muʿāwiyah wrote to him, "Come to me and we will examine that with which you were entrusted and that which happened under your administration. If the matter is straightened out between us, so be it; if not, you
[13] may return to your place of safety." When Ziyād (still) did not come to Muʿāwiyah, Busr seized Ziyād's oldest sons—ʿAbd al-Raḥmān, ʿUbaydallāh, and ʿAbbād—imprisoned them, and wrote to Ziyād, "You had better go to the Commander of the Faithful or I will surely kill your sons." Ziyād wrote (back) to him, "I'm not leaving this place where I am until God decides between me and your master. If you kill any son of mine in your possession, then the outcome is up to God, Praise Him, and we will face the reckoning 'and those who do evil will know such a destiny that they will be utterly overthrown.'"[72]

When Busr intended to kill them, Abū Bakrah came to him saying, "You seized my sons and nephews as innocent youths although al-Ḥasan had made peace with Muʿāwiyah on condition of a guarantee of safe-conduct for ʿAlī's companions, wherever they might be. So you don't have any way to get at them or their father." Busr said, "Your brother has wealth which he took, and he refused to deliver it." Abū Bakrah replied, "He doesn't have anything, so leave my nephews alone until I bring you a letter from Muʿāwiyah [telling you] to release them." Busr granted him a few days' delay, saying, "I shall kill them unless you bring me Muʿāwiyah's letter to release them, or Ziyād goes to the Commander of the Faithful." When Abū Bakrah came to Muʿāwiyah, he interceded with him for Ziyād and his sons. Muʿāwiyah wrote to Busr to leave them alone and let them go, so he did.

I was told by Aḥmad b. ʿAlī[73]—ʿAlī—a shaykh of Thaqīf—Busr b. ʿUbaydallāh: When Abū Bakrah went to Muʿāwiyah at al-Kūfah, Mu'āwiyah asked him, "O Abū Bakrah, have you come to visit or because you need something?" He replied; "To tell you the truth, I only came out of necessity." Mu'āwiyah said, "Intercede, O Abū Bakrah, and we will consider favoring

72. Qur'ān 26: 228.
73. Cario reads: Aḥmad b. Zuhayr.

you with regard to [your request] since you deserve that. What is it?" He answered, "Give my brother, Ziyād, a guarantee of safe-conduct and write to Busr to release his children and to stop bothering them" Muʿāwiyah replied, "As far as the sons of [14]
Ziyād are concerned, we shall write for you what you have asked on their behalf. As far as Ziyād is concerned, he has wealth belonging to the Muslims. When he pays it, we will have no way to get at him." Abū Bakrah said, "O Commander of the Faithful, if he had anything, he would not withhold it from you, God willing." So Muʿāwiyah wrote on Abū Bakrah's behalf to Busr telling him not to interfere with any of Ziyād's children.

Muʿāwiyah then said to Abū Bakrah "Will you make a pact with us, O Abū Bakrah?" The latter replied, "Yes, I entrust you, O Commander of the Faithful, to watch over yourself and your flock and to act virtuously. For you have taken a great thing upon yourself—the Caliphate of God over His creation. So fear God, for you have a goal which you will not avoid, while behind you there is a slow but persistant Pursuer.[74] You are about to reach the destination. The Pursuer will overtake you, and you will come to One who will ask you about what you were doing, while He knows more about it than you. Instead it will be an accounting and an apprehension. You will certainly not prefer anything over the satisfaction of God, Almighty and Great."

I was told by Aḥmad—ʿAlī—Salamah b. ʿUthmān: Busr wrote to Ziyād, "If you don't present yourself, I shall surely crucify your sons." Ziyād wrote back to him, "If you do, that would be worthy of you, because the son of the eater of livers[75] sent you." Abū Bakrah then rode to Muʿāwiyah and said, "O Muʿāwiyah, the people did not give you their allegiance for the killing of children." He asked, "How's that, O Abū Bakrah?" The latter replied, "Busr intends to kill the children of Ziyād." Muʿāwiyah then wrote to Busr, "Release any children of Ziyād you have."

Muʿāwiyah had written to Ziyād after ʿAlī's assassination,

74. Qur'ān 7: 72.

75. That is, Muʿāwiyah, whose mother, Hind, had eaten the liver of Muḥammad's uncle, Ḥamzah, in revenge at the Battle of ʿUḥud.

threatening him. I was told by ʿUmar b. Shabbah—ʿAlī—Ḥabbān b. Mūsā—al-Mujālid—al-Shaʿbī:[76] When ʿAlī was killed,
[15] Muʿāwiyah wrote to Ziyād threatening him. So he got up to speak, saying, "How amazing is the son of the eater of livers, cavern of hypocrisy, and head of the factions. He wrote to me threatening me, while there are two nephews of the Messenger of God—that is, Ibn ʿAbbās and al-Ḥasan b. ʿAlī—between me and him. They have ninety thousand men who put their swords on their shoulders, unbending. If I were free of this business, he would feel the most biting of heavy sword blows." Ziyād remained as governor of Fārs until al-Ḥasan made peace with Muʿāwiyah, and Muʿāwiyah had arrived at al-Kūfah. Ziyād fortified himself in a stronghold which is called the Fortress of Ziyād.

In this year Muʿāwiyah put ʿAbdallāh b. ʿĀmir in charge of al-Baṣrah and of military matters in Sijistān[77] and Khurāsān[78]

ʿAbdallāh b. ʿĀmir Put in Charge of al-Baṣrah

I was told by Abū Zayd[79]—ʿAlī: When Muʿāwiyah intended to send ʿUtbah b. Abī Sufyān to be in charge of al-Baṣrah, Ibn ʿĀmir spoke with Muʿāwiyah, saying, "I have wealth and deposits there, and if you don't put me in charge of it, I shall leave." Muʿāwiyah then put him in charge of al-Baṣrah, Khurāsān, and Sijistān. He wanted to put Zayd b. Jabalah in charge of his police force, but the latter refused. So he put Ḥabīb b. Shihāb al-Shaʾmī[80] in charge of his police— according to another report it was Qays b. al-Haytham al-Sulamī. He also appointed ʿAmīrah b. Yathribī al-Ḍabbī, the brother of ʿAmr b. Yathribī al-Ḍabbī, as judge (*qāḍī*).

76. Abū ʿAmr ʿĀmir b. Sharāḥīl al-Shaʿbī (19/20–110[640/41–728]) was a Kūfan official, agent for his tribe of Ḥamdān (75–81[694–700]), envoy for ʿAbd al-Malik, and judge. See *EI*[1], s.v. al-Shaʿbī.

77. Sijistān is the province of Sīstān in the Helmand Valley of western Afghanistan. See Le Strange, *Lands*, 344–51.

78. Khurāsān is the province in northwestern Iran. See Le Strange, *Lands*, 382–434.

79. Abū Zayd al-Anṣārī, Saʿīd b. Aws (d. 214[830] or 215[831]) was a Baṣran grammarian and lexicographer. See *EI*[2], s.v. Abū Zayd al-Anṣārī.

80. O reads: al-Shibāmī; C reads: al-Taymī.

I was told by Abū Zayd—'Alī b. Muḥammad: When Ibn 'Āmir was governor for Mu'āwiyah, Yazīd b. Mālik al-Bāhilī, The Broken-nosed, rebelled. He was called The Broken-nosed [16] because of a blow which he had received on his face. When he rebelled with Sahm b. Ghālib al-Hujaymī and went to Jisr[81] in the morning, they met 'Ibādah b. Qurṣ al-Laythī[82] worshipping there. He belonged to the Banū Bujayr, and had been a Companion (of Muḥammad). They rebuked him, killed him,[83] and then asked for a guarantee of safe-conduct afterwards. Ibn 'Āmir guaranteed their safety and wrote to Mu'āwiyah, "I gave them your guarantee of protection." Mu'āwiyah wrote back to him, "You may violate that guarantee of protection, (since) you weren't asked for it." They thus remained in guaranteed security until Ibn 'Āmir was dismissed.[84]

In this year 'Alī b. 'Abdallāh b. 'Abbās[85] was born. According to another report he was born in the year 40 (660/661) before 'Alī was killed, and this is what al-Wāqidī says.

'Utbah b. Abī Sufyān led the people in the pilgrimage in this year according to Abū Ma'shar.[86] I was told that by Aḥmad b. Thābit—whoever told him—Isḥāq b. 'Īsā. As for al-Wāqidī, Aḥmad reported according to his informant that he used to say: 'Anbasah b. Abī Sufyān led the people in the pilgrimage this year.

---

81. That is, "the bridge." According to Ibn Khayyāṭ, *Ta'rīkh*, I, 235, this was the subdistrict (*nāḥiyah*) called Jisr al-Baṣrah.

82. Or 'Ibādah b. Qurt al-Laythī. See Ibn al-Athīr, *Usd*, III, 107.

83. According to Ibn al-Athīr, *Usd*, III, 107, 'Ibādah was killed in al-Ahwāz. Ibn Khayyāṭ, *Ta'rīkh*, I, 235, reports that Sahm also killed Sa'd, a mawlā of Qudāmah b. Maẓ'ūn, and that Ibn 'Āmir killed several of their comrades but granted them both safe-conducts.

84. They were killed after Ziyād became governor of al-Baṣrah in 45(665). See Ibn al-Athīr, *Usd*, III, 108.

85. 'Alī b. 'Abdallāh b. 'Abbās (41–117[661–735/6]) was the ancestor of the 'Abbāsid caliphs. See *EI²*, s.v. 'Alī b. 'Abd Allāh b. al-'Abbās.

86. Abū Ma'shar, Najīḥ b. 'Abd al-Raḥmān (d. 170[787]) was a former slave from Yaman who lived in al-Madīnah until 160(776/7) when he moved to Baghdad. His book on early Muslim campaigns was based on Madinan authorities. See *EI²*, s.v. Abū Ma'shar.

The Events of the Year 42

(April 26, 662–April 14, 663)

During this year the Muslims raided the Alāns.[87] They also raided the Byzantines and inflicted a shocking defeat on them, reportedly killing several generals (*baṭāriqah*).[88]

It was said that al-Ḥajjāj b. Yūsuf[89] was born in this year.

In this year Muʿāwiyah made Marwān b. al-Ḥakam[90] governor of al-Madīnah, and Marwān appointed ʿAbdallāh b. al-Ḥārith b. Nawfal as judge. Khālid b. al-ʿĀṣ b. Hishām was (the governor) in charge of Mecca; al-Mughīrah b. Shuʿbah was in
[17] charge of al-Kūfah on his[91] behalf, while Shurayḥ[92] super-

---

87. The Alāns were an Iranian people living north of the Caucasus, the ancestors of the modern Ossets. See *EI²*, s.v. Alān.

88. *Baṭrīq* (pl. *baṭāriqah*) in Arabic comes from the Latin *patricius* via the Greek *patrikios*. In Arabic usage a *baṭrīq* meant to the Byzantines what a *qāʾid* (general, leader) meant to the Arabs.

89. Al-Ḥajjāj b. Yūsuf (42–95[662–714]) was a member of the Thaqīf from al-Ṭāʾif and governor of Iraq and the East, 75–95(694–714). According to Ibn Khayyāṭ, *Taʾrīkh*, I, 236, al-Ḥajjāj was born in 41(661/2) See *EI²*, s.v. al-Ḥadjdjādj.

90. Marwān b. al-Ḥakam (d. 65[685]) was Muʿāwiyah's cousin and founded the Marwānid dynasty of caliphs. See *EI²*, s.v. Marwān b. al-Ḥakam.

91. Most probably Muʿāwiyah is meant here.

92. Shurayḥ b. al-Ḥārith al-Kindī (d. bet. 78[697] and 80[699]). He had been

vised rendering judgment there. ʿAbdallāh b. ʿĀmir was in charge of al-Baṣrah, while ʿAmr b. Yathribī was in charge of rendering judgment, and Qays b. al-Haytham was in charge of Khurāsān on behalf of ʿAbdallāh b. ʿĀmir.

(According to) ʿAlī b. Muḥammad—Muḥammad b. al-Faḍl al-ʿAbsī—his father: ʿAbdallāh b. ʿĀmir sent Qays b. al-Haytham to be in charge of Khurāsān when Muʿāwiyah appointed the former to be governor of al-Baṣrah and Khurāsān. Qays remained in Khurāsān for two years. Another report about the governorship of Qays is that of Ḥamzah b. Ṣāliḥ[93] al-Sulamī —Ziyād b. Ṣāliḥ: When his affairs were settled, Muʿāwiyah sent Qays b. al-Haytham to Khurāsān. He then added Khurāsān to (the territory under) Ibn ʿĀmir, who left Qays in charge of it.

During this year the Khārijites who had separated from those Khārijites who were (later) killed at al-Nahrawān were stirred into action, along with those who had been carried, wounded, from the battlefield at al-Nahrawān. Having recovered from their wounds the latter had been forgiven by ʿAlī b. Abī Ṭālib.

What Happened to the Khārijites

(According to) Hishām b. Muḥammad[94]—Abū Mikhnaf[95]—al-Naḍr b. Ṣāliḥ b. Ḥabīb—Jarīr b. Mālik b. Zuhayr b. Jadhīmah al-ʿAbsī—Ubayy b. ʿUmārah al-ʿAbsī: Ḥayyān b. Ẓabyān[96] al-Sulamī held the view of the Khārijites and was among the wounded who were carried from the battlefield at al-Nahrawān. ʿAlī included him among the four hundred of those who were wounded at the Battle of al-Nahr whom he forgave. Ḥayyān stayed with his family and clan, waiting for about a

---

sent to Iraq by the caliph ʿUmar as judge in 19(640). See Ibn Saʿd, *Ṭabaqāt*, VI, 90–100.

93. Cairo reads: Ḥamzah b. Abī Ṣāliḥ.

94. Hishām b. Muḥammad b. al-Sāʾib, Abū al-Mundhir, al-Kalbī (120–204 [737–819] or 206[821]) was a Shīʿite native of al-Kūfah. credited with over one hundred fifty works on all subjects. See *EI*², s.v. al-Kalbī.

95. Abū Mikhnaf, Lūṭ b. Yaḥyā b. Saʿīd b. Mikhnaf al-Azdī (ca. 70–132 [689–745]) was an early collector of historical traditions at al-Kūfah. See U. Sezgin, *Abū Miḫnaf*.

96. O consistently has *Ṭaybān*.

month or so. Then he left for al-Rayy[97] with men who held Khārijite views. They stayed at al-Rayy until they heard about ʿAlī's assassination. At that, Ḥayyān summoned his compan-
[18] ions—they were about ten men, one of whom was Sālim b. Rabīʿah al-ʿAbsī—and they came to him.

After Ḥayyān praised and extolled God, he said, "O Brothers of the Muslims. I have heard that your brother, Ibn Muljam,[98] brother of the Murād, lay in wait to kill ʿAlī b. Abī Ṭālib in the pre-dawn darkness opposite the door of the congregational mosque [*masjid*]. He remained motionless, waiting for ʿAli to come out, until he did come out when it was time for the dawn worship. (Then) he attacked ʿAlī and struck his head with his sword. ʿAlī only lasted two nights until he died." Sālim b. Rabīʿah al-ʿAbsī exclaimed, "May God not cut off the right hand of whoever struck his skull with the sword!" The folk began to praise God for ʿAlī's death, may peace be upon him and may God be satisfied with him and not be satisfied with them.

Al-Naḍr b. Ṣāliḥ (said): Afterwards, during the governorship (*imārah*) of Muṣʿab b. al-Zubayr,[99] I asked Sālim b. Rabīʿah about what he had said with regard to ʿAlī. He confirmed it for me, saying, "I held their view for a while, but I have since abandoned it." We agreed that he had abandoned it. Whenever that was mentioned to him, he was consumed (with regret).

Then Ḥayyān b. Ẓabyān said to his companions:

> By God, no one lives forever. Nights and days and years and months will not continue indefinitely for a son of Adam until he tastes death and will part from the virtuous brothers and leave the world over which only weaklings weep, a world which is always harmful for whoever has concern and worry. Then let us be off, may God have mercy upon you, to our city [*miṣr*].[100] Let us join our brothers and summon them to commanding good and forbid-

---

97. Al-Rayy was a city in northern Iran. See Le Strange, *Lands*, 214–15. Balādhurī, *Ansāb*, IV A, 143, adds that he went to fight the Daylām.

98. ʿAbd al-Raḥmān b. Muljam al-Murādī assassinated ʿAlī in 40(661). See *EI*², s.v. Ibn Muljam.

99. Muṣʿab b. al-Zubayr was governor of al-Baṣrah for his brother, the counter-Caliph, ʿAbdallāh, 67–72(686–91). See *EI*¹, s.v. Muṣʿab b. al-Zubair.

100. That is, al-Kūfah.

ding evil[101] and to striving [*jihād*][102] against the factions. For we have no excuse for being inactive while our rulers are oppressive, and while guiding precedent [*sunnah*] is abandoned and our vengeance remains unexacted against those who killed our brothers in the assemblies.[103] If God gives us victory over them, let us turn afterwards to that which is more correct and satisfying and upright. God will thereby heal the hearts of believers. If we are killed, we would have repose in parting from the oppressors, while our forefathers have set an example for us. [19]

So they said to him, "We all say the same, and praise the view that you expressed. Then lead us to the city, for we are satisfied with your guidance and your command."

Ḥayyān left and they left with him, proceeding to al-Kūfah. That was when he said:[104]

My friend, I have neither solace nor composure,
nor skill after the victims[105] at al-Nahr,
Only camels rising[106] with numerous squadrons.
You will call upon God and in Him you will prevail.
My mule has left Qusṭānat al-Rayy[107] behind;
I shall never approach it again.
But I am leaving soon, even if my supporters are few,
so I would not shame you two,[108] with whom he goes.

Ḥayyān proceeded until he settled at al-Kūfah where he remained until Muʿāwiyah came to power and sent al-Mughīrah b. Shuʿbah to be governor there. Al-Mughīrah liked things to

---

101. Qur'ān 3:104, 110. The Khārijites were among the first Muslims to emphasize this responsibility.

102. See above, n. 57.

103. That is, the assemblies (*al-majālis*) of the Khārijites.

104. These lines are ascribed to Sālim b. Rabīʿah al-ʿAbdī in Balādhurī, *Ansāb*, IV A, 143.

105. The text reads: *muṣābīn*, "the victims"; O reads: *muṣallīn*, "worshippers."

106. The text reads: *nahaḍāt*, "camels rising"; C reads: *nahaghāt*, "scouting parties."

107. Qusṭanāh or Qisṭānah was a village one day's journey from al-Rayy on the road to Sāwah. See Yaqūt, *Muʿjam*, IV, 94–5.

108. O reads: "spur on you two."

run smoothly; he behaved well with people and did not ask sectarians about their sects. People would be brought to him,
[20] and he would be told that so-and-so holds Shīʿite views, and so-and-so holds Khārijite views. But he would say, "God has decided that you will continue to disagree. And God will judge between His creatures concerning that in which they disagree."[109] So people felt safe with him.

The Khārijites would meet each other, and recalling the circumstances of their brethren at al-Nahrawān, they would consider deceit and ruin to lie in staying, while merit and reward lay in striving (*jihād*) against the people of the *qiblah*.[110]

(According to) Abū Mikhnaf—al-Naḍr b. Ṣāliḥ—Ubayy b. ʿUmārah: In the days of al-Mughīrah b. Shuʿbah the Khārijites turned to three persons, one of whom was al-Mustawrid b. ʿUllifah. The latter rebelled with three hundred men and headed toward Jarjarāya[111] on the banks of the Tigris. (According to) Abū Mikhnaf—Jaʿfar b. Ḥudhayfah of the family of ʿĀmir b. Juwayn—al-Muḥill b. Khalīfah: In the days of al-Mughīrah b. Shuʿbah the Khārijites turned to three persons: al-Mustawrid b. ʿUllifah al-Taymī of Taym al-Ribāb, Ḥayyān b. Ẓabyān al-Sulamī, and Muʿādh b. Juwayn b. Ḥuṣayn al-Ṭāʾī al-Sinbisī, who was the nephew of Zayd b. Ḥuṣayn. Zayd was one of those whom ʿAlī killed at the Battle of al-Nahrawān. This Muʿādh b. Juwayn was among the four hundred wounded who were carried off the battlefield and pardoned by ʿAlī.

The Khārijites assembled at the dwelling of Ḥayyān b. Ẓabyān al-Sulamī and deliberated about whom they should appoint to be in charge. Al-Mustawrid addressed them, "O Muslims and believers, may God give you what you desire and remove from you what you hate. Appoint whomever you like over you. By Him who knows the secret in one's eyes and what

109. See Qurʾān 42:10. Deferring to God's judgment in order to avoid conflict in this way amounts to the position later identified as Murjiʾite. See W. Montgomery Watt, *The Formative Period of Islamic Thought*, 119–28.

110. The *qiblah* is the direction of the Kaʿbah in Mecca toward which Muslim's face when they worship. The Khārijites called nominal Muslims "people of the *qiblah*."

111. Jarjarāyā was a town near the place where the Nahrawān Canal emptied into the Tigris River. See Le Strange, *Lands*, 37.

is hidden in one's heart, I don't care which of you would govern me. We do not seek[112] the glory of this world, and there is no way to remain in it. We desire only immortality in the abode of [21] immortality." At that, Ḥayyān b. Ẓabyān said, "As for me, I have no need to rule, and I am satisifed with every one of my brethren. Look, then, upon whomever of you that you wish and name him. I shall be the first to render allegiance." Muʿādh b. Juwayn b. Ḥuṣayn then spoke to them, "Since you both say you are thus [content to follow another] while you are both leaders of the Muslims and possessors of their lineages as regards virtue, religion, and standing, who shall lead the Muslims? For they are not all virtuous enough for that command. However, when Muslims are equal in virtue, the most perspicacious of them in war, the most learned of them in religion, and the most capable of them in carrying out strongly that which is imposed must take charge. Both of you, God be praised, are among those who are satisfactory for this command. Let one of you two take charge." They both replied, "You be in charge for we have been satisfied with you, for you, praise God, are perfect in your religion and your views." He then responded to both of them, "You are both older than I, let one of you two take charge."

At that moment, a group of the Khārijites who were present said, "We are satisfied with the three of you. Put in charge whomever of you that you prefer." At that, each of the three men said to his companion, "You be in charge, for I am satisfied with you and I have no desire for rule." After that had continued among (the three of) them for a long time, Ḥayyān b. Ẓabyān declared, "Since Muʿādh b. Juwayn said, 'Don't put me in charge of both of you since you are both older than I,' I say the same to you that he said to us. Hold out your hand that I may render allegiance to you." So al-Mustawrid held out his hand and Ḥayyān rendered allegiance to him, followed by Muʿādh b. Juwayn and then by the entire group. That was in Jumāda II (August 22–September 20, 662). The folk agreed to equip and prepare themselves, and to be ready. They were to

112. The text reads: *nurīdu*; O reads: *yazīdu*, that is, "the glory of this world does not increase."

rebel at the beginning of the new moon, that is, the new moon of Shaʿbān 43 (November 8, 663). So they were equipped and ready.

[22] It was said that in this year Busr b. Abī Arṭāt al-ʿĀmirī set out for al-Madīnah, Mecca, and al-Yaman. He killed various Muslims during that journey, according to al-Wāqidī. I have (previously) mentioned those who differ with him about the time Busr made that journey. Al-Wāqidī claimed that he was told by Dāwūd b. Ḥayyān—ʿAṭā' b. Abī Marwān: Busr b. Abī Arṭāt stayed at al-Madīnah for a month investigating the people. He killed everyone who was said to have helped against ʿUthmān. (According to) ʿAṭā b. Abī Marwān—Ḥanẓalah b. ʿAlī al-Aslamī: Busr found some of the Banū Kaʿb and their youths at one of their wells, so he threw them in it.

In this year Ziyād came to Muʿāwiyah. This is according to what I was told by ʿUmar—Abū al-Ḥasan[113]—Sulaymān b. Abī Arqam:[114] Ziyād came to Muʿāwiyah from Fārs and reached a settlement with him in return for the wealth which he brought to Muʿāwiyah. The reason why he came after having refused at one of the strongholds of Fārs is (in) the following account that I was told by ʿUmar—Abū al-Ḥasan—Maslamah b. Muḥārib: ʿAbd al-Raḥmān b. Abī Bakrah used to be in charge of Ziyād's property in al-Baṣrah. Muʿāwiyah learned that Ziyād had wealth with ʿAbd al-Raḥmān. When Ziyād feared for things which ʿAbd al-Raḥmān held for him, he wrote to ʿAbd al-Raḥmān ordering him to safeguard his property. When Muʿāwiyah sent to al-Mughīrah b. Shuʿbah to investigate Ziyād's wealth, al-Mughīrah came and took ʿAbd al-Raḥmān aside saying, "Your father may have done me wrong, but Ziyād treated me well." He then wrote to Muʿāwiyah, "I didn't find anything in ʿAbd al-Raḥmān's possession which I am free to take." Muʿāwiyah wrote back to al-Mughīrah to torture him. Some authorities reported that al-Mughīrah tortured ʿAbd al-Raḥmān b. Abī
[23] Bakrah when Muʿāwiyah wrote to him, although he wanted to be excused. When Muʿāwiyah learned of this, he said, "Perse-

113. That is, ʿAlī b. Muḥammad al-Madā'inī.

114. Cairo reads: Sulaymān b. Arqam. Sulaymān's father was commonly called al-Arqam b. Abī al-Arqam. See *EI*², s.v. al-Arḳam.

vere in what your kinsman ordered you to do." So al-Mughīrah covered ʿAbd al-Raḥmān's face with silk, and moistened it with water so that it would stick, and the latter fainted. Al-Mughīrah did that three times, released him, and wrote back to Muʿāwiyah, "I tortured him but did not get anything from him." Thus he earned Ziyād's gratitude.

I was told by ʿUmar—Abū al-Ḥasan—ʿAbd al-Malik b. ʿAbdallāh al-Thaqafī—shaykhs of the Thaqīf: Al-Mughīrah b. Shuʿbah entered Muʿāwiyah's presence, and upon seeing him Muʿāwiyah said:

The place of a man's secret, if
he reveals the secret, is his sincere brother.
So if you reveal a secret, let it be to
someone sincere who will keep it secret, or don't disclose it.

Al-Mughīrah replied, "O Commander of the Faithful, if you should place your trust in me, you would do so with someone who is sincere, sympathetic, Godfearing, and dependable. What is it, O Commander of the Faithful?" Muʿāwiyah replied, "I remembered Ziyād clinging to the land of Fārs and his defiance there, and I didn't sleep last night." Al-Mughīrah wanted to downplay Ziyād, so he asked, "What is Ziyād over there, O Commander of the Faithful?" Muʿāwiyah replied, "What a miserable, low, incompetent, trickster of an Arab. He holds wealth fortified in a fortress of Fārs. He contrives subterfuges and lies in wait. I am not reassured that he won't acknowledge a man belonging to the people of this house.[115] If so he will have renewed the war against me deceitfully." Al-Mughīrah then asked, "Do you give me permission to go to him, O Commander of the Faithful?" He answered, "Yes. Go to him and be polite."

Al-Mughīrah then came to Ziyād, and when he learned about al-Mughīrah's approach, Ziyād remarked, "He only came on an [24]
important mission." Then he admitted al-Mughīrah, who entered his presence, while Ziyād was in his reception hall facing

115. The text reads: *ahl hādhā al-bayt*, that is, a member of Muḥammad's family, in particular a relative of ʿAlī. See *EI*², s. v. Ahl al-Bayt.

the sun. Ziyād greeted him saying, "May the visitor prosper." To which al-Mughīrah replied, "The news ends with you, Abū Mughīrah.[116] Muʿāwiyah was so carried away with fear that he sent me to you. He didn't know anyone who attempted this matter[117] except al-Ḥasan. Since the latter has already rendered allegiance to Muʿāwiyah, take [something] for yourself before settling down [somewhere]. Muʿāwiyah has no need of you." Ziyād responded, "Confidentially, give me the best practical advice you can." Al-Mughīrah answered, "A frank opinion might be distasteful but there is no use watering it down.[118] I think you should attach your rope to Muʿāwiyah's and travel to him." Ziyād replied, "I will see, and God will decide."

I was told by ʿUmar—ʿAlī—Maslamah b. Muḥārib: When Ziyād had remained in the fortress for over a year, Muʿāwiyah wrote to him, "Why do you destroy yourself? Come to me and tell me how much wealth you collected as taxes, what you spent, and what remained with you; you will be guaranteed a safe-conduct. If you would like to remain with us, then do so; and if you prefer to return to your place of safety, then return." At that, Ziyād left Fārs. When al-Mughīrah b. Shuʿbah learned that Ziyād had decided to come to Muʿāwiyah, he set out for Muʿāwiyah before Ziyād set out from Fārs. Ziyād set out from Iṣṭakhr to Arrajān[119] and came to Māh Bahrādhān.[120] Then he took the Ḥulwān[121] Road until he reached al-Madā'in. ʿAbd al-
[25] Raḥmān then left for Muʿāwiyah, to inform him of Ziyād's coming. Then, when Ziyād had reached Syria, and al-Mughīrah arrived a month later, Muʿāwiyah said to the latter, "O Mughīrah, Ziyād's journey was a month longer than yours and you left before he did, and yet he arrived before you." Al-Mughīrah replied, "O Commander of the Faithful, if one clever person

116. That is, "You are the object of my visit."

117. This probably means attempting to resist him.

118. The text reads: *al-madhīq*, that is, milk mixed with water.

119. Arrajān was a town and district in northwestern Fārs. See Le Strange, *Lands*, 268–69.

120. Māh Bahrādhān was the district of Nihāwand in the Jibāl, also called Māh Dīnār. See Ṭabarī, I, 2633–34; Yāqūt, *Muʿjam*, IV, 406; and *EI*[1], s.v. Nihāwand.

121. Ḥulwān was a town on the main road at the border of the Jibāl and Iraq. See Le Strange, *Lands*, 91.

speaks with another, his argument will silence him." Mu'āwiyah responded, "Watch out! Keep your secret from me." So al-Mughīrah said, "Ziyād came hoping for gain [*ziyādah*], while I came fearing loss, so that explains how we traveled."

Mu'āwiyah questioned Ziyād about the wealth of Fārs that he had collected. So Ziyād told him how much he had sent to 'Alī and how much he had spent properly on necessary expenses. Mu'āwiyah believed him concerning what he had spent and what he had left, and he collected the remainder from Ziyād, saying, "You have been the most reliable of our deputies [*khulafā'*]."

I was told by 'Umar—'Alī[122]—'Abū Mikhnaf, Abū 'Abd al-Raḥmān al-Iṣfahānī, Salamah b. 'Uthmān, a shaykh of the Banū Tamīm, and others who may be trusted: When Mu'āwiyah wrote to Ziyād while the latter was in Fārs asking him to come to him, Ziyād set out from Fārs with al-Minjāb b. Rāshid al-Dabbī and Ḥārith b. Badr[123] al-Ghudānī. Mu'āwiyah also dispatched 'Abdallāh b. Khāzim to Fārs with a contingent, saying, "Should you meet Ziyād en route, seize him." Ibn Khāzim journeyed to Fārs—some said that he met Ziyād at Sūq al-Ahwāz;[124] others (said that) he met him at Arrajān. When they met, Ibn Khāzim seized the reins of Ziyād ('s horse) demanding, "Dismount, O Ziyād!" At that, al-Minjāb b. Rāshid shouted to him, "Let go, O son of a black, or I shall tie[125] your hand in the reins!" It is also said that Ibn Khāzim caught up with them while Ziyād was sitting and spoke to him rudely, whereupon al-Minjāb reviled Ibn Khāzim. Ziyād then asked him, "What do [26]
you want, O Ibn Khāzim?" He answered, "I want you to come to al-Baṣrah." When Ziyād replied, "Indeed, I am going there," Ibn Khāzim went off embarrassed by him.

(According to) some authorities: Ziyād and Ibn Khāzim met at Arrajān and quarreled. Ziyād told Ibn Khāzim, "I have received Mu'āwiyah's safe-conduct, so I intend to go to him. This is his letter to me." Ibn Khāzim replied, "If you intend to go to the Commander of the Faithful, there is no way to get at you."

---

122. C reads: Abū al-Ḥasan.
123. C reads: Zayd.
124. Sūq al-Ahwāz was a city in Khuzistān. See Le Strange, *Lands*, 232–34.
125. The text reads: '*allaqtu*; C reads: '*aqaltu*, "hobble."

Ibn Khāzim then departed for Sābūr,[126] while Ziyād left for Māh Bahrādhān, and came to Muʿāwiyah who asked him about the wealth of Fārs. Ziyād answered, "I spent it, O Commander of the Faithful, on provisions, stipends, and campaigns. I deposited the remainder with folk for safekeeping."

Ziyād thus kept putting off Muʿāwiyah while he wrote letters to folk, among whom was Shuʿbah b. al-Qilʿim, "You know how I trust you, so consider the verse of the Book of God, Almighty and Great, 'We offered the trust to the heavens and the earth and the mountains . . .'[127] Take care of what you can." He also designated in the letters the amount which he had confirmed for Muʿāwiyah, and he concealed the letters with his messenger, ordering him to pass by some (people) who would inform Muʿāwiyah. So his messenger did that until (word of) it spread and he was seized and brought to Muʿāwiyah. Muʿāwiyah then told Ziyād, "If you are not going to deceive me, I need these letters." So Muʿāwiyah read them, and (the amount) was indeed the same as Ziyād had confirmed for him. Muʿāwiyah said, "I fear that you may have (already) deceived me. Make peace with me in return for whatever you wish." At that, Ziyād made peace with him for part of what he told Muʿāwiyah he had, and delivered it. Ziyād then said, "O Commander of the Faithful, I had wealth before becoming governor. I would like to keep that wealth and to give up what I acquired as governor."

Then Ziyād asked Muʿāwiyah's permission to settle at al-Kūfah. When he gave it, Ziyād proceeded to al-Kūfah.[128] Al-Mu-
[27] ghīrah would honor and praise Ziyād, and Muʿāwiyah wrote to al-Mu-ghīrah, "Urge Ziyād, Sulaymān b. Ṣurad,[129] Ḥujr b. ʿAdī[130]

---

126. Sābūr was the city of Bishāpūr in Fārs. See Le Strange, *Lands*, 262–63.

127. Qurʾān 33:72.

128. C adds: "So he settled in it after he gave permission."

129. Sulaymān b. Ṣurad al-Khuzāʿī (d. 65[685]) had settled in al-Kūfah with his tribe. He had been among those who protested the land policy of Saʿīd b. al-ʿĀs, there. He fought on ʿAlī's side at the Battle of Ṣiffīn, but had objected to the arbitration agreement. See Dīnawarī, *Akhbār*, 182, 198, 210; *EI*[1], s.v. Sulaimān b. Ṣurad al-Khuzāʿī; S. H. M. Jafri, *Shiʿa Islam*, 82.

130. Ḥujr b. ʿAdī al-Kindī (d. 50[70]) had commanded the Muslim right wing at Jalūlāʾ. He was among those who protested the land policy of Saʿīd b. al-ʿĀṣ, and had pursuaded the Kūfans to join ʿAlī before the Battle of the Camel. He

Shabath b. Ribʿī,[131] Ibn al-Kawwāʾ,[132] and ʿAmr b. al-Ḥamiq[133] to worship with the assembly." Consequently they would be present with him at worship.[134]

I was told by ʿUmar b. Shabbah—ʿAlī—Sulaymān b. Arqam:[135] I learned that Ziyād arrived at al-Kūfah, and, when it was time for worship, al-Mughīrah said to him, "Come forward and lead the worship." Ziyād replied, "I won't. You have more right than I to lead worship during your regime [*sulṭānikum*]." Ziyād also entered al-Mughīrah's presence while Umm Ayyūb bt. ʿUmārah b. ʿUqbah was with him. Al-Mughīrah seated her in front of Ziyād, saying, "You will not be concealed from Abū al-Mughīrah." When al-Mughīrah died, Ziyād married her, while she was (still) young. Ziyād would order that an elephant of his be made to stand and Umm Ayyūb would look at it. As a result (that place) was called Bāb al-Fīl.[136]

ʿAnbasah b. Abī Sufyān led the people in the pilgrimage this year. I was told this by Aḥmad b. Thābit—someone—Isḥāq b. ʿĪsā—Abū Maʿshar.

---

was wounded at Ṣiffīn, witnessed the arbitration agreement, commanded ʿAlī's right wing at al-Nahrawān, and was a potential rival of the family of al-Ashʿath b. Qays for the leadership of the Kindah at al-Kūfah. See Dīnawarī, *Akhbār*, 135, 154, 176, 187, 209, 223, 238; *EI*², s.v. Ḥudjr b. ʿAdī al-Kindī; Jafri, *Shiʿa Islam*, 82. For his disruption of worship see below.

131. Shabath b. Ribʿī al-Tamīmī, who had followed the false prophetess Sajāḥ as a youth, fought on ʿAlī's side at Ṣiffīn, was put in charge of fighting by the Ḥarūriyyah, but commanded ʿAlī's left wing at al-Nahrawān. He became the chief of the Banū Ḥanẓalah at al-Kūfah. See Dīnawarī, *Akhbār*, 223, 243; Ṭabarī, I, 1919, 3270, 3349, 3380, 3388.

132. ʿAbdallāh b. al-Kawwāʾ al-Yashkūrī had favored judgment according to the Qurʾān at Ṣiffīn. He was put in charge of worship by the Ḥarūriyyah, and was one of the Khārijite leaders who fought at al-Nahrawān. See Dīnawarī, *Akhbār*, 176, 209; Ṭabarī, I, 2921.

133. C reads: ʿUmar b. al-Ḥamiq. ʿAmr b. al-Ḥamiq al-Khuzāʿī was one of the notables who had opposed ʿUthmān in 33(653/4) and had helped to kill ʿUthmān. He fought on ʿAlī's side at Ṣiffīn, and witnessed the arbitration agreement. See Dīnawarī, *Akhbār*, 176, 209; and Ṭabarī, I, 2921.

134. The point is that all of those whose loyalty was suspect were required to attend public worship led by the governor as a sign that they accepted the current regime.

135. C reads: Abū al-Ḥasan b. Arqam.

136. That is, "the Gate of the Elephant." See also Balādhurī, *Futūḥ*, 288.

The Events of the Year 43

(April 15, 663–April 3, 664)

Among these events was Busr b. Abī Arṭāt's[137] campaign against the Byzantines. Al-Wāqidī claimed that Busr spent the winter in their territory until he reached Constantinople. But some experts in historical matters have denied that, saying that Busr never spent the winter in Byzantine territory.

In this year ʿAmr b. al-ʿĀṣ died in Egypt on Yawm al-Fiṭr[138]
[28] (January 6, 664). He had been its governor for ʿUmar b. al-Khaṭṭāb for four years, and for ʿUthmān for four years minus two months, and for Muʿāwiyah for two years minus one month.

In this year Muʿāwiyah appointed ʿAbdallāh b. ʿAmr b. al-ʿĀṣ governor of Egypt after the death of his father. Al-Wāqidī claimed that he was it's governor for about two years.

In Ṣafar of this year (May 15–June 12, 663) Muḥammad b. Maslamah[139] died in al-Madīnah. Marwān b. al-Ḥakam led the prayers over him.

---

137. Ibn Khayyāṭ, *Ta'rīkh*, I, 238, calls him Busr b. Arṭāt.

138. Yawm al-Fiṭr is the day celebrating the end of the month-long fast of Ramaḍān.

139. Muḥammad b. Maslamah b. Khālid b. ʿAdī was an early Muslim convert

In this year al-Mustawrid b. ʿUllifah, the Khārijite, was killed, as Hishām b. Muḥammad claimed. Others have claimed that he was killed in the previous year.

The Killing of al-Mustawrid b. ʿUllifah[140]

We have already reported[141] the meeting of the remaining Khārijites who were carried off wounded at the Battle of al-Nahr, those who withdrew to al-Rayy and others. They met with the three persons whom I named previously, one of whom was al-Mustawrid b. ʿUllifah. We reported how they rendered allegiance to him and gathered for revolt at the beginning of the new moon of Shaʿban 43 (November 8, 663).

(According to) Hishām—Jaʿfar b. Hudhayfah al-Ṭāʾī—al-Muhill b. Khalīfah: Qabīṣah[142] b. al-Dammūn,[143] who was in charge of the police came to al-Mughīrah b. Shuʿbah, saying, "Shimr b. Jaʿwanah al-Kilābī came and informed me that the Khārijites have gathered at the house of Ḥayyān b. Ẓabyān al-Sulamī, and have agreed among themselves to rebel against you at the beginning of Shaʿbān (November 8, 663)." Al-Mughīrah b. Shuʿbah then told Qabīṣah b. al-Dammūn, who was an ally of the Thaqīf (they claimed that he came from al-Ṣadif in Ḥadramawt), "Take the police to surround the house [29]
of Ḥayyān b. Ẓabyān, and bring him to me." They were convinced that he was the commander of those Khārijites. Qabīṣah took the police and many other people, and, before Ḥayyān b. Ẓabyān realized it, they were at his house at noon.[144] Muʿādh b. Juwayn and about twenty of their companions were with Ḥayyān at that time. Ḥayyān's wife, an *umm walad* of his,[145]

---

who had fought at the Battle of Badr. He helped to kill Kaʿb b. al-Ashraf; killed the Jew, Marḥab, after the conquest of Khaybar; and had been put in charge of al-Madīnah when Muḥammad went to Tabūk. See Ibn Hishām, *Sīrah*, I, 492, 550–51, 761, 896.

140. This account is summarized by Balādhurī, *Ansāb*, IV A, 143–47.

141. O begins: "Abū Jaʿfar, may God have mercy on him, said."

142. O and Cairo read: Qubayṣah.

143. O reads: al-Dammūr; C reads: al-Zanbūr.

144. O adds: *ṣakkahu ʿammī* "my uncle locked it."

145. C reads: "and an *umm walad* of his." An *umm walad* was a slave woman who had borne a child to her master. Such a woman was normally freed and her child recognized as legitimate after their master died.

jumped up, and took their swords which she threw under the bedding. Some of the folk sought to defend themselves with their swords, but, when they did not find them, they surrendered. Qabīṣah took them away to al-Mughīrah b. Shuʿbah who asked them, "What prompted you to want to split the stick of the Muslims?" They replied, "We didn't want anything of the sort," to which he responded, "Yes indeed! I heard that about you, and then your gathering confirmed it for me." They answered, "As far as our gathering in that house is concerned, Ḥayyān b. Ẓabyān taught us to recite the Qur'ān, so we meet with him in his house in order to recite it to him." Al-Mughīrah ordered, "Take them to the prison." They remained there for about a year.

When their brethren heard about their arrest, they were (more) cautious.[146] Al-Mustawrid b. ʿUllifah, their leader (*ṣāḥib*), left (al-Kūfah) and settled at a house in al-Ḥīrah next to the Qaṣr al-ʿAdasiyyīn[147] of the Kalb. He sent to his brethren, who would visit him frequently, and equip[148] themselves. When their frequent visits increased, their leader, al-Mustawrid b. ʿUllifah al-Taymī, said to them, "Let us leave this place, for I fear that you will be discovered." Some of them said to each other, "Let us go to this place;"[149] others said, "that
[30] place."

Ḥajjār b. Abjar looked down upon them from a house in which he and a group of his family were staying. Suddenly they would see two horsemen arrive and enter that house in which the folk were (gathered). Then, before long, two others would come and enter, and shortly afterwards another would come and enter, then still another who would enter. That would concern him.[150] They would also leave close together. So Ḥajjār said to the lady of the house in which he was staying, while she was

146. O reads: *jaddadū*, "they started over."

147. The Qaṣr al-Adasiyyīn was one of the fortified enclosures at the town of al-Ḥīrah, about six km from al-Kūfah. It belonged to the Banū ʿAmmār b. ʿAbd al-Masīh, and was named after their ancestress, ʿAdasah bt. Mālik b. ʿAwf al-Kalbī. See Balādhurī, *Futūḥ*, 244; Ibn al-Faqīh, *Buldān*, 183; and Yāqūt, *Muʿjam*, IV, 116.

148. C reads: *yajtahidū*, "exerted."

149. C reads: "to what place does he bid us go?"

150. C reads: "all that bothered him."

nursing a boy[151] of hers, "Woe unto you! Who are these horsemen whom I see entering this house?" She replied, "By God, I don't know who they are except that men visit this house frequently and continuously, on foot and on horseback. We have disapproved of that for days, but we don't know who they are."

Ḥajjār then rode out on his horse, accompanied by one of his young servants (*ghulām*). He proceeded until he reached the door of their house, where one of their men was in charge. Whenever one of their men came to the door, the doorkeeper went in to his master and informed him, and the latter admitted the visitor. But if a man well-known to them came to the doorkeeper, he would enter without asking permission. When Ḥajjār came to the doorkeeper, the latter did not recognize him, so he asked, "Who are you, may God have mercy on you, and what do you want?" Ḥajjār replied, "I want to meet my comrade."[152] The doorkeeper then asked, "And what is your name?" He told him, "Ḥajjār b. Abjar." He said, "Stay as you are until I inform them about you, then I will come out to you." So Ḥajjār said to him, "Enter, rightly guided." At that the man entered, and Ḥajjār followed him quickly until he reached the door of a large *ṣuffah*[153] where they were. The doorkeeper had entered their presence meanwhile and said, "This man asks permission to see you. I refused him, saying, 'Who are you?' He replied, 'I am Ḥajjār b. Abjar.'" Ḥajjār then heard them becoming alarmed and exclaiming, "Ḥajjār b. Abjar! By [31]
God! Ḥajjār b. Abjar did not come for any good purpose." When he heard what they said,[154] he wanted to leave, having confirmed his suspicion about what they were doing. But he wouldn't let himself leave until he saw them for himself. Approaching until he stood between the curtains of the door of the *ṣuffah*, he said, "Peace be upon you!" He looked, and there before him was a large group of men, weapons in full view, and coats of mail. Ḥajjār exclaimed, "O God! May He gather them for some good purpose. Who are you, God save you?" ʿAlī b. Abī Shimr b. al-Ḥusayn of the Taym al-Ribāb recognized him.

151. C reads: "boys."
152. O reads: "I want to meet al-Riyāḥī."
153. A *ṣuffah* was a covered place attached to a house and open on one side.
154. O reads: "what was said about him."

This ʿAlī was one of the eight Khārijites who were put to flight at the Battle of al-Nahr. He was a horseman of the Arabs and one of their pious ascetics, and he was among the best of them. ʿAlī said to him, "O Ḥajjār b. Abjar, if you came looking for information,[155] then you have found it, and if you came for something else, then enter and tell us why you came." Ḥajjār replied, "I don't need to enter." And he left.

At that, they said to each other, "Catch and hold him, for he is going to inform on you." A group of them went out right after him—that was just at sunset. When they caught up with him while he rode his horse, they said to him, "Tell us your story and why you came." He replied, "I didn't come for anything which should alarm or frighten you." So they said to him, "Wait until we draw near you and speak with you or until you draw near to us. Inform us, and we will let you know our business and state our concern." He then told them, "I won't draw near to you, and I don't want you to draw near to me." At that ʿAlī b. Abī Shimr b. al-Ḥuṣayn asked him, "Can we trust you not to inform on us for tonight, which would be charitable of you, because we share kinship and a just claim?" Ḥajjār replied, "Yes, you are safe from me for tonight and all nights forever." Then he hurried off and entered al-Kūfah, taking his
[32] family with him. The others, meanwhile, said to each other, "We aren't certain that he won't inform on us, so let's leave this place at once."

After they had performed the sunset worship, they left, dispersing from al-Ḥīrah. Their leader told them, "Join me at the house of Sulaym b. Maḥdūj al-ʿAbdī of the Banū Salamah." He then left al-Ḥīrah and proceeded until he came to the ʿAbd al-Qays. When he came to the Banū Salamah, he sent to Sulaym b. Maḥdūj, who was related to him by marriage. When he came to him, Sulaym took him in along with five or six of his companions. Meanwhile, Ḥajjār b. Abjar returned to his dwelling, and they expected to hear that he had reported them to the authorities or to the people. But he reported them to neither one, and the Khārijites did not hear anything about him that they disliked in that respect.

155. The text reads: *khabar*; C reads: *khayr*, "good."

During his term as governor, al-Mughīrah b. Shuʿbah learned that the Khārijites were rebelling against him, and that they had rallied to one of their men. So al-Mughīrah b. Shuʿbah rose before the people, and after praising and extolling God, he continued:

> Now then, you know, O people, that I have always desired well-being for your community and have averted harm from you. You also know, by God, that I feared that that would be[156] an evil example for the impudent [*sufahā*ʾ] among you, but not for the forbearing [*ḥulamā*ʾ] and Godfearing. By God, I feared lest I would ever find that the forbearing and Godfearing were punished for the crime of impetuous fools. So restrain the impudent among you, O people, before misfortune overcomes the general public. It has been reported to me that some men among you desire to foment divisions and controversy openly in the city.[157] By God, they will not rebel in any Arab district in this city, but I shall destroy them and make them an exemplary warning for whomever comes after them. So let folk look to themselves before [they] regret [it]. I have taken this stand desiring proof and excuses. [33]

At that, Maʿqil b. Qays al-Riyāḥī rose before him, saying "O amīr, was any one of those folk named to you? If so, then let us know who they are. If they should belong to us, we would satisfy you with respect to them. If they should belong to others, order those who are obedient among the people of our city to have every tribe bring you its impudent ones." Al-Mughīrah replied, "None of them was named to me, but I have been told that a group intends to rebel in the city." Maʿqil then told him, "May God make you prosper, I shall go among my folk and satisfy you about those who belong to them. Let every man among the leaders thus satisfy you about his folk."

Al-Mughīrah b. Shuʿbah then descended[158] and sent to summon the leaders of the people. Then he told them, "You al-

---

156. The text reads: *yakūna*; C reads: *takrahūna*, "that you would detest."
157. That is, al-Kūfah.
158. The text reads: *nazala*; C reads: *taraka*, "left."

ready know what has taken place regarding this matter, and you have heard what I have said, so let every man among the leaders satisfy me with regard to his folk. If not, then by Him than whom there is no other god! I shall surely change from someone you like into someone you will hate. For a vile person only disgraces himself, while he who admonishes is absolved from guilt."

The leaders then left for their clans, and implored them by God and Islām to point out whomever they thought intended to incite discord or to withdraw from the community. Ṣaʿṣaʿah b. Ṣūḥān also came and stayed among the ʿAbd al-Qays.

(According to) Hishām—Abū Mikhnaf—Al-Aswad b. Qays al-ʿAbdī—Murrah b. al-Nuʿmān: Ṣaʿṣaʿah b. Ṣūḥān stayed with us, and, by God, some news had reached him that al-Taymī[159] and his companions were staying at the house of Sulaym b. Maḥdūj. But in spite of his differences with them and his hatred for their views, he detested having them seized while they were with his clan. He also detested the evil treatment of the People of the House[160] by his folk. So he said something nice. At that time we had many notables and there were a good number of us.

[34] Ṣaʿṣaʿah stood before us after he performed the afternoon worship, saying:

> O assemblage of God's worshippers, when God, much praise be unto him,[161] distributed merit among the Muslims, He bestowed the best part of it on you. So you decided in favor of God's religion, which He chose for Himself and was satisfied with for his angels and messengers [*rusul*]. Then you adhered to it until God took His Messenger.[162] Then, afterwards, the people quarreled, one faction standing firm, while another apostatized. One faction were hypocrites, while another waited. You, however, persevered in God's religion, and had faith in Him and His Messenger. You fought the apostates until the religion was

159. That is, al-Mustawrid.
160. See above, n. 115.
161. C reads: "to whom be praise [and] much wealth."
162. That is, he died.

established and God destroyed the evildoers. In return, God continued to increase the good He bestowed on you in everything and in every circumstance, until the community quarreled among its members. One faction said, "We want Ṭalḥah, al-Zubayr, and ʿĀʾishah,[163] while another faction said, "We want the people of the West."[164] Yet another faction said, "We want ʿAbdallāh b. Wahb al-Rāsibī, [that is, the] Rāsib of the Azd."[165] But you said, "We only want the People of the House, through whom God first gave us dignity," [hoping for] a reward from God to you and a settlement. You thus continued to be in the right, adhering to it, and observing it, until God destroyed by means of you and those whose guidance and views were similar to yours, the faithless at the Battle of the Camel[166] and the renegades at the Battle of al-Nahrawān.

He said nothing about the Syrians because the government was theirs at that time.

No folk are worse enemies of God, you, the family of your Prophet, and the community of the Muslims, than these mistaken renegades who separated from our Imām[167] and allowed our blood to be shed, and who accuse us of unbelief. Beware lest you shelter them in your houses or be secretive about them, for no Arab alive should be worse enemies of them than you. By God, it has been reported to me that some of them are among the living. I am investigating [35]
that and asking questions. If I should find that out, truly I

163. Ṭalḥah b. ʿUbaydallāh (d. 36[656]) had led ʿAlī's opponents along with al-Zubayr b. al-ʿAwwām (d. 36[656]) and ʿĀʾishah bt. Abī Bakr (ca. 614–78), Muḥammad's favorite wife, at the Battle of the Camel where both Ṭalḥah and al-Zubayr were killed. See N. Abbott, *Aishah the Beloved of Mohammad*; *EI*², s.v. ʿĀʾisha Bint Abī Bakr; *EI*¹, s.v. Ṭalḥa b. ʿUbaydallāh; and al-Zubair b. al-ʿAwwām.

164. That is, Muʿāwiyah and the Syrians.

165. ʿAbdallāh b. Wahb al-Rāsibī (d. 38[658]) had led the Khārijites at the Battle of al-Nahrawān where he was killed. See *EI*², s.v. ʿAbd Allāh b. Wahb al-Rāsibī.

166. The Battle of the Camel was fought outside al-Baṣrah in Jumādā II 36 (December 656). See *EI*², s.v. al-Djamal.

167. That is, ʿAlī b. Abī Ṭālib.

> would win favor with God by shedding their blood, for that is permitted.

Then he continued:

> O assemblage of the ʿAbd al-Qays, these governors of ours know you and your views better than anyone, so don't give them grounds to take action against you, for they would be swifter than anything toward you and those like you.[168]

Then he stepped aside and sat down, and all his folk said, "God curse them!" and "May God be rid of them! By God, we shall not shelter them, and should we know where they are we shall surely point them out to you." The only exception was Sulaym b. Maḥdūj who didn't say anything. But he returned to his folk depressed and despondent, not liking to evict his companions from his dwelling. They would blame him, for they were related by marriage and relied on each other. He also disliked having them sought in his house, for they would perish and he with them. When he had arrived, he entered his dwelling. The companions of al-Mustawrid also arrived, coming to him. Every one of them informed al-Mustawrid of what al-Mughīrah b. Shuʿbah had done with the people and of how their leaders had come to them and stood before them. They told him, "Let us leave. By God, we aren't certain we won't be taken in our clans."

Al-Mustawrid asked them, "Don't you think that the head of the ʿAbd al-Qays stood before them just as the heads of the [other] clans stood before their clans?" They replied, "Yes, by God, we think so." He remarked, "Indeed, my host hasn't mentioned anything to me." They said, "We think, by God, that he is embarrassed by you." So he called Sulaym and he came to al-Mustawrid who said, "O Ibn Maḥdūj, I have learned that the heads of the clans stood before them and approached them concerning me and my companions. Did anyone stand before you[169] reporting anything of that to you?" He replied, "Yes, Ṣaʿṣaʿah b. Ṣūḥān stood before us requesting us not to shelter anyone

---

168. The text reads: *amthalikum*; C reads: *qatlikum*, "and for killing you."
169. C adds: "Summoning you."

sought by them, and they said many things which I disliked mentioning to you. You may consider that something of your business was a burden for me." Al-Mustawrid told him, "You [36] have honored your dwelling and acted well. Now we, God willing, shall depart from you." At that, Sulaym exclaimed, "By God, if they want [to take] you in my dwelling, they won't reach you or one of your companions until I die first." Al-Mustawrid replied,[170] "God protect you from that."

Those in al-Mughīrah's prison learned that the people of the city had agreed to expel and to seize the Khārijites among them. Concerning that Mu'ādh b. Juwayn b. Ḥuṣayn said:

Indeed, O Sellers![171] the time has come for one,
who sells himself to God, to depart.

Will you remain out of ignorance in the house of those who err,
while everyone of you is hunted down to be killed?

For the enemies[172] assaulted the folk and they
set you up for slaughter by a mistaken opinion.

Indeed, O folk, strive for the goal which,
when it is mentioned is more righteous and more just.

If only I were with you on the back of a swimmer [*sābiḥ*],[173]
powerful, short-legged, armored, not defenseless.

If only I were with you opposing your enemy,
for I am given first the cup of fate to drink.

It is hard for me that you are afraid and driven out.
When I draw out [my sword] unsheathed among the
violators,

---

170. O reads: "they said to him."
171. *Shārūn* was a term the Khārijites used for themselves, referring to the doctrine that they sold themselves to God for the reward of heaven.
172. The text reads: *'udāh*; C and O read: *ghadāh*, "this morning they."
173. Swimmer is a metaphor for a horse on a battlefield.

When every glorious [person] scatters their group,
when you would say he had turned away and fled, he would come back,

Showing the blade of the sword in the heat[174] of the tumult,
he regards steadfastness as exemplary in some places.

It is hard for me that you are wronged and decrease,
and I become sorrowful as a prisoner[175] in chains.

If I were with you while they headed for you,
then I would stir up dust between the two factions,

For many a group have I broken up, and many an attack
have I experienced, and many an opponent have I left dead on the ground.

Al-Mustawrid sent word to his companions, telling them,
[37] "Leave this tribe. Let no Muslim person be disgraced unwittingly because of us." Among them[176] were some who shared their views. They agreed (to go to) Sūrā,[177] and they left for that town, four, five, and ten at a time. Three hundred men in all presented themselves at Sūrā. Then they set out for the Ṣarāt[178] and spent the night there."

When al-Mughīrah b. Shuʿbah was informed about them, he summoned the leaders of the people, saying, "Destruction and an evil opinion have sent forth these wretches, so whom do you think I should send against them?" ʿAdī b. Ḥātim[179] stood

---

174. The text reads: *ḥamas*; O reads: *hawmah*, "in the turmoil of battle."

175. The text reads: *asīr*; C reads: amīr, "a commander in chains."

176. That is, among the ʿAbd al-Qays.

177. Sūrā was an old Jewish town on the upper Nahr Sūrā (the modern Shaṭṭ Hindiyyah branch of the Euphrates) where there was a bridge across the river for the main road from al-Kūfah to al-Madā'in, near the later site of Qaṣr Ibn Hubayrah. See Ibn al-Faqīh, *Buldān*, 183–84; and Yāqūt, *Muʿjam*, III, 184.

178. The Ṣarāt Canal was the section of the Nahr Sūrā below the bridge of al-Qāmighān. See Suhrāb, *ʿAjā'ib*, 25; and Yāqūt, *Muʿjam*, III, 377–78.

179. ʿAdī b. Ḥātim b. ʿAbdallāh b. Saʿd al-Ṭā'ī (d. 68[687/88]) was the son of the famous poet, Ḥātim al-Ṭā'ī, and had converted to Islam from Christianity. He was the leader of the Ṭayyi' tribe at al-Kūfah, and he fought on ʿAlī's side at the Battle of the Camel and at Ṣiffīn. See *EI*², s.v. ʿAdī b. Ḥātim.

up, saying, "We are all their enemy, consider their opinion to be foolish,[180] and remain obedient to you, so whomever of us you wish will set out for them." Maʿqil b. Qays then arose, saying, "You should only send against them one of the notables of the city whom you see around you, whom you find to be attentive and obedient, who differs with them and desires their destruction. I don't think, may God preserve you, that you would send anyone of the people against them who is a greater enemy of their's and more violently against them than I am. So send me against them, and, with God's permission, I will protect you from them." Al-Mughīrah replied, "Go in God's name." Three thousand men were then equipped for his expedition. Al-Mugīrah told Qabīṣah b. al-Dammūn, "Bring me ʿAlī's faction, and send them out with Maʿqil b. Qays, because he was one of the leaders of his companions." When word was sent to the members of his faction who were known, they gathered together. They were also the strongest in allowing the blood of these renegades to be shed, and were more courageous against them than others, as they had fought them previously.

(According to) Abū Mikhnaf—al-Aswad b. Qays—Murrah b. Munqidh b. al-Nuʿmān: I was among those assigned (to go) with him[181] at that time. He continued: Ṣaʿṣaʿah b. Ṣūḥān had stood up after Maʿqil b. Qays, saying, "Send me against them, O amīr. By God, I permit their blood to be shed and think [38]
lightly of bearing responsibility for it." But al-Mughīrah replied, "Sit down! You are [only] an orator," and that offended Ṣaʿṣaʿah.

Indeed al-Mughīrah said that because he heard that Ṣaʿṣaʿah would censure ʿUthmān b. ʿAffān,[182] and would constantly mention ʿAlī and prefer him. He had summoned him previously, saying, "As for you, I have heard that you censure ʿUthmān to one of the people, and I have also heard that you openly proclaim something of ʿAlī's superiority. But you do not mention any superiority of ʿAlī about which I am ignorant. Moreover, I

---

180. The text reads: *musfih*; C reads: *mubshid*, "detestable."

181. That is, Maʿqil b. Qays.

182. That is, ʿUthmān b. ʿAffān, the third Commander of the Faithful (23–35 [644–55]).

know more about that [than you]. But this regime has appeared, and we have been ordered to announce ʿAlī's faults to the people. So we leave out much of that which we are supposed to do, and mention [only] what we must in order to protect ourselves from these folk by means of dissimulation. If you discuss ʿAlī's superiority, do it secretly among your companions in your homes. As far as [doing this] publicly in the mosque is concerned, the Caliph does not permit this to us, nor does he forgive us for it." Ṣaʿṣaʿah would then tell al-Mughīrah, "Yes, I will do so." But then al-Mughiirah would hear that Ṣaʿṣaʿah had resumed doing what he had forbidden him to do.

Thus, when Ṣaʿṣaʿah stood before him, saying, "Send me against them," al-Mughīrah found that the former's dispute with him had aroused his hatred towards Ṣaʿṣaʿah. So he said, "Sit down! You are [only] an orator." When al-Mughīrah thus offended him, Ṣaʿṣaʿah replied, "Am I nothing but an orator? Yes indeed, by God! I favor orators [who are] firm leaders. By God! If you had seen me under the banner of the ʿAbd al-Qays at the Battle of the Camel, where the lances clashed splitting the shafts lengthwise and making the heads fall off,[183] you would have known that I am the lion, the beast." At that, al-
[39] Mughīrah said, "That's enough now. By my life, you were granted an eloquent tongue." Qabīṣah b. al-Dammūn lost no time in sending out the army with Maʿqil. They were three thousand (men who were) the pick of the Shīʿah and their horsemen.

(According to) Abū Mikhnaf—Abū al-Naḍr b. Ṣāliḥ—Sālim b. Rabīʿah: I was sitting with al-Mughīrah b. Shuʿbah when Maʿqil b. Qays came to pay his respects and bid him farewell. Al-Mughīrah told him, "O Maʿqil b. Qays, I have sent with you horsemen whom I ordered to be selected from the people of the city. So go against this renegade band who withdrew from our community and accused it[184] of unbelief. Summon them to repent and to [re]join the community. If they do so, then accept them and hold back from them; and if they do not, then fight them and seek God's help against them." Maʿqil b. Qays re-

183. The text reads: *tukhtalā*; O reads: *takhtallu*, "totter."
184. C reads: "us."

plied, "We shall summon them and excuse them. But, by God, I don't think they will accept, and if they don't accept the truth, we won't accept the false from them. Have you found out, may God cause you to prosper, where the folk are camped?" Al-Mughīrah answered, "Yes, Simāk b. 'Ubayd al-Absī"[185]—who was his governor over al-Madā'in—"wrote to me informing me that they set out from the Ṣarāt and proceeded until they halted at Bahurasīr,[186] and that they intended to cross over to al-Madīnah al-'Atīqah,[187] which contains the residences of the Khusraws and the White [Palace] of al-Madā'in. When Simāk prevented them from crossing, they stayed in the city of Bahurasīr. So take the field against them and pursue them until you catch them. Don't give up on them. They are forbidden to stay for more than an hour in any territory where you summon them. So if they accept, fine, and if not, then oppose them; for they would not stay in a territory for two days without corrupting everyone who associates with [40] them."

Ma'qil left that very day and spent the night at Sūrā. Meanwhile, al-Mughīrah ordered his mawlā, Warrād, and the latter went out to the people in the congregational mosque and announced, "O people, Ma'qil b. Qays has gone against these renegades and has spent[188] the night at Sūrā. Let none of his companions[189] do differently, lest the amīr go out against every Muslim among them. He adjures them not to spend the night at al-Kūfah. Whoever was assigned to this expedition whom we find at al-Kūfah after today will have outlawed himself."[190]

(According to) Abū Mikhnaf—'Abd al-Raḥmān b. Ḥabīb[191]—'Abdallāh b. 'Uqbah al-Ghanawī: I was among those who

---

185. O reads: al-Qaysī.

186. Bahurasīr or Behrasīr was the round, walled, Sasanian city of Veh-Artakhshatr west of the Tigris which formed the western part of al-Madā'in. See G. Gullini, "Problems of an excavation in northern Babylonia," 25.

187. "The Old City" was the Arabic name for Ctesiphon, the northernmost part of al-Madā'in on the east bank of the Tigris. See S. El-'Alī, "Al-Madā'in and its surrounding area in Arabic literary sources," 422–25.

188. O reads: "is spending."

189. That is, those men assigned to go with him.

190. That is, they will have made it permissible to have their blood shed.

191. C reads: Jundab.

went out with al-Mustawrid b. ʿUllifah, and I was the youngest man among them. We went out until we came to the Ṣarāt and stayed there until everyone in our group had arrived. Then we went forth until we reached and entered Bahurasīr. Simāk b. ʿUbayd al-ʿAbsī, who was in al-Madīnah al-ʿAtīqah, had been warned about us, so when we were about to cross the floating bridge to them, he fought us for it, and then he cut it. As a result, we stayed at Bahurasīr.

Al-Mustawrid b. ʿUllifah summoned me, saying, "Can you write, O my nephew?" I replied that I could, so he called for parchment and an inkwell for me, and said to write as follows:

> From God's Servant [ʿAbdallāh],[192] al-Mustawrid, Commander of the Faithful, to Simāk b. ʿUbayd. Now then, we take revenge on behalf of our folk for tyranny in judgment, failure to enforce prescriptions,[193] and the monopolization of the *fay*'.[194] I summon you to the Book of God, Almighty and Great, and the example [*sunnah*] of His Prophet, and the rule [*wilāyah*] of Abū Bakr and ʿUmar.[195] I also call upon you do disavow ʿUthmān and ʿAlī for their innovation in religion [*iḥdāth fī al-dīn*] and their abandonment of the
> [41] judgment of the Book. If you accept, you will have come to your senses; and if you do not, we will have run out of excuses for you, and we will permit war against you, and will reject you for your disgraceful act. 'Indeed, God does not love disloyal people.'[196]

---

192. ʿAbdallāh (Servant of God) was used as a prefix for the names of caliphs in Muʿāwiyah's inscription near al-Ṭā'if (58[677/8]), on coins of ʿAbd al-Malik, al-Ṣaffāh, and al-Manṣūr, and on the official weights and commodity stamps of Sulaymān, Yazīd b. ʿAbd al-Malik, al-Manṣūr, and al-Mahdī. See Lavoix, *Catalogue*, 17–24, 26; Miles, "Early Islamic Insciptions," 237; id., *Early Arabic Glass Weights and Stamps, Supplement*, 4, 8; id., *Contributions to Arabic Metrology*, I, i, 43–9; id., *Numismatic History of Rayy*, 23; id., *Excavation Coins from the Persepolis Region*, 64–7. It also occurs in the heading of a letter ascribed to ʿUmar I by Balādhurī, *Futūḥ*, 350.

193. The text reads: *al-ḥudūd*, that is, the punishments explicitly prescribed in the Qur'ān.

194. See above, n. 51.

195. That is, to recognize that Abū Bakr and ʿUmar had been legitimate rulers.

196. Qur'ān 8:58.

Al-Mustawrid said, "Go off to Simāk with this letter, deliver it to him, and remember what he says to you, and meet me." Al-Ghanawī continued: I was a callow and inexperienced youth when I reached puberty, and did not have much practical knowledge. I replied, "May God cause you to prosper, if you ordered me to throw myself into the Tigris, I would cast myself into it without disobeying you, but can you guarantee to me that Simāk won't detain me and prevent me from [returning to] you? In that case, the *jihād* I look forward to would elude me." At that, he smiled and said, "O my nephew, indeed you are an envoy, and nothing happens to them. If I feared that would happen, I would not send you. You could not take better care of yourself than I would for you."

So I left and crossed over to them at a ford. When I came to Simāk, there were many people around him, and when I drew near they weren't looking at me.[197] But when I approached them, about ten (of them) intercepted me. I supposed, by God, that they intended to seize me and that they did not respect envoys as my master had told me. At that, I drew my sword, exclaiming, "No! By Him in Whose hand is my soul, don't tangle with me or else God will absolve me of guilt concerning you." They asked me, "O servant of God, who are you?" I replied, "I am a messenger from the Commander of the Faithful, al-Mustawrid b. ʿUllifah." They then asked, "So why did you draw your sword?" I answered, "Because you were rushing at me, and I feared that you would bind me and be treacherous to me." They answered, "You are safe, and indeed, we came to you to go to your side, to hold the top of your sword,[198] and to see why you came and what you ask." I then asked them, "Will [42]
I be safe until you return me to my companions?" They replied, "Of course," so I watched my sword. Then I approached until I stood before Simāk b. ʿUbayd. His companions had already crowded around me. Some of them were holding the top of my sword, and some of them were holding my upper arm.

197. O reads: "they started to look at me."

198. That is, to make certain that he would not draw it. This was diplomatic protocol.

I presented my master's letter to him, and when he had read it, he looked up at me, saying, "Al-Mustawrid would not be my choice for Caliph because of what I have seen of his hypocrisy and baseness in drawing his sword against the Muslims. Al-Mustawrid presents me with the denunciation of ʿAlī and ʿUthmān and calls me to [recognize] his rule. By God, what a wretched shaykh I would be then." He looked at me and said, "O my son, go to your master and tell him, 'Fear God and desist from your views and enter into the community of the Muslims. If you so wish, I will write to al-Mughīrah requesting a guaranteed safe-conduct for you, for you will find him quick to put things right and one who enjoys well-being.'"

I replied to him, "I know what will happen to them on that day.[199] Far from that, indeed we seek security with God on the Day of Resurrection through that which makes you fear us in the temporal world." At that, Simāk responded, "You miserable wretch, how can I be merciful to you?" Then he addressed his companions, "They abandoned [the right way] by what they did. Then they began to recite the Qur'ān to him, pretended to humble themselves, and pretended to weep. So he thought thereby that they had something of the truth. 'Indeed they are only like cattle, nay, rather they are straying from the way.'[200] By God! I never saw folk who were in more manifest error nor a more obvious calamity than those whom you see." I replied, "Say, I did not come to you to revile you, nor to hear your account or that of your companions. Tell me, you give me
[43] your answer to what is in this letter; if not, I shall return to my master." At that, he looked at me. Then he said to his companions, "Aren't you astonished at this youth? By God, indeed, he seems greater to me than his father when he says to me 'Are you going to give me your answer to what is in this letter?' Off you go, my son, to your master, however, you may regret [it] if the cavalry should surround you all and the lances are aimed at your breasts. You may wish then you were in your mother's house."

I left him then, and crossed over to my companions. When I

199. That is, what will happen to non-Khārijites on the Day of Judgment.
200. Qur'ān 25:44.

approached my master,[201] he asked, "What did he reply to you?" I answered, "He did not reply positively. I said thus to him, and he said thus to me." I then told him the (whole) story. Al-Mustawrid then said, "It makes no difference to unbelievers whether you warn them or not. They will not believe. God has sealed their hearts and their hearing, and there is a veil concealing their sight. An awful punishment will be theirs."[202]

We stayed in that place of ours for two or three days. Then we realized that Maʿqil b. Qays was marching against us. Al-Mustawrid assembled us, and after praising and extolling God, he said, "Now then, indeed, this senile Maʿqil b. Qays has headed for us. He is one of the weak, lying Sabāʾiyyah[203] and is an enemy of God and of you, so give me your advice." Some of us told him, "By God, we only went forth desiring God and to fight against [*jihād*] whomever attacks God. But they have come to us, so where should we go to escape from them? Let us stand our ground instead, so that God will decide between us and them, for He is the best of judges." Another group said, "Let us withdraw instead and turn aside. Let us summon the [44]
people and protest against [our rulers] with supplication." He responded: "O assemblage of Muslims, by God, I did not go forth seeking the temporal world, nor its renown, glory or survival in it. I do not want any of it for myself, and that goes double for the things people compete for in it. I value such things less than the toe of my shoe. I went forth seeking only martyrdom, and that God would guide me to honor by humbling some of those who err. I have considered what I consulted you about. I do not think that I should wait for them to attack me, while they are exceedingly numerous, but I thought that I should move on until I go too far. For when they learn of that, they will go forth in search of me, and will thus become isolated and scattered. We should fight them in those circumstances. So let us go forth in the name of God, Almighty and Great."

---

201. C reads: "our companions."

202. Qurʾān 2:6–7.

203. The Sabāʾiyyah were ostensibly named by their enemies after ʿAbdallāh b. Sabaʾ, an extremist supporter of ʿAlī. See *EI*², s.v. ʿAbd Allāh b. Sabaʾ.

At that, we went forth and proceeded along the bank of the Tigris until we reached Jarjarāyā. We then crossed the river and continued as if we were in the territory of Jūkha[204] until we reached Madhār,[205] where we remained. News of our location reached ʿAbdallāh b. ʿĀmir, so he asked al-Mughīrah b. Shuʿbah how he was doing with the army which he had sent against the Khārijites and how many of them there were. He was informed of their number, and was told that al-Mughīrah had considered a leading man of high standing who had fought against the Khārijites along with ʿAlī, and had been among the latter's companions. He sent this man along with ʿAlī's faction because of their hostility to the Khārijites. ʿAbdallāh remarked, "He had the right idea." He then sent to Sharīk b. al-Aʿwar al-Ḥārithī, who shared ʿAlī's views, telling him, "Go forth against this renegade, and choose three thousand men[206] from the people. Then pursue them until you drive them out of the Baṣran
[45] territory or kill them." He also told him privately, "Go forth against the enemies of God with those Baṣrans who consider killing them to be lawful." Sharīk supposed that ʿAbdallāh meant ʿAlī's faction by this, but that he disliked naming them. So he chose people, and urged the horsemen of the Rabīʿah who held Shīʿite views, and their leaders agreed. Then he went forth with them, heading for al-Mustawrid at al-Madhār.

(According to) Abū Mikhnaf—Ḥuṣayrah b. ʿAbdallāh b. al-Ḥārith—his father ʿAbdallāh b. al-Ḥārith: I was among those who went forth with Maʿqil b. Qays, and I accompanied him. By God, I did not leave him for an hour of the day from the time I left. The first place we stopped was Sūrā. We remained there for a day until most of his men joined him, then we left hurrying swiftly toward our enemy lest he elude us. After we dispatched a vanguard, we departed. Stopping at Kūthā, we spent a day until whoever lagged behind joined us. Then, after

---

204. Jūkhā was an administrative district east of the Tigris which included the region of the Diyala River and the Nahrawān Canal. See M. Morony, "Administrative geography," 18–21.

205. Al-Madhār was a town across the southeastern border of Jūkhā in the territory of al-Baṣrah. See Le Strange, *Lands*, 42–3.

206. C reads: "cavalry."

part of the night had passed, he marched us from Kūthā.

We advanced until we drew near al-Madā'in, where the people received us and informed us that the Khārijites had already left. By God, that grieved us; we were certain of trouble and a lengthy search. Maʿqil b. Qays advanced until he halted at the gate of the city of Bahurasīr, without entering it. Simāk b. ʿUbayd went out to him, greeted him, and ordered his servants (*ghilmān*) and mawālī to bring Maʿqil carrots (*jazar*),[207] barley, and fodder. They brought enough for him and the army which accompanied him. Maʿqil b. Qays stayed at al-Madā'in for three nights; then he assembled his men, saying, "These misguided renegades have left, going their own directions and hoping that [46] you will hurry after them. Thus you would be isolated and scattered, and you would only overtake them after you were tired and worn out. But nothing of that sort is going to happen to you unless the same happens to them."

Maʿqil then marched us out from al-Madā'in, and sent Abū al-Rawwāgh al-Shākirī ahead with three hundred horsemen. He followed after the Khārijites, while Maʿqil followed him. Abū al-Rawwāgh began to ask about them and to pursue the direction they had taken, until his force crossed over (at) Jarjarāyā in pursuit of them. They followed the direction which the Khārijites had taken and pursued them. He continued persistently until he caught up with them when they were staying at al-Madhār. When he approached them, he took counsel with his men whether or not they should encounter and fight them before Maʿqil's arrival. Some of them told him, "Attack them with us, so we may fight them." Others said, "By God, we don't think you should be in a hurry to fight them until our commander comes and we encounter them with our entire force."

(According to) Abū Mikhnaf—Tulayd b. Zayd b. Rāshid al-Fā'isī told me that his father was with Abū al-Rawwāgh that day. He said: Abū al-Rawwāgh told us, "When Maʿqil b. Qays sent me ahead of him, he, indeed, ordered me to follow them, and when I caught up with them not to be in a hurry to fight

207. C reads: *khubz*, "bread."

them until he joined me." All his men then answered him, "So matters are clear now. Draw us aside,[208] so we may be near them until our leader reaches us." He then had us draw aside—that was in the evening.

We spent the entire night on guard until morning. At mid-
[47] morning they came out against us. So we went out to meet them. There were three hundred of them and three hundred of us. When they advanced and assaulted us, by God, none of us withstood them. We were put to flight for a while, but then Abū al-Rawwāgh shouted to us, "O horsemen of evil, may God shame you the rest of today! Return! Return!" At that, he attacked, and we attacked with him. When we drew near the folk, he wheeled us about and we turned away, while they turned to attack us.[209] They got the better of us for a long time. We were on excellent trained horses; none of us was hit, and our wounds were slight. Abū al-Rawwāgh then told us, "May your mothers be bereaved of you! Let us turn away and wheel around close to them. Let us not separate from them until our commander arrives. For it would be more disgraceful for us to return to the army having been put to flight by our enemy, without having withstood them until the battle had become fierce and many of you had died fighting."

At that, one of our men answered him, "God will not be ashamed of the truth. By God, they routed us." Abū al-Rawwāgh responded, "May God not increase your kind among us! If we don't leave the battle, we won't be routed. As long as we are engaged in close combat with them and keep near them, we will be in good shape until the army arrives. That is, provided we do not turn back, by God, lest it be said, 'Abū Ḥumrān b. Bujayr al-Hamdānī was routed.' I would only care if it is said, 'Abū al-Rawwāgh was routed.' So stay close, and if they come to you, and you can't fight them, then withdraw. And if they attack you, and you are unable to fight them, stay a while, then withdraw to a safe place. When they return against you,

208. C adds: "but not leave our position."

209. The text reads: *karrū ʿalaynā*; C reads: *kabarū*, "they were too difficult for us."

engage them in close combat and keep near them, for the army will arrive in a while."

Whenever the Khārijites were charged, they began to withdraw, and took a defensive position. When they began to counterattack, and their group broke up, Abū al-Rawwāgh and his men pursued them on horseback. The Khārijites saw that they would not break off from them, having pursued them thus from the early morning until the first time of worship. When it was time for the noon worship, al-Mustawrid dismounted to worship, and Abū al-Rawwāgh and his men withdrew a *mīl*[210] or two away. His men dismounted and performed noon worship, while they appointed two men to stand guard. They held their position until they performed afternoon worship. [48]

A youth then brought them a dispatch from Maʿqil b. Qays to Abū al-Rawwāgh. The villagers and passers-by on the road would pass by them and see them fighting. Those who left them heading in the direction from which Maʿqil was coming, met Maʿqil and informed him about his men's encounter with the Khārijites. He would ask, "How do you think they are doing?" They would reply, "We think the Ḥarūriyyah are driving off your men." So he would inquire, "Do you think my men are engaged in close combat with them, and are fighting them?" They would answer, "Yes, they are engaged in close combat with them and are being routed." So he said, "If my opinion of Abū al-Rawwāgh was correct, he would never approach you having been routed." Then Maʿqil halted them, and sent for Muḥriz b. Shihāb b. Bujayr b. Sufyān b. Khālid b. Minqar al-Tamīmī, and said to him, "Stay behind with the weak people, then set out with them slowly until you reach me." Then he called out to the able-bodied, "Everyone who is able-bodied hurry along with me. Hasten to your brothers for they have encountered their enemy, and I hope that God will destroy the enemy before you reach them."

Maʿqil gathered some seven hundred able-bodied, stalwart men, people with excellent horses, and set out hurriedly. When

---

210. The *mīl* was four thousand standard *dhirāʿ*, or two km. See Hinz, *Islamische Masse und Gewichte*, 63.

[49] he approached Abū al-Rawwāgh, the latter said, "This cavalry is covered with dust. Let us advance towards our enemy so that the army will reach us while we are near them. Thus they won't see that we withdraw from them or fear them." Abū al-Rawwāgh then advanced until he halted opposite al-Mustawrid and his companions, and Maʿqil joined them with his men. When he had drawn near them, the sun set, so he dismounted and worshipped with his men, and Abū al-Rawwāgh dismounted and worshipped with his men on the other side, while the Khārijites worshipped as well. Then Maʿqil b. Qays advanced with his men. When he came up to Abū al-Rawwāgh, he summoned him. When the latter came, Maʿqil told him, "Well done, Abū al-Rawwāgh. You have a reputation for steadfastness and persistence." He replied, "May God cause you to prosper. They are tough and disagreeable, so don't get close to them yourself, but send[211] someone to fight them in front of you. You, yourself, stay behind the people in support of them." At that, Maʿqil remarked, "What an excellent idea you have." By God, no sooner had he said it than they charged him and his men.[212] When they came upon Maʿqil, most of his men broke away from him in fear, but he stood firm, and dismounting, he shouted, "The ground! The ground! O people of Islām!" Abū al-Rawwāgh al-Shākirī and many of the horsemen and guards, some two hundred men, dismounted with him. When al-Mustawrid and his companions came upon them, they met them with lances and swords, Maʿqil's cavalry having broken away in panic temporarily. Then Miskīn b. ʿĀmir b. Unayf b. Shurayḥ b. ʿAmr b. ʿUdas, who was among the most courageous and bravest people that day, shouted to them saying, "O people of Islām! Where would you flee while your commander has dismounted? Aren't you ashamed? Indeed flight is disgraceful, dishonorable, and base." Then he returned to the attack and a
[50] large troop of cavalry returned with him and assaulted the Khārijites. Meanwhile Maʿqil b. Qays fought the latter under his banner with those steadfast people who had dismounted with

211. C reads: "select."
212. C adds: "and he stood firm."

him. Together they assaulted the Khārijites until they forced them to the houses. Shortly thereafter Muḥriz b. Shihāb joined them with the people who had stayed behind. When they arrived, Ma'qil had them dismount. Then he formed them into a line, with a right and a left wing. He put Abū al-Rawwāgh in charge of the right wing and Muḥriz b. Bujayr b. Sufyān in charge of the left wing, while Miskīn b. 'Āmir was in charge of the cavalry. Then he told them, "Do not leave your battle lines until morning, and when morning comes, let us rise up against them and do battle with them." The people thus remained at their stations in their battle lines.

(According to) Abū Mikhnaf—'Abd al-Raḥmān b. Jundab—'Abdallāh b. 'Uqbah al-Ghanawī: When Ma'qil b. Qays caught up with us, al-Mustawrid told us, "Don't leave Ma'qil alone so that he can marshal the cavalry and infantry against you. Assault them in earnest. Perhaps God will bring him down thereby." At that, we attacked them in earnest. They were defeated and scattered, and then broke in panic. However, Ma'qil leapt from his horse when he saw the flight of his men, and raised his banner, and some of his men dismounted with him. They fought for a long time, and they held their own against us. Then they summoned each other against us and pressed upon us from every side. So we retreated until we had the houses at our backs. We had fought them for a long time, but only a few of us were wounded and killed.

(According to) Abū Mikhnaf—Ḥuṣayrah b. 'Abdallāh—his father: 'Umayr b. Abī Ashā'ah al-Azdī was killed that day. He was a leader, and he was among those who dismounted with Ma'qil b. Qays. I was among those who dismounted with him. By God![213] I shall not forget the words of 'Umayr b. Abī Ashā'ah [51]
while we were fighting together, and he was striking them boldly with his sword:

She knew that I—when they scattered
From me, and the base, the low [were] tormented and tarnished[214]—

213. C reads: "By Him Who has my soul in His hand."
214. The text reads: *wuḍḍa'u*; C reads: *ruḍḍa'u*, "ignoble.

[Am] a courageous man, more imposing, for whom fear[215] is insignificant.

He fought fiercely. I never saw anyone fight like him. He wounded many men and was killed. I only know that he killed one person whom he had seized by the neck. ʿUmayr fell upon the man's chest and slaughtered him. While he was cutting off the man's head, one of their men attacked him and thrust his lance through the hollow of ʿUmayr's throat. He fell down from the man's chest and lay dead on the ground. We assaulted them and drove them back to the village, before withdrawing to our battlefield. I then went to ʿUmayr hoping that a spark of life was still in him, but he had expired. So I returned to my companions and remained with them.

(According to) Abū Mikhnaf—ʿAbd al-Raḥmān b. Jundab—ʿAbdallāh b. ʿUqbah al-Ghanawī: We had stationed ourselves in the early part of the night when a man came to us whom we had dispatched at the beginning of the night. Some of those who passed by on the road had informed us that an army was approaching us from al-Baṣrah, but we had paid no attention. We said to a local man whom we employed, "Go and find out if an army has come against us from the direction of al-Baṣrah." He returned while we were waiting for the Kūfans, and told us, "Yes, Sharīk b. al-Aʿwar has come to you. I met a squadron a
[52] *farsakh*[216] (six km) away at the time of the first (morning) worship. I don't think they will camp where you are until tonight or early tomorrow morning." We were bewildered at his words. Al-Mustawrid then said to his companions, "What do you think?" We replied, "We think as you do." He said, "I don't think that I can resist all of them. Let us return in the direction from which we came. The Baṣrans will not pursue us into the territory of al-Kūfah. Only the people of our own city will pursue us then." We then asked him, "Why is that?" And he replied, "Fighting the people of one city is easier for us than fighting the people of both." We responded "Lead us wherever you like." He said, "Dismount so your animals may rest a

215. The text reads: *rawʿ*; C reads: *hayj*, "combat."
216. A *farsakh* was three *mīl* or six km. See Hinz, *Islamische Masse und Gewichte*, 62.

while, and feed them; then pay attention to what I command you to do."

At that, we dismounted and fed our animals. Then there was a respite for a while between us and the Kūfans. They had withdrawn from the village for fear that we would attack them at night. When we had rested our mounts and fed them, al-Mustawrid gave the order and we mounted our animals. Then he said, "Enter the village, then leave at the rear of it, taking a lout [*ʿilj*] with you who will bring you out the back way. Then he will double back with you until he brings you back to the road by which you came. Leave [Maʿqil's men] where they are; they will not notice you for most of the night or until morning." Then we entered the village. After taking a lout, we left with him leading us, and said, "Take us around behind this line so that we may return to the road by which we came." He did so, bringing us back until we stood on the road by which we had come. Then we returned by that road and advanced until we halted at Jarjarāyā.

(According to) Abū Mikhnaf—Ḥuṣayrah b. ʿAbdallāh—his father ʿAbdallāh b. al-Ḥārith: I was the first one who noticed their departure.[217] I said, "May God make you prosper. Dealing with this enemy has made me suspicious for a long while. They were stationed; we saw their shape. Then it disappeared [53]
after a while. I fear that they are abandoning their position in order to deceive the people." At that, Maʿqil inquired, "What do you fear their strategem is?" I replied, "I fear that they will attack the people at night." When he answered, "By God, I do not feel safe from that," I told him to be prepared for it. He responded, "Stay as you are until I take a look. O ʿAttāb, set out with whomever you like so that you may get close to the village, and observe whether you see any of them or hear word of them.[218] Ask the villagers about them." At that he went off with a fifth of the raiders galloping until he observed the village. He began to notice that no one spoke to him. When he shouted to the villagers, some of them came out to him. So he

217. The text reads: *dhahābihim*; O reads: *dahā'ihim*, "their cunning."
218. Cairo reads: "hear a sound from them."

asked them about the Khārijites, and they replied, "They left, and we don't know how they went."

When ʿAttāb returned to Maʿqil and told him the news, Maʿqil said, "I don't feel safe from night attacks. Where are the Muḍar?" So the Muḍar came, and he said, "Stay here." Then he asked, "Where are the Rabīʿah?" He set the Rabīʿah, the Tamīm, and the Hamdān facing different directions, while the rest of the Yaman faced another direction. Each of those quarters faced a different direction while its back was near the back of the other quarter. Maʿqil made rounds among them until he had stopped at every quarter, saying, "O people, if they come to you, let the others know, and fight them. Don't abandon your position under any circumstances until you receive my order. None of you is to abandon his sector until morning. Then we shall see what we think." They remained on guard until morning, fearing a night attack by the Khārijites. When morning came, they dismounted and worshipped. People came and told them that the Khārijites had returned by the road on which they had come, going back to their starting point.

Sharīk b. al-Aʿwar arrived with an army of Baṣrans and dismounted where Maʿqil b. Qays was. He met Sharīk, and they questioned each other for a while. Then Maʿqil told Sharīk, "I am going to follow in their track until I overtake them. Per-
[54] haps God will destroy them, but I am not certain that, if I fail to search for them, their [numbers] will not multiply." Sharīk then got up and assembled some of his outstanding men, including Khālid b. Maʿdān al-Ṭāʾī and Bayhas b. Ṣuhayb al-Jarmī. He proposed to them, "O men, would you like to go with our Kūfan brothers in search of this common enemy of ours until God annihilates them? Then we will return." At that, Khālid b. Maʿdān and Bayhas al-Jarmī replied, "No, by God! We won't do it. We approached them to drive them out from our territory, and to prevent them from entering it. God spare us their inconvenience! We are going back to our city. It is for the Kūfans to defend their own territory from these dogs." He responded, "Woe unto you! Obey me with regard to them, for they are evil folk. There are wages and favor with the regime[219]

219. C reads: "with God."

for you in fighting them." Bayhas al-Jarmī then told him, "By God! then we are as the brother of the Banū Kinānah[220] said:

Like a wet-nurse for other's children who lets
her own sons perish, so she doesn't patch her tatters thereby.

Haven't you heard that the Kurds have rebelled in the mountains of Fārs?" Sharīk replied, "I have heard that." Bayhas continued, "So you order us to go off with you to protect the territory of the Kūfans, to fight their enemy, and to abandon our land." Sharīk responded, "What are the Kurds? Indeed a squadron of you will be enough for them." At that, Bayhas retorted, "And a squadron of Kūfans will be sufficient for this enemy whom you appoint us to deal with. Upon my life! If they were obliged to help us, then we would have to help them, but they don't need us any more. There is strife in our territory similar to that in theirs. Let them take care of what is before them, and we must do likewise. Upon my life! If we obey you with regard [55] to pursuing them, and you pursue them, you will have made bold with your commander. You did what was proper. You should find out his opinion about what he permits you to do."

When he saw that, Sharīk said to his companions: "Go and depart." And he went himself to meet Maʿqil—both of them were sympathetic to Shīʿite views. Sharīk said, "Indeed, by God, I have tried to get those who are with me to follow me so that I can march with you against your enemy, but they prevailed over me." Maʿqil replied, "May God do as much for you. We don't need that. Indeed, by God, had they made an effort, I hope none of them[221] would have escaped to tell the tale."

(According to) Abū Mikhnaf—al-Ṣaqʿab b. Zuhayr—Abū Imāmah ʿUbaydallāh[222] b. Junādah—Sharīk b. al-Aʿwar: When he said, "By God, had they made an effort, I hope none of them would have escaped to tell the tale," by God, I detested it. I felt sorry for him, and considered[223] such talk[224] to be wrong. By

220. That is, Ibn Jadhl al-Ṭiʿān al-Kinānī. See Jāḥiẓ, *Hayawān*, I, 197; Buḥturī, *Hamāsah*, 171; Marzūqī, *Sharḥ Dīwān al-Hamāsah*, 736.
221. That probably is, the Khārijites.
222. C reads: Abū Ramlah ʿAbdallāh.
223. The text reads: *ḥasibtu*; O reads: *khashaytu*, "I feared."
224. The text reads: *shibh*; C reads: *sabab*, "the reason for."

God, there were no unjust people among us.

(According to) Abū Mikhnaf—Ḥuṣayrah b. ʿAbdallāh—his father, ʿAbdallāh al-Ḥārith al-Azdī: We were happy when we learned that al-Mustawrid b. ʿUllifah and his companions had doubled back, saying, "Let's pursue them and confront them at al-Madā'in, and if they draw near to al-Kūfah it would be even more destructive for them. Maʿqil b. Qays then summoned Abū al-Rawwāgh, telling him, "Pursue him with the men who were with you [before] and pin him down for me until I catch up with you."[225] He said, "Give me more men than that, for it will make me stronger against the Khārijites if they want to fight with me before your arrival. We have had trouble with them." Maʿqil then increased his force by three hundred men. Abū al-Rawwāgh thus pursued the enemy with six hundred men.

The Khārijites advanced rapidly until they halted at Jarjarāyā. Abū al-Rawwāgh also advanced quickly on their heels until he caught up with them at Jarjarāyā where they had camped. He also camped there at sunrise. When they saw that it was Abū al-Rawwāgh with the vanguard, they told each other, "Fighting these will be easier than fighting whoever comes after them." They came out against us, sending ten and twenty of their horsemen at a time. We did likewise, and the two troops attacked each other for a while, being mingled together. When they saw that, the Khārijites united and assaulted us in earnest with a single charge. They drove us back until we left the field to them. Then Abū al-Rawwāgh called to his men saying, "O evil horsemen! O evil defenders! How miserably you fought the folk. To me! To me!" He then prevailed upon about one hundred horsemen and engaged the Khārijites in close combat, while saying:

Indeed the youth, every youth, who is not dismayed,
when the coward turned away from the blow of the spear point,
She knew that I, when the injury alighted,
would frighten, on the day of battle, a bold hero.

---

225. C reads: "follow you."

When he engaged with them, he fought them for a long time. Then his men engaged them from every side, fighting earnestly with them until they drove the enemy back to their former position. When al-Mustawrid and his companions saw that, they thought that if Maʿqil came to them at that time, he would certainly destroy them. So al-Mustawrid and his companions departed until they crossed the Tigris and entered the territory of [57]
Bahurasīr. Abū al-Rawwāgh crossed after them and pursued them, and Maʿqil b. Qays arrived, following Abū al-Rawwāgh, and crossed the Tigris after him. Al-Mustawrid advanced towards al-Madīnah al-ʿAtīqah, but when Simāk b. ʿUbayd learned of that, he went out and crossed over to it. Then he brought out his men and the people of al-Madāʾin. He lined them up at (the city) gate, and set archers on the wall. When the Khārijites learned of that, they went off until they halted at Sābāṭ.[226] Abū al-Rawwāgh also advanced in search of the folk until he passed Simāk b. ʿUbayd at al-Madāʾin. When the latter informed him of the direction which they had taken, Abū al-Rawwāgh pursued them until he halted where they were at Sābāṭ.

(According to) Abū Mikhnaf—ʿAbd al-Raḥmān b. Ḥabīb—ʿAbdallāh b. ʿUqbah al-Ghanawī: When Abū al-Rawwāgh halted where we were, al-Mustawrid summoned his companions, saying, "These men who have halted here with Abū al-Rawwāgh are the noble companions of Maʿqil. By God, he only sent his defenders and horsemen ahead against you. By God, if I knew that when I hurried to him, racing with these men of his,[227] I would take Maʿqil by surprise while they were still some way off,[228] I would do so. Let one of you go out, and ask about Maʿqil. Where is he and how far has he gotten?"

I went out myself and met some louts who came from the direction of al-Madāʾin. I asked them, "What have you heard

---

226. Sābāt was a bridgehead on the Kūfan side of the Nahr al-Malik, near the point where that canal emptied into the Tigris, on the main road from al-Kūfah to al-Madāʾin. See El-ʿAlī, "Madāʾin," 435; Yāqūt, *Muʿjam*, IV, 569.

227. The text reads: *bādartu aṣḥabahu hāʾulāʾi ilayhi.*

228. The text reads: *yuqārifūhu bi-sāʿatin*; O and Cairo read: *yufāriqūhu bi-sāʿatin*, "were still some distance [lit. "a while"] away from him." See text, p. [62].

about Maʿqil b. Qays?" They replied, "A messenger came to Simāk b. ʿUbayd from Maʿqil. Simāk had sent him to meet Maʿqil, and to see how far he had gotten and where he wished to halt. The messenger returned to Simāk and said 'I left him camping at Daylamāyā' "[229]—it is one of the villages of Bahurasīr on an inlet[230] of the Tigris which belonged to Qudāmah b. al-ʿAjlān al-Azdī. I asked him, "How far is this place between
[58] us and them?" They responded, "Three *farsakhs* [eighteen km] or thereabouts."

When I returned to my master and told him the news, he said to his companions, "Ride!" So they did, and al-Mustawrid advanced until he brought them to the Sābāṭ Bridge. This was the bridge over the Nahr al-Malik.[231] He was on the side of the bridge leading toward al-Kūfah, while Abū al-Rawwāgh and his men were on the side leading toward al-Mada'in. We advanced until we stopped at the bridge. Then al-Mustawrid told us, "Let a detachment of you halt." So when about fifty of us halted, he said, "Cut this bridge." So we dismounted and cut it. When Abū al-Rawwāgh's men saw us stopping on horseback, they thought that we wanted to cross over to them. They lined up opposite us and marshalled themselves thereby distracting us from our cutting of the bridge.

We then took a guide from the people of Sābāṭ and told him, "Lead us to Daylamāyā." So he led us, moving quickly, and off we went with our horses taking us swiftly[232] at the amble and the gallop. Shortly afterwards we looked down upon Maʿqil and his men while they were getting underway. When he saw us his men had already separated from him and his vanguard and men were not with him. One squadron of them had been summoned and another squadron had withdrawn. They were taken by surprise. Upon seeing us, Maʿqil set up his standard and dismounted, calling out, "O servants of God! The ground! The

229. C reads: *Dīlmayāthā.*

230. The text reads: *jānit*; Cairo reads: *jānib,* "beside."

231. The Nahr al-Malik was a canal linking the Euphrates and Tigris Rivers, west of al-Madā'in. See Le Strange, *Lands,* 68.

232. The text reads: *talmaʿu binā,* lit. "flashing us"; C reads: *ḥatta balagha binā,* "until our horses brought us."

ground!" At that, about two hundred men dismounted with him.

When we began to attack them, they met us with the tips of their lances, while kneeling on their knees, and we could not overpower them. Al-Mustawrid then said to us, "Leave these alone since they have dismounted, and attack their horses so that you may come between them and their horses. If you strike their horses, they will be [like] slaughter-camels for you after a while." So we attacked their horses, separating them [59] from the men and cutting their reins. They had tied the horses together, but they now went off in all directions. Then we turned against the people, who were withdrawing[233] and advancing.[234] We attacked them so that we divided them up. Then we advanced toward Ma'qil b. Qays and his men, who were still on their knees. We attacked them, but they did not budge. We attacked them again, but they still did not budge.[235]

At that, al-Mustawrid told us, "Fight them at close quarters. Half of you take the field against them." Half of us dismounted and the rest remained on horseback with him. I was among those on horseback. By God, we wanted to get at them. By God, we fought them, and we believed we had overwhelmed them when the vanguard[236] of Abū al-Rawwāgh's men, who were his noble companions and horsemen, burst upon us. Upon drawing near, they charged us, and at that we all dismounted, and fought them until our master and theirs were both hit. I don't believe there was anyone who escaped from them on that day except me. By God, I believe I was the youngest man there.

(According to) Abū Mikhnaf—'Abd al-Raḥmān b. Ḥabīb—'Abdallāh b. 'Uqbah al-Ghanawī: My informant related this account to me on two occasions, once during the governorship of Muṣ'ab b. al-Zubayr[237] at Bājumayrā, and once while we were

233. The text reads: *mutazaḥḥilīn*; C reads: *mutarajjalīn*, "going on foot."

234. The text reads: *mutaqaddamīn*; C reads: *munfariqīn*, "separating."

235. C reads: "They did not budge, so we attacked them, but they were steadfast. Then we attacked them again, but they were steadfast."

236. O reads: "reinforcements from their vanguard."

237. Muṣ'ab b. al-Zubayr was governor of al-Baṣrah, 67–72(686–91).

with ʿAbd al-Raḥmān b. Muḥammad b. al-Ashʿath[238] at Dayr al-Jamājim.[239] He said, "By God, he was killed that day at Dayr al-
[60] Jamājim, the day of the rout, while I saw him coming against the enemy, striking them with his sword." I said to him at Dayr al-Jamājim, "You related this account to me at Bājumayrā with Muṣʿab b. al-Zubayr, but I did not ask you how you [alone] escaped among your companions." He replied, "I tell you, by God, when our master was killed, all except five or six of his men were killed."

He continued: We assaulted a group of about twenty men of the enemy until they gave way. I reached a horse standing with its saddle and bridle on it. I did not know what the story was with its master, whether he had been killed, or had dismounted to fight and left it. I went up to it and, taking its bridle, I put my foot in the stirrup and seated myself firmly upon it. By God, Maʿqil's men assaulted me, and reached me, but when I touched the side of the horse, by God, it was better than serviceable. Some of them[240] galloped after me, but they did not keep up with me. I then proceeded, galloping the horse, and that was in the evening. When I knew that I had discouraged them, and felt safe, I began to ride (at a) trot. I continued at that pace, and when I met a lout, I told him, "Lead me quickly to where I can leave the main road, the Kūfah Road." He did so, and, by God, shortly afterwards I reached Kūthā. I went on until I came to a wide part of the river. I plunged the horse into it and crossed it. Then I rode onward. When I came to Dayr Kaʿb, I halted. I hobbled my horse and let him rest, and took a nap myself. Then I awoke quickly and mounted upon the horse. Thus I traveled for part of the night, (rested), and spent the rest of the night travelling. I worshipped in the early morning at al-

238. ʿAbd al-Raḥmān b. Muḥammad b. al-Ashʿath b. Qays al-Kindī was to lead a major revolt against al-Ḥajjāj, 80–82(699–701) or 83(703) See *EI*², s.v. Ibn al-Ashʿath.

239. Dayr al-Jamājim, the "monastery of the skulls", was the place near al-Kūfah where al-Ḥajjāj defeated Ibn al-Ashʿath for the first time in Shaʿbān 82 (September 701). See Yāqūt, *Muʿjam*, II, 652; and *EI*² s.v. Ibn al-Ashʿath.

240. C reads: "a group of them."

Muzāḥimiyyah, two *farsakhs* (twelve km) distant from Qubbayn.[241]

I then proceeded until I entered al-Kūfah in broad daylight. After a while I came to Sharīk b. Namlah al-Muḥāribī, and I informed him about myself and about his companions. I also asked him to meet al-Mughīrah b. Shuʿbah and get a guarantee of safe-conduct from him for me. He told me, "You will obtain the guarantee of safe-conduct, God willing, and you have come with good news." By God, I spent the night grieved by the affairs of the people. Sharīk b. Namlah al-Muḥāribī went quickly until he came to al-Mughīrah, asked his permission (to enter), and was admitted. Sharīk said, "I have good news and a request, so grant my request and then I shall announce my good news to you." Al-Mughīrah replied, "Your request is granted, so give your good news." Sharīk continued, "Grant a guarantee of safe-conduct to ʿAbdallāh b. ʿUqbah al-Ghanawī, for he was with the folk." He answered, "I grant him a guarantee of safe-conduct. By God, I wish that you would bring me all of them so that I could grant them a guarantee of safe-conduct." Sharīk said, "I announce that all of the folk have been killed. My friend was with the folk, and according to what he told me, none of them but he escaped." Al-Mughīrah asked, "So how did Maʿqil b. Qays do?" Sharīk replied, "May God cause you to prosper, he doesn't know anything about our companions." [61]

Before he had finished his speech, Abū al-Rawwāgh and Miskīn b. ʿĀmir b. Unayf arrived bringing good news of the victory. They related that Maʿqil b. Qays and al-Mustawrid b. ʿUllifah each sent against his opponent, a lance in al-Mustawrid's hand and a sword in Maʿqil's hand. Thus they encountered each other, and when al-Mustawrid thrust his lance at Maʿqil's breast so that the spearhead went out his back, Maʿqil struck him with the sword on his head so that it sank into the midst of his brain. Thus they both fell dead.

(According to) Abū Mikhnaf—Ḥuṣayrah b. ʿAbdallāh—his father: When al-Mustawrid b. ʿUllifah saw us halting at Sābāṭ

241. Qubbayn was a village just across the bridge of Sūrā. See Yāqūt, *Muʿjam*, IV, 35.

where he was, he approached the bridge and cut it. We were thinking that he wanted to cross to us. We went up from the dark cultivated land of Sābāṭ to the desert that was between al-
[62] Madā'in and Sābāṭ. We were arrayed and deployed. But we waited a long time without seeing them coming out to us. Abū al-Rawwāgh then said, "Indeed they are up to something. Is there someone who will inform us about them?" At that, I said, "I and Wuhayb b. Abū Ashā' al-Azdī will inform you about that and bring you news about them." When both of us went close to the bridge on our horses and found it severed, we supposed that the folk had only cut it out of fear of us and out of alarm at us. We then returned galloping quickly until we reached our master and informed him about what we saw. Abū al-Rawwāgh asked, "What do you suppose?" We replied, "They only cut the bridge in fear of us and out of alarm at us which God put in their hearts." He remarked, "By my life! The folk did not rebel[242] desiring flight, but they have deceived you. Do you hear? By God, I certainly think they said that Maʿqil sent Abū Rawwāgh against you only with his noble companions. If you could leave the latter where they are and make a forced march[243] toward Maʿqil and his men, you may find them peacefully unguarded when you come upon them. Thus they cut the bridge in order to divert you from catching up with them until they come upon your commander by surprise. To the rescue! Rescue lies in searching." We took it to heart that it was as he had said. We shouted to the people of the village, and when they came quickly, we told them, "Tie the bridge quickly." We urged them on, and in a short while they were finished with it. Then we crossed over it and pursued (the enemy) quickly without caring about anything else. We kept after them, and, by God, we did not cease to ask about them. We were told, "So far they have been ahead of you."

By God, we did not cease to seek them fervently, desiring to
[63] catch up with them, until the first person who fled from them met us. Maʿqil's men had been routed without one person caring about another. When Abū al-Rawwāgh met them, he

242. O reads: "gather."
243. C reads: "begin to march."

shouted to the people, "To me! To me!" The people came to him and took refuge with him. He then said, "Woe unto you! Why are you coming?" They replied, "We don't know. We were certainly surprised. The folk were with us among our army while we were separated from each other. For they assaulted us and split us up." Abū al-Rawwāgh asked, "What did the commander do?" Someone told him, "He dismounted and was fighting." Someone else said, "I certainly saw him killed." Abū al-Rawwāgh told them, "O People! Return with me. If we reach our commander alive, we shall fight along with him. And if we find that he has perished, we shall fight them. For we are horsemen of the people of the city selected for this enemy. Let neither the opinion of your commander, nor those of the people of the city about you be spoiled[244] there. I swear by God, if you should see the Khārijites after they had killed Maʿqil, it would not be proper for you to disengage from them until you take revenge on them or perish. Set out with God's blessing." He then set out and we did likewise. He began to shout to each person he met, bringing him back. He summoned his outstanding men, saying, "Strike the faces of the people and turn them back."

We advanced turning the people back until we reached the army. Suddenly we were where the standard of Maʿqil b. Qays was set up. Two hundred or more cavalrymen of the people were with him while their outstanding men were only with them on foot. They were fighting the fiercest battle that people ever heard of. When we burst upon them, suddenly we were among the Khārijites who had almost overwhelmed our companions, while the latter, holding out against that, were fighting them. When they saw us, they returned to the attack, and then assaulted the Khārijites. The Khārijites withdrew a short [64] distance from them, and we reached our companions.

Abū al-Rawwāgh looked at Maʿqil, and saw that he was summoning, encouraging, and inciting his men. He asked Maʿqil, "Are you alive? May all my uncles be your ransom." He replied that he was and then assaulted the folk. At that, Abū al-Rawwāgh called out to his men, "Don't you see your com-

244. The text reads: *yafsudanna*; O reads: *yuqbalna*, "be disapproved."

mander is alive? Assault the folk!" He attacked and we attacked the folk all together. We delivered a jolting shock to their cavalry, while Maʿqil and his men assaulted them.

At that, al-Mustawrid dismounted and shouted to his companions, "O band of Sellers! The ground! The ground! By God, besides Whom there is no god save He, Paradise belongs to whomever is killed with the genuine intention of *jihād* against these oppressors and their expression of enmity." They all dismounted then, and we did likewise. We then advanced against al-Mustawrid with unsheathed swords and clashed with them[245] for much of the day. It was as violent as any battle the people had ever fought. However al-Mustawrid called out to Maʿqil, saying, "O Maʿqil, show yourself to me!" So Maʿqil went out to him, and we said to Maʿqil, "We implore you not to go out against this dog of whose soul God has despaired." He replied, "No, by God, no man ever challenged me to a duel that I shrank from." So he marched against him with a sword while the other went out against him with a lance. We shouted to Maʿqil to meet his opponent with a lance like his but he refused. Al-Mustawrid approached him and transfixed him so that the spearhead went out his back, while Maʿqil struck him with his sword so that it sank into the midst of his (opponent's) brain. Al-Mustawrid fell down dead, and Maʿqil was killed.

Maʿqil had said to us when he showed himself to al-Mustawrid, "If I perish, your commander is to be ʿAmr b. Muḥriz b. Shihāb al-Saʿdī, then al-Minqarī"[246] So when Maʿqil perished, ʿAmr b. Muḥriz took the standard, and said, "If I am killed, Abū al-Rawwāgh is to be in charge of you, and if Abū al-Rawwāgh is killed, your commander is to be Miskīn b. ʿĀmir b.
[65] Unayf," who at that time was a raw youth. Then he charged with his standard and ordered the people to assault the enemy. Before long they had killed the Khārijites.

The events of this year included the appointment of ʿAbdallāh b. Khāzim b. Ẓabyān as governor of Khurāsān by ʿAbdallāh b. ʿĀmir, and the departure of Qays b. al-Haytham from that post. According to what Abū Mikhnaf reported from Muqātil b.

245. That is, with the swords.
246. That is, belonging to the Minqarī subdivision of the Banū Saʿd.

Ḥayyān, the cause of that was that Ibn ʿĀmir wanted to dismiss Qays b. al-Haytham because he considered him to be slow in (delivering) the tax revenues. Ibn Khāzim told him, "Appoint me governor of Khurāsān, and I will satisfy you with regard to it and with regard to Qays b. al-Haytham." Qays learned that Ibn ʿĀmir disapproved of him because of his contempt for him and his suspension of gifts, and that he had appointed Ibn Khāzim governor. When he feared that Ibn Khāzim would make trouble for him and go over his accounts, he abandoned Khurāsān and approached (Ibn ʿĀmir at al-Baṣrah). As a result, Ibn ʿĀmir's anger at him increased, and he said, "You abandoned the frontier region." He beat and imprisoned Qays and sent a man belonging to the Banū Yashkur to be in charge of Khurāsān. (According to) Abū Mikhnaf: Ibn ʿĀmir sent Aslam b. Zurʿah al-Kilābī when he dismissed Qays b. Al-Haytham.

(According to) ʿAlī b. Muḥammad—Abū ʿAbd al-Raḥmān al-Thaqafī—his shaykhs: Ibn ʿĀmir put Qays b. al-Haytham in charge of Khurāsān during the rule of Muʿāwiyah. Ibn Khāzim told Ibn ʿĀmir, "You sent a weak man to Khurāsān. I fear that if he encounters war that he will be put to flight with the people. You would thus destroy Khurāsān, and your uncles[247] would be dishonored." Ibn ʿĀmir asked, "What would you suggest?" He replied, "Write a pledge for me that if Qays abandons your enemy I will take his place." Ibn ʿĀmir wrote that for him. When a group from Ṭukhāristān[248] rose up, Qays b. al- [66]
Haytham sought advice, and Ibn Khāzim advised him to draw back (his forces) until his outposts joined him. Thereupon, he drew back. When he had marched one or two days' journey from his position, Ibn Khāzim made his pledge public, took over the affairs of the people, encountered the enemy, and put them to flight. The news reached the two cities[249] and Syria. At that, the Qaysiyyah[250] became angry, saying, "Ibn Khāzim deceived Qays and Ibn ʿĀmir." Their anger increased until they complained to Muʿāwiyah. When the latter sent for Ibn Khā-

247. That is, Ibn ʿĀmir's family.

248. Ṭukhāristān is the region to the south of the upper Oxus River. See Le Strange, *lands*, 426–7.

249. That is, al-Baṣrah and al-Kūfah.

250. That is, the faction of Qays b. Haytham.

zim, he came and apologized for what was said about him. Muʿāwiyah told him, "Stand up and apologize to the people tomorrow." Ibn Khāzim returned to his companions and said, "Indeed, I was put in charage of the sermon (*khuṭbah*), but I am not a master of speech. So sit around the pulpit (*minbar*), and when I speak, show your approval." He then stood up on the morrow and after praising and extolling God, he spoke, "Indeed, a leader of worship (*imām*) must either deliver the sermon, finding no escape from it, or he stupidly pours [it] out from his head heedless of what goes forth from him. I am neither kind. Whoever is acquainted with me knows that I am aware of opportunities, leaping at them, stopping at dangers, penetrating with the raiding party, and distributing with equality. I implore you, by God, whoever has known that about me, say that I am right." His companions around the pulpit responded, "You are right." He then said, "O Commander of the Faithful, indeed, you are among those I implored. Say what you know." Muʿāwiyah replied, "You are right."

(According to) ʿAlī—a shaykh of the Banū Tamīm called Muʿammar—some knowledgeable people: Qays b. al-Haytham came to Ibn ʿĀmir from Khurāsān unwillingly because of Ibn Khāzim. So Ibn ʿĀmir beat him one hundred (times), shaved him, and imprisoned him. When his mother interceded for him, he released him.

[67] According to what is said, Marwān b. al-Ḥakam led the people in the pilgrimage this year, while he was in charge of al-Madīnah. Khālid b. al-ʿĀṣ b. Hishām was in charge of Mecca and al-Mughīrah b. Shuʿbah was in charge of al-Kūfah, while Shurayḥ was in charge of rendering judgment. ʿAbdallāh b. ʿĀmir was in charge of al-Baṣrah, Fārs, Sijistān, and Khurāsān, while ʿUmayr b. Yathribī was in charge of rendering judgment there.[251]

251. Most probably at al-Baṣrah. C reads: *quḍā'i Baṣratan*, "rendering judgment at al-Baṣrah."

The Events of the Year 44

(April 4, 664–March 24, 665)

Among the events that occured during this year was the invasion of Byzantine territory by the Muslims led by ʿAbd al-Raḥmān b. al-Walīd, their winter campaign there, and Busr b. Abī Arṭāt's raid at sea.

In this year Muʿāwiyah also dismissed ʿAbdallāh b. ʿĀmir (as governor) of al-Baṣrah. The reason for this was that Ibn ʿĀmir was easy-going and generous and would not restrain the impudent. Al-Baṣrah was ruined because of that while he was governor there for Muʿāwiyah. (According to) ʿUmar b. Shabbah —Yazīd al-Bāhilī: Ibn ʿĀmir complained to Ziyād about the corruption of the people and the manifestation of evildoing. When Ziyād advised, "Unleash the sword among them," Ibn ʿĀmir responded, "Indeed, I hate to reform them by my own corruption."

(According to) ʿUmar—Abū al-Ḥasan: Ibn ʿĀmir was gentle and easy-going, governing smoothly; he would not punish (anyone) during his regime, nor cut off (the hand of) a thief. When he was spoken to about that, he replied, "I am on intimate terms with the people. How can I look at a man whose father's or brother's hand I have cut off?"

(According to) ʿUmar—ʿAlī—Maslamah b. Muhārib: Ibn al-Kawwā'—Ibn al-Kawwā''s name was ʿAbdallāh b. Awfah[252]—visited Muʿāwiyah. When the latter asked him about the peo-
[68] ple Ibn al-Kawwā' said, "As far as the people of al-Baṣrah are concerned, the impudent among them have prevailed over them while their governor is weak." When Ibn ʿĀmir learned what Ibn al-Kawwā' had said, he appointed Ṭufayl b. ʿAwf al-Yashkurī governor of Khurāsān. At that time there was a mutual estrangement between him and Ibn al-Kawwā'. At that Ibn al-Kawwā' remarked, "Indeed, this Ibn Dajājah[253] doesn't know me very well. Did he think that the governorship of Ṭufayl over Khurāsān would displease me? I would like for every Yashkurī remaining on earth to be hostile to me as long as he appointed them as governors." Muʿāwiyah then dismissed Ibn ʿĀmir and sent al-Ḥārith b. ʿAbdallāh al-Azdī.

(According to) al-Qaḥdhamī: Ibn ʿĀmir asked, "Who among the people is the worst enemy of Ibn al-Kawwā'?" When he was told that it was ʿAbdallāh b. Abī Shaykh, Ibn ʿĀmir appointed him governor of Khurāsān, and Ibn al-Kawwā' said what he did.

(According to) ʿUmar—Abū al-Ḥasan—a shaykh of the Thaqīf and Abū ʿAbd al-Raḥmān al-Iṣbahānī: Ibn ʿĀmir sent a delegation to Muʿāwiyah, so they were there at the same time as a delegation of Kūfans, among whom was Ibn al-Kawwā' al-Yashkurī. When Muʿāwiyah asked them about Iraq and especially about al-Baṣrah, Ibn al-Kawwā' told him, "O Commander of the Faithful, indeed, impudent persons have devoured the people of al-Baṣrah while their government was too weak to deal with them, and it has paralyzed and weakened Ibn ʿĀmir." At that Muʿāwiyah told him, "You talk about the Baṣrans while they are present." When the delegation returned to al-Baṣrah, and informed Ibn ʿĀmir of that, he was angry and asked, "Who among the people of Iraq[254] is the worst enemy of Ibn al-Kawwā'?" When he was told that it was ʿAbdallāh b. Abī Shaykh al-Yashkurī, Ibn ʿĀmir appointed him governor of Khurāsān. When Ibn al-Kawwā' heard about it, he said what he did.

252. Cairo reads: Abū Awfāh.

253. Ibn ʿĀmir's mother was Dajājah bt. Asmā' b. al-Ṣalt Sulamī. See Ibn al-Athīr, *Usd*, III, 191.

254. O reads: "of the Arabs."

(According to) ʿUmar—ʿAlī: When Ibn ʿĀmir was too weak for his job, and the (disruptive) conditions spread in al-Baṣrah, Muʿāwiyah wrote to him, asking him to visit. ʿUmar (said): Abū al-Ḥasan told me that that was in this year, and that Ibn [69] ʿĀmir appointed Qays b. al-Haytham as his deputy over al-Baṣrah. He came to Muʿāwiyah, and the latter returned him to the (same) position. When Ibn ʿĀmir took leave of him, Muʿāwiyah told him, "Indeed I would ask three things from you, so say 'they are yours.'" He replied, "They are yours as I am Ibn Umm Ḥakīm." Muʿāwiyah said, "Return my position to me and don't be angry." Ibn ʿĀmir replied, "I have done so." Muʿāwiyah said, "Give me your property at Arafat." Ibn ʿĀmir responded as before. Muʿāwiyah said, "Give me your houses at Mecca." Ibn ʿĀmir answered the same way. Muʿāwiyah remarked, "You were attached by kinship." Ibn ʿĀmir then said, "O Commander of the Faithful, I ask three things from you, so say 'they are yours.'" Muʿāwiyah replied, "They are yours as I am Ibn Hind." Ibn ʿĀmir said, "Return my property at Arafat to me." Muʿāwiyah replied, "I have done so." Ibn ʿĀmir said, "Don't investigate anyone who was an official of mine when I was governor and don't investigate me." Muʿāwiyah answered as before. Ibn ʿĀmir said, "Marry me to your daughter, Hind." Muʿāwiyah replied the same way. It is also said that Muʿāwiyah told him, "Choose whether I should investigate you and ask you for an accounting of what you got and return you to your position, or whether I should allow you to keep what you got and dismiss you." So Ibn ʿĀmir chose to be allowed to keep what he got and be dismissed.

In this year Muʿāwiyah also attached the lineage of Ziyād b. Sumayyah to his own father, Abū Sufyān, as it is said. (According to) ʿUmar b. Shabbah: They claimed that a man belonging to the ʿAbd al-Qays accompanied Ziyād when he visited Muʿāwiyah. The man said to Ziyād, "Indeed, I have influence with Ibn ʿĀmir, and if you permit me I would go to him. Ziyād replied, "On condition that you report to me what happens between you and him." When the man agreed to do so, Ziyād gave his permission, and the man went to Ibn ʿĀmir who told him, "Hey! Hey! Ibn Sumayyah investigates me and exposes my officials. Indeed, it grieved me to bring witnesses from Qu-

raysh swearing that Abū Sufyān never saw Sumayyah." When the man returned, Ziyād questioned him, but he refused to in-
[70] form him. Ziyād didn't leave him alone until the man informed him.

Ziyād then told Muʿāwiyah about it, who instructed his chamberlain (*ḥājib*), "When Ibn ʿĀmir comes, turn the face of his mount away from the most distant gates." When the chamberlain did so, Ibn ʿĀmir came to Yazīd and complained to him about it. Yazīd asked him, "Did you mention Ziyād?" Ibn ʿĀmir replied that he had, whereupon Yazīd rode with him so that he had him enter. But when Muʿāwiyah noticed him, he got up and went inside. Yazīd told Ibn ʿĀmir, "Sit here, you might stay a long time at home away from his audience." After a long time, Muʿāwiyah came out with a stick in his hand with which he struck the gates while he was quoting:

We have a reputation and you have one too,
which the companions have known.

Then he sat down and said, "O Ibn ʿĀmir, you were saying what you were about Ziyād. Indeed, by God, the Arabs knew that I was more noble than they during the Jāhiliyyah[255] and that Islām only increased my nobility, and that I was not increased from insignificance by Ziyād and did not become noble from baseness through him. But I understood his right, so I set him in his place." Ibn ʿĀmir replied, "O Commander of the Faithful, we will do what Ziyād likes." Muʿāwiyah responded, "Then we will do what you like." Ibn ʿĀmir then went off to Ziyād and tried to appease him.

I was told by Aḥmad b. Zuhayr—ʿAbd al-Raḥmān b. Ṣāliḥ—ʿAmr b. Hāshim—ʿUmar b. Bashīr[256] al-Hamdānī—Abū Isḥāq: When Ziyād came to al-Kūfah, he said, "I have come to you about a matter for which I sought only you." They replied, "Call upon us for whatever you wish." Ziyād said, "Attach my lineage to Muʿāwiyah." They replied, "As far as false testimony is concerned, no." He then came to al-Baṣrah and someone testified for him.

255. The Jāhiliyyah was the time of lawless ignorance before Islam. See *EI*², s.v. Djāhiliyya.

256. C reads: Bishr.

Mu'āwiyah led the people in the pilgrimage this year.

In this year Marwān made the *maqṣūrah*,[257] and Mu'āwiyah also made one in Syria according to what was reported.

The officials in the provincial capitals during this year were the same officials whom we mentioned for the previous year. [71]

---

257. A *maqṣūrah* was a protective lodge in the mosque for the ruler or governor during public worship.

The Events of the Year 45

(March 24, 665–March 13, 666)

Among these events was Mu'āwiyah's appointment of al-Ḥārith b. 'Abdallāh al-Azdī as governor over al-Baṣrah. I was told by 'Umar—'Alī b. Muḥammad: Mu'āwiyah dismissed Ibn 'Āmir and made al-Ḥārith b. 'Abdallāh al-Azdī governor of al-Baṣrah at the beginning of this year. Al-Ḥārith stayed at al-Baṣrah four months, then Mu'āwiyah dismissed him. He was said to be al-Ḥārith b. 'Amr and Ibn 'Abd and Ibn 'Amr,[258] and he was a Syrian. Mu'āwiyah had dismissed Ibn 'Āmir in order to make Ziyād governor, so he made al-Ḥārith governor as the stalking horse. Al-Ḥārith put 'Abdallāh b. 'Amr b. Ghaylān al-Thaqafī in charge of his police. Then Mu'āwiyah dismissed al-Ḥārith and put Ziyād in charge of al-Baṣrah.

Ziyād's Governorship over al-Baṣrah[259]

I was told by 'Umar—'Alī—some knowledgeable people: When Ziyād came to al-Kūfah, al-Mughīrah supposed that he came as governor over al-Kūfah. Ziyād stayed in the house of Salmān b.

---

258. Cairo reads: Ibn 'Abd 'Amr.

259. C reads: "In this year Mu'āwiyah dismissed al-Ḥārith from al-Baṣrah and made Ziyād governor."

Rabī'ah al-Bāhilī, and al-Mughīrah sent Wā'il b. Ḥujr al-Ḥaḍramī, Abu Hunaydah to him, saying, "Inform me about him." Wā'il came to Ziyād, but wasn't able to get anything out of him, so he left for al-Mughīrah. He was superstitious, and when he saw a crow cawing, he returned to Ziyād, saying, "O Abū al-Mughīrah, this crow urges you to depart from al-Kūfah." Then he returned to al-Mughīrah, and Mu'āwiyah's [72] messenger came to Ziyād that very day (saying), "Go to al-Baṣrah."

As for 'Abdallāh b. Aḥmad al-Marwazī, he told me—his father—Sulaymān—'Abdallāh—Isḥāq, that is, Ibn Yaḥyā—Ma'bad b. Khālid al-Jadalī: Ziyād who is called Ibn Abī Sufyān came to us from Mu'āwiyah. He stayed at the house of Salmān b. Rabī'ah al-Bāhilī, waiting for Mu'āwiyah's instructions. When al-Mughīrah b. Shu'bah was governor over al-Kūfah, he heard that Ziyād expected that his own appointment as governor over al-Kūfah would arrive. So al-Mughīrah summoned Qaṭan b. 'Abdallāh al-Ḥārithī, and asked, "Would you be good enough to take care of al-Kūfah for me until I come back to you from the Commander of the Faithful?" He replied, "I am not the one for that." Al-Mughīrah then summoned 'Uyaynah[260] b. al-Nahhās al-'Ijlī, and asked him. When he agreed, al-Mughīrah went to Mu'āwiyah. Upon arriving, he asked Mu'āwiyah to dismiss him and grant him settlements at Qarqīsiyā[261] between both "backs" of the Qays.[262] When Mu'āwiyah heard that, he feared he might revolt and replied, "By God, indeed, you shall certainly return to your office, O Abū 'Abdallāh." When Mu'āwiyah refused him, al-Mughīrah's suspicion only increased. Mu'āwiyah returned him to his office, and he reached us at night while I was on top of the citadel, guarding it. He struck the gate, but we refused to acknowledge him. When he feared that we might drop bricks on him, he told us his name. So I went down to him, welcoming and greeting him, and he quoted:

---

260. Cairo reads: 'Utaybah.

261. Qarqīsiyā was a town on the left bank of the Euphrates just above its confluence with the Khābūr River. See *EI*², s.v. Ḳarḳīsiyā.

262. The tribe of Qays 'Aylān had occupied the territory around Qarqīsiyā after the Muslim conquest. See *EI*², s.v. Ḳays 'Aylān.

Be startled, O Umm ʿAmr, by the likes of me,
whenever a distant journey is imposed on him.[263]

[73] "Go to Ibn Sumayyah and make him leave, so that he is beyond the bridge by morning." So we went off[264] and brought Ziyād and took him out until we had removed him beyond the bridge before morning came.

I was told by ʿUmar—ʿAlī—Maslamah and al-Hudhalī and others: Muʿāwiyah appointed Ziyād governor over al-Baṣrah, Khurāsān, and Sijistān. Then he included al-Hind, al-Baḥrayn, and ʿUmān in his (territory). Ziyād arrived at al-Baṣrah at the end of Rabīʿ II or on the first of Jumādā I 45 (July 20, 665). There was open depravity in al-Baṣrah, so he delivered a "free" (*al-batrā'*) speech (*khuṭbah*) in which he did not praise God. It was also said that he praised God, saying:

> Praise be to God for His virtues and His goodness, and we ask Him for the utmost of His blessings. O God, since You have provided us with blessings, inspire us with gratitude for your blessing upon us.[265] Now then, indeed, the terrible things that the impudent among you commit and in which the wise among you are implicated are extreme ignorance, blind error, and the immorality for the perpetrators of which the eternal fire kindles its blazing flame. The young grow up in them, and the old do not abstain from them, as if you did not hear God's signs[266] nor recited the Book of God, nor heard of the generous reward which God reck-

---

263. In Ṭarafah, *Dīwān*, 154, this line reads:

So know, O Umm ʿAmr, that the likes of me,
whenever a distant journey is imposed on him. . .

264. O reads: "I went off."

265. Other versions of this *khuṭbah* are quoted with minor differences by Jāḥiẓ, *Bayān*, II, 56–8, according to Abū al-Ḥasan al-Madā'inī; by Ibn Qutaybah, *ʿUyūn*, II, 241–3, according to al-Haytham b. ʿAdī; by Ibn A 'tham al-Kūfī, *Futūḥ*, IV, 177–80; by Ibn ʿAbd Rabbihi, *ʿIqd*, IV, 110–12, according to Abū al-Ḥasan al-Madā'inī from Maslamah b. Muḥārib from Abū Bakr al-Hudhalī; and by Ibn Abī al-Ḥadīd, *Sharḥ Nahj al-balāghah*, XVI, 200–3, according to ʿAlī b. Muḥammad al-Madā'inī. There is a partial English translation by I. Lichtenstadter in "From Particularism to Unity," 268; and a complete translation of the version in Jāḥiẓ by K. A. Fariq in "Ziyād Ibn Abih," 2–4.

266. *Āy* are signs, miracles or tokens, also used of the verses of the Qur'ān.

oned for people who obey Him, and the painful punishment for unending eternity for people who disobey Him. Are you like someone whose eyes have been dazzled by the world, and whose ears have been closed by desires, and who has preferred the transitory over the permanent? Don't you recall that you have inaugurated misdeeds in Islām that you did not do before, including your abandonment[267] of these established brothels, and the weak women snatched in broad daylight, whose number is not few? Are there not censors among you to restrain the seducers from prowling at night and attacking by day? You have advanced kinship and kept religion away. You excuse yourselves inexcusably, and you condone the thief. Every man [74]
among you defends on behalf of his fool an act of one who does not fear punishment,[268] and does not expect the return [to God]. You are not wise, while you follow the foolish and what you regard as shielding them continues, so that they violate the inviolable of Islām.[269] Then they duck behind you as coverts in suspicious hiding places. Food and drink be forbidden to me until I level them to the ground by destruction and burning. Indeed, I think that the end of this business will only be reformed by what was right at first: flexibility[270] without weakness and strength without compulsion and violence.[271] Indeed, I swear by God that unless you straighten yourselves out for me, I shall certainly take the guardian for the ward,[272] the one who stays for the one who leaves, the one who approaches for the one who turns away,[273] the healthy for the sick, until anyone among you who meets his brother shall say, "Save yourself

---

267. Jāḥiẓ, *Bayān*, II, 57, inserts: "of the weak to be oppressed and his wealth to be taken."

268. The text reads: *ʿiqāban*; C reads: *ʿāqībatahu*, "its consequences."

269. The text reads: *ḥuram al-Islāmī*; O reads: *ḥurrat al-Muslimīn*, "a free woman of the Muslims."

270. The text reads: *līnin*; O reads: *kays*, "intelligence."

271. The text reads: *jabariyyat*^{in} *wa ʿanf*^{in}; C reads: *jabarūtiyyati ʿanf*^{in}, "tyranny of violence."

272. The text reads: *al-walī*; Ibn ʿAbd Rabbihi, *ʿIqd*, IV, 111 reads: *al-mawlā*, "the client."

273. Jāḥiẓ, *Bayān*, II, 58, adds: "the obedient for the disobedient."

Saʿd, for Saʿīd has perished!" Indeed, lies from the pulpit[274] remain well-known, so if you catch me in a lie it is permissible for you to disobey me.[275] Whoever among you is burglarized, I will be guarantor for whatever of his was stolen. Beware of night-prowling too, for no prowler will be brought to me but I shall shed his blood. I will postpone this for you for as long as it takes for the news to reach al-Kūfah and return to me.[276] Beware also of the summoning of the Jāhiliyyah,[277] for I shall cut out the tongue of anyone I find appealing to it. You have also invented misdeeds which did not exist [before], and we have invented a punishment for every crime. Whoever drowns folk, I shall drown; whoever burns folk, we shall burn; whoever breaks into a house, I shall break into his heart; and whoever digs
[75] up a grave, I shall bury him alive. So spare me your hands and tongues, and I shall spare you my hand and my harm.[278] I shall behead anyone of you who seems contrary to your belief in general. There have been hatreds between me and some folks, but I have put all that behind me.[279] Whoever of you was beneficent, let him increase his beneficence; and whoever was offensive, let him renounce his offense. Indeed, if I should know that one of you was overcome with incurable hatred toward me, I would not expose him nor disclose him unless he shows [it] to me openly. If he does so, I shall not argue with him. So resume your affairs, and help yourselves. Perhaps someone who is worried by our arrival may be pleased, and someone who is pleased with our arrival may be grieved.

O people, we have become your rulers and protectors. We rule you by the authority [*sulṭān*] of God, which He

274. Ibn ʿAbd Rabbihi, *ʿIqd*, IV, 111 reads: "of the amīr."

275. Jāḥiẓ, *Bayān*, II, 58, adds: "And if you hear it from me disparage me for it, and know that it is the same with me.

276. C reads: "to Syria and return to al-Baṣrah and to you."

277. The "summoning of the Jāhiliyyah" was the pre-Islamic custom of calling upon relatives for support or revenge.

278. The text reads: *'adhāya*. Jāḥiẓ, *Bayān*, II, 58; Ibn ʿAbd Rabbihi, *ʿIqd*, IV, 112; Ibn Abī al-Ḥadīd, *Nahj*, XVI, 202 read: *lisānī*, "my tongue."

279. Lit: "behind my ears and beneath my foot."

gave us, and protect you with the *fay'*[280] of God, which He bestowed on us. So you owe us obedience in whatever we desire, and we owe you justice in whatever we were assigned. So be worthy of our justice and our *fay'* by your loyalty. Know also that whatever I may fail to do, I shall not fail to do three [things]: I shall not be unavailable to anyone of you who has a request, even if he comes to me knocking at night; nor delay payment of provisions and stipends; nor prolong your expeditions. So pray to God for the righteousness of your leaders, for they are your rulers. They set the example for you, and [they are] your shelter[281] whence you take refuge. As long as you are righteous, they will be righteous.[282] Do not let your hearts imbibe hatred for them, for your rage will be aggravated and your grief lengthened thereby, and you will not achieve your desire. Even if [your desire] were granted to you, it would be evil for you. I ask God to help everyone for everyone's sake,[283] and if you see me give an order then carry it out literally. I swear by God that I have many [potential] victims among you, so let every man among you beware lest he be among [76]
them.

At that, ʿAbdallāh b. Ahtam stood up, saying, "O amīr, I testify that you have been granted wisdom and unmistakable judgment." Ziyād responded, "You have lied. That was the prophet of God, David."[284] Al-Aḥnaf[285] said, "You have spoken and did it well, O amīr. But praise [comes] after performance and commendation after the stipend. We should not praise until we experience." Ziyād replied, "You have spoken the truth." At that Abū Bilāl, Mirdās b. Udayyah,[286] got up mut-

---

280. C reads: *taqwā*, "piety." Concerning *fay'*, see above, n. 51.

281. Lit: "cave."

282. Jāḥiẓ, *Bayān*, II, 59; Ibn ʿAbd Rabbihi, *ʿIqd*, IV, 112 read: "as long as they are righteous, you are righteous."

283. The text reads: *ʿalā kullin*; O reads: *maʿa kullin*, "with everyone."

284. Referring to Qur'ān 38:20.

285. Al-Aḥnaf, "the deformed", was Abū Baḥr Ṣakhr b. Qays b. Muʿāwiyah al-Tamīmī al-Saʿdī (d. 67[686/7]), who was the leader of the Banū Tamīm at al-Baṣrah. See *EI*², s.v. al-Aḥnaf b. Ḳays.

286. Mirdās b. Udayyah (d. 61[680/81]) was a Khārijite leader at al-

tering and saying, "God imparted differently from what you said. God, Almighty and Great, said, 'And Abraham who fulfilled his mission. One sinner shall not bear the burden of another and a man will only have what he achieved [himself].'[287] So God promised us better than what you did, O Ziyād." Ziyād responded, "Indeed we cannot find a way to what you and your companions want until we plunge into blood for it."

(According to) ʿUmar—Khallād b. Yazīd—someone—al-Shaʿbī: Every time I heard someone speaking well, I wanted him to be silent for fear that he would spoil it except for Ziyād. For whenever he would continue, his speech was most excellent.

I was told by ʿUmar—ʿAlī—Maslamah: Ziyād appointed ʿAbdallāh b. Ḥiṣn to be in charge of his police. He then granted the people a respite until the news reached al-Kūfah and (word of) the arrival of the news at al-Kūfah came back to him. He also used to delay the evening worship so that he was the last to worship. Then he would worship, commanding someone to recite slowly the *sūrah* of "the Cow" or something similar from the Qur'ān. When he had finished, Ziyād granted a respite for as long as it would take for a man to reach al-Khuraybah.[288] Then he ordered the commander of his police to go forth. So he went forth and killed every man he saw. One night he caught a bedouin and brought him to Ziyād, who asked, "Did you hear
[77] the announcement?" He replied, "No, by God, I arrived with my milch-camel, and when the night descended upon me, I lacked a place for her. I waited for morning to come, without knowing what the amīr had done." Ziyād declared, "By God, I believe you are telling the truth, but there will be a good example for this community in your death." Then he gave the order and the man was beheaded.

Ziyād was the first one who consolidated the government's

Baṣrah who had fought at Nahrawān but opposed the use of violence afterwards. He is considered to be one of the first of the inactive Khārijites. See *EI*[1], s.v. Mirdās b. Udaiya.

287. Qur'ān 53:37–38.

288. Al-Khuraybah was the location of two deserted Persian forts on the outskirts of al-Baṣrah where the original Muslim settlement had been. See Balādhurī, *Futūḥ*, 341, 346.

business and secured the monarchy for Muʿāwiyah. He compelled the people to obey, implemented punishment, unsheathed the sword, arrested on (mere) suspicion, and meted out dubious punishment. The people feared his government greatly so that some of them felt safe with each other. If a man or woman dropped something, no one would touch it until its owner came and picked it up. Women spent the night without locking their doors. He ruled the people with an administration the like of which had never been seen. The people feared him with a dread that they never had of anyone before him. He also lavished stipends and built the provision depot.

When Ziyād heard a sound from the house of ʿUmayr, he asked, "What's that?" He was told that it was a watchman, so he said, "Desist from this! I will be guarantor for whatever of his may be lost as far away as Iṣṭakhr." Ziyād also established the police force at four thousand men, headed by ʿAbdallāh b. Ḥiṣn, one of the Banū ʾUbayd b. Thaʿlabah, owner of the Cemetery of Ibn Ḥiṣn, and by al-Jaʿd b. Qays al-Tamīmī,[289] the owner of the Arch of al-Jaʿd. They were both in charge of his police force together. One day while Ziyād was going along, they both went in front of him with two spears, competing (with each other). Ziyād ordered, "O Jaʿd, throw down your spear." So he threw it down, and Ibn Ḥiṣn remained in charge of his police until Ziyād died. It was said that Ziyād put al-Jaʿd in charge of dealing with the evil doers, and that he would [78]
pursue them.

When Ziyād was told that the roads were dangerous, he said, "My efforts are confined to the city until I prevail over it and reform it. If the city should prevail over me, victory over anything else would be more difficult. When the city has been brought under control, what is outside of it will be tackled." Thus he consolidated his control. He would say, "If a rope should be lost between me and Khurāsān, I would know who took it." He also inscribed five hundred of the Baṣran shaykhs among his companions, and provided them with three hundred to five hundred dirhams. So Ḥārith b. Badr al-Ghudānī said of him:

289. C reads: al-Numayrī.

Who will tell Ziyād about me?
what a wonderful brother of the Caliph and Amīr!

For you are an imām of justice and aspiration,
and determination when the affairs attend you.

Your brother is the Deputy of God,[290] son of Ḥarb,
and you his assistant,[291] what a wonderful assistant!

You obtain what is desired and there comes
To your friend that which the conscience conceals for us.

Victorious by God's command, helping,
when the flock goes astray, you do not oppress.

Plentiful milk streams through your hands
of what they wanted from the world for themselves.

You apportion equally, and neither rich
nor poor complains to you about injustice.

You were energetic, and came at a wicked
time when evils were manifest.

When men divided its desire among themselves,
and the breasts would not disguise their grudges,

And city-dwellers feared and every one in the desert,
remaining out of fear or going.

So when the sword of God arose among them,
Ziyād arose bright, illuminated,

Powerful, not inexperienced among the young,
nor anxious, nor very old.

---

290. *Khalīfat Allāh.*
291. Wazīr.

I was told by ʿUmar b. Shabbah—ʿAlī b. Muḥammad: Ziyād sought help from a number of Companions of the Prophet, among whom were ʿImrān b. al-Ḥusayn al-Khuzāʿī, whom he put in charge of rendering judgment at al-Baṣrah, al-Ḥakam b. ʿAmr al-Ghifārī, whom he put in charge of Khurāsān, Samurah b. Jundab, Anas b. Mālik, and ʿAbd al-Raḥmān b. Samurah. When ʿImrān asked to resign from his position, Ziyād relieved him and appointed ʿAbdallāh b. Faḍālah al-Laythī as judge, then his brother, ʿĀṣim b. Faḍālah, then Zurārah b. Awfā al-Jurashī, whose sister, Lubābah, was with Ziyād. It was also said that Ziyād was the first to have people go in front of him with spears and walk in front of him with clubs. He made use of the guard, a unit of five hundred men, and appointed Shaybān, owner of the Cemetery of Shaybān among the Banū Saʿd, to be in charge of them. They were stationed at the mosque. [79]

I was told by ʿUmar—ʿAlī: Ziyād divided Khurāsān into four parts and appointed ʿUmayr b. Aḥmar al-Yashkurī over Marw, Khulayd b. ʿAbdallāh al-Ḥanafī over Abrashahr, Qays b. al-Haytham over Marw al-Rūdh, al-Fāryāb and al-Ṭāliqān, and Nāfiʿ b. Khālid al-Ṭāḥī over Harāt, Bādhghīs, Qādis, and Bushanj.

I was told by 'Umar—ʿAlī—Maslamah b. Muḥārib and Ibn Abī ʿAmr, shaykh of the Azd: Ziyād rebuked Nāfiʿ b. Khālid al-Ṭāḥī, imprisoned him, and made him sign a note for one hundred thousand dirhams—some say, eight hundred thousand. The reason for Ziyād's bad feeling towards him was that Nāfiʿ had sent him a table with gem-encrusted legs by means of a servant (*ghulām*) of his, called Zayd, who was Nāfiʿ's steward [80] over all his affairs. But Zayd slandered Nāfiʿ, and told Ziyād, "He has cheated you and taken one of the legs of the table, and substituted a leg of gold for it." Some of the leading men of the Azd then went to Ziyād. Among them was Sayf b. Wahb al-Maʿwalī, who was noble and about whom the poet says:

> Apply to Sayf for generosity and liberality,
> and apply to Ṣabrah[292] for the greatest deeds.

292. Ṣabrah b. Shaymān b. ʿUkayf b. Kuyyūm was a leader of the Azd at the Battle of the Camel. See Ibn Durayd, *Ishtiqāq*, 299.

They entered Ziyād's presence while he was brushing his teeth, and when Ziyād saw them he quoted:

Recall for us the stopping place of our horses,
at the bend,[293] since you are in need of us.

As far as the Azd are concerned, they say, "No, Sayf b. Wahb Abū Ṭalḥah al-Maʿwalī quoted that line instead, when he entered Ziyād's presence." So Ziyād replied, "Yes." However, it reminded Ziyād of the time when Ṣabrah had protected him, so he called for the note and erased it with his toothbrush and released Nāfiʿ.

I was told by ʿUmar b. Shabbah—ʿAlī—Maslamah: Ziyād dismissed Nāfiʿ b. Khālid al-Ṭāḥī, Khulayd b. ʿAbdallāh al-Ḥanafī, and ʿUmayr b. Aḥmar al-Yashkurī, and appointed al-Ḥakam b. ʿAmr b. Mujaddah[294] b. Ḥidhyam[295] b. al-Ḥārith b. Nuʿaylah[296] b. Mulayk.[297] Nuʿaylah was the brother of Ghifār b. Mulayk but they were few so they wound up with Ghifār. According to Maslamah:[298] Ziyād ordered his chamberlain, saying, "Invite al-Ḥakam to come to me," meaning al-Ḥakam b. Abī al-ʿĀṣ al-Thaqafī. So the chamberlain went out and upon seeing al-Ḥakam b. ʿAmr al-Ghifārī, he admitted him. Ziyād remarked, "Here is a man with nobility who has companionship
[81] with the Messenger of God," and appointed him over Khurāsān. Then Ziyād said, "I did not want you, but God, Almighty and Great, wanted you."

I was told by ʿUmar—ʿAlī—Abū al-Raḥmān al-Thaqafī and Muḥammad b. Fuḍayl—his father: When Ziyād became governor of Iraq, he appointed al-Ḥakam b. ʿAmr al-Ghifārī as governor over Khurāsān. He also appointed men along with him over the districts and ordered them to obey al-Ḥakam. They were in charge of collecting the tax revenue. They were Aslam b. Zur-

293. See Yāqūt, *Muʿjam*, II, 349–50.

294. C reads: Muhaddaj; O reads, Makhdūj. Mukhaddaj is given as an alternative by Ibn al-Athīr, *Usd*, II, 154.

295. C reads: Jurthum; O reads: Khulaym b. Ḥulwān; Ibn al-Athīr, *Usd*, II, 36, 153 reads: Jidhyam.

296. Ibn Hajar, *Iṣābah*, I, 346 reads: Thaʿlabah.

297. Ibn al-Athīr, *Usd*, II, 154; Ibn Hajar, *Iṣābah*, I, 346 read: Mulayl b. Damrah b. Bakr b. ʿAbd Manāt b. Kinānah.

298. O adds: "Salamah told us."

ʿah, Khulayd b. ʿAbdallāh al-Ḥanafī, Nāfiʿ b. Khālid al-Ṭāḥī, Rabīʿah b. ʿIsl al-Yarbūʿī, ʿUmayr b. Aḥmar al-Yashkurī, and Ḥātim b. al-Nuʿmān al-Bāhilī. Al-Ḥakam b. ʿAmr died after he had raided Ṭukhāristān taking great booty and had appointed Anas b. Abī Unās b. Zunaym as his deputy. He had written to Ziyād, "Indeed I have recommended him to God, to the Muslims, and to you." Ziyad remarked, "O God, indeed I do not approve of him for Your religion, nor for the Muslims, nor for me." Ziyād wrote to Khulayd b. ʿAbdallāh al-Ḥanafī about the governorship of Khurāsān. Then he sent al-Rabīʿ b. Ziyād al-Ḥārithī to Khurāsān with fifty thousand men, twenty-five thousand from al-Baṣrah and twenty-five thousand from al-Kūfah. Al-Rabīʿ was in charge of the Baṣrans and ʿAbdallāh b. Abī ʿAqīl was in charge of the Kūfans, while al-Rabīʿ b. Ziyād was in charge of the entire group.

It is also said that in this year Marwān b. al-Ḥakam led the people in the pilgrimage while he was in charge of al-Madīnah. The previously mentioned governors and officials in charge of the provincial capitals during this year were al-Mughīrah b. Shuʿbah in charge of al-Kūfah, while Shurayḥ was in charge of rendering judgment there, and Ziyād in charge of al-Baṣrah, and the (other) officials whom I have mentioned previously.

During this year ʿAbd al-Raḥmān b. Khālid b. al-Walīd led the winter raid against Byzantine territory.

The Events of the Year 46

(March 13, 666–March 2, 667)

[82] Among these events was the winter raid of Mālik b. ʿUbaydallāh against Byzantine territory. According to alternative accounts this raid was led by ʿAbd al-Raḥmān b. Khālid b. al-Walīd or by Mālik b. Hubayrah al-Sakūnī.

During this year, ʿAbd al-Raḥmān b. Khālid b. al-Walīd departed from Byzantine territory to Homs. Ibn Uthāl al-Naṣrānī[299] is said to have slipped him a poisoned drink, and when he drank it, it killed him.

The Death of ʿAbd al-Raḥmān b. Khālid b. al-Walīd

The reason for that was what I was told by ʿUmar—ʿAlī—Maslamah b. Muḥārib: ʿAbd al-Raḥmān b. Khālid b. al-Walīd had become great in Syria and the Syrians favored him because of the reputation among them of his father, Khālid b. al-Walīd, and because of his usefulness to the Muslims in Byzantine territory, as well as his bravery. They favored him so much that

299. "The Christian."

Muʿāwiyah feared him. He was afraid for himself with regard to ʿAbd al-Raḥmān, because of the affection of the people for him. So he ordered Ibn Uthāl to plot to kill him, and guaranteed to Ibn Uthāl that, if he did so, his tax (*kharāj*) would be revoked for as long as he lived and that he would be put in charge of the collection of the tax revenues (*kharāj*) of Homs. As a result, when ʿAbd al-Raḥmān b. Khālid reached Homs, returning from Byzantine territory, Ibn Uthāl slipped him a poisoned drink with some of his slaves. He drank it and died at Homs. Muʿāwiyah then fulfilled for Ibn Uthāl what he had guaranteed to him. He put Ibn Uthāl in charge of (collecting) the tax revenues (*kharāj*) of Homs and revoked his own tax (*kharāj*). Khālid b. ʿAbd al-Raḥmān b. Khālid b. al-Walīd came to al-Madīnah, and one day he sat with ʿUrwah b. al-Zubayr. When Khālid greeted him, ʿUrwah asked him who he was. When he replied, "I am Khālid b. ʿAbd al-Raḥmān b. Khālid b. al-Walīd," ʿUrwah [83]
asked him, "What did Ibn ʿUthāl do?" At that, Khālid got up from his presence and departed, heading for Homs. Then he lay in wait for Ibn Uthāl there. When he saw Ibn Uthāl riding one day, Khālid b. ʿAbd al-Raḥmān stood in his way and struck him with his sword, killing him. When he was brought to Muʿāwiyah, the latter imprisoned him for several days and fined him Ibn Uthāl's blood price, so that no one retaliated against Khālid for killing him. When Khālid returned to al-Madīnah, he came to ʿUrwah and greeted him. When ʿUrwah asked him, "What did Ibn Uthāl do?" he replied, "I took care of Ibn Uthāl for you, but what did Ibn Jurmūz do?" At that, ʿUrwah became silent. When Khālid b. ʿAbd al-Raḥmān struck Ibn Uthāl, he said:

I am the descendent of the Sword of God, so know me!
Only my noble descent and my religion last,
And a trenchant sword with which my right hand assailed.

During this year al-Khaṭīm and Sahm b. Ghālib al-Ḥujaymī rebelled, proclaiming, "Judgment belongs only to God."[300] I was

---

300. The text reads: *ḥakkama*, which means "to say the Khārijite slogan, *la ḥukmah illa li-llāhi*."

told about their affair by ʿUmar—ʿAlī: When Ziyād became governor, Sahm b. Ghālib al-Ḥujaymī and al-Khaṭīm, who was Yazīd b. Mālik al-Bāhilī, feared him. As for Sahm, he went off to al-Ahwāz and caused mischief, proclaiming, "Judgment belongs only to God." Then he returned, hid, and sought a guarantee of safe-conduct. Ziyād did not grant him that, but sought him, killed him, and crucified him on his door. As for al-Khaṭīm, Ziyād exiled him to Baḥrayn, then he allowed him to come back, saying to him, "Stay in your city." Ziyād also told Muslim b. ʿAmr to vouch for him, but Muslim refused, saying, "If he spends the night away from his house, I shall let you know." Muslim then came to Ziyād and said, "Al-Khaṭīm did
[84] not spend the night in his house." At that, Ziyād ordered him to be killed and (his corpse) thrown into (the district of) the Bāhilah (tribe).[301]

ʿUtbah b. Abī Sufyān led the people in the pilgrimage this year. The officials and governors were the same as during the previous year.

---

301. C reads: "the gate of his kinsmen."

The Events of the Year 47

(March 3, 667–February 19, 668)

The winter campaign of Mālik b. Hubayrah against Byzantine territory occurred during this year, as well as the winter campaign of Abū ʿAbd al-Raḥmān al-Qaynī against Anṭākiyah.

In this year also, ʿAbdallāh b. ʿAmr b. al-ʿĀṣ was dismissed from (the governorship of) Egypt, and Muʿāwiyah b. Ḥudayj was put in charge there. According to al-Wāqidī, Muʿāwiyah b. Ḥudayj set out westward; he was an ʿUthmānī.[302] ʿAbd al-Raḥmān b. Abī Bakr, who had come from al-Iskandariyyah, marched past him, saying to him, "O Muʿāwiyah, indeed, by my life, you took your reward from Muʿāwiyah. You killed Muḥammad b. Abī Bakr in order to be made governor of Egypt, and you have become its governor." Muʿāwiyah b. Ḥudayj replied, "I only killed Muḥammad b. Abī Bakr for what he did to ʿUthmān." At that ʿAbd al-Raḥmān replied, "However, if you were seeking [revenge for] the blood of ʿUthmān, you would not have participated in what Muʿāwiyah did, since ʿAmr b. al-ʿĀṣ

302. An ʿUthmānī was one of those who demanded revenge for the death of ʿUthmān and the punishment of his murderers during the first civil war.

treated al-Ashʿarī the way he did.[303] You were the first person to jump up and declare allegiance to Muʿāwiyah.

Some of the biographers said that in this year Ziyād sent al-Ḥakam b. ʿAmr al-Ghifārī to Khurāsān as governor. He raided the mountain of al-Ghūr and Farāwandah. He defeated the people there with the sword by force, conquered the territory, and acquired much booty and captives. I shall mention those who
[85] differ with this account later if God Most High wills. The one who told this account mentioned that al-Ḥakam b. ʿAmr returned from this raid of his and died at Marw.

There is disagreement over who led the people in the pilgrimage this year. Al-Wāqidī said ʿUtbah b. Abī Sufyān was put in charge of the pilgrimage in this year. Others said the one who led the pilgrimage in this year was ʿAnbasah b. Abī Sufyān. The governors and officials in charge of the provincial capitals were the same as those whom I mentioned for the preceding year.

---

303. This refers to ʿAmr's deception of Abū Mūsā al-Ashʿarī during the arbitration at Adhrūḥ.

The Events of the Year 48

(February 20, 668–February 8, 669)

The winter campaign of ʿAbd al-Raḥmān al-Qaynī against Anṭākiyah occurred during this year, as well as the summer campaign of ʿAbdallāh b. Qays al-Fazārī, the sea raid of Mālik b. Hubayrah al-Sakūnī, and the joint sea raid of ʿUqbah b. ʿĀmir al-Juhanī with the Egyptians and the people of al-Madīnah. Al-Mundhir b. al-Zuhayr was in charge of the people of al-Madīnah, and Khālid b. ʿAbd al-Raḥmān b. Khālid b. al-Walīd was in charge of them all.

According to some authorities, Ziyād sent Ghālib b. Faḍālah al-Laythī to be in charge of Khurāsān. Ghālib had been a Companion of the Messenger of God.

Marwān b. al-Ḥakam led the people in the pilgrimage this year, according to most biographers. He expected to be dismissed due to Muʿāwiyah's ill will towards him and because Muʿāwiyah had taken back Fadak after having granted it to him. The governors of the provincial capitals and their officials during this year were the same as those during the preceding year.

[86] # The Events of the Year 49

(February 9, 669–January 28, 670)

The winter campaign of Mālik b. Hubayrah al-Sakūnī into Byzantine territory occurred during this year.

The raid of Faḍālah b. ʿUbayd against Jarabbah also occurred during this year. He spent the winter at Jarabbah, conquered it, and took many captives there.

The summer campaign of ʿAbdallāh b. Kurz al-Bajalī occurred during this year.

The sea raid of Yazīd b. Shajarah al-Rahāwī occurred during this year. He spent the winter with the Syrians.

The sea raid of ʿUqbah b. Nāfiʿ occurred during this year, and he spent the winter with the Egyptians.

The raid of Yazīd b. Muʿāwiyah against the Byzantines occurred during this year. He reached Qusṭanṭīniyyah accompanied by Ibn ʿAbbās, Ibn ʿUmar, Ibn al-Zubayr, and Abū Ayyūb al-Anṣārī.

[87] In this year Muʿāwiyah discharged Marwān b. al-Ḥakam from al-Madīnah, in the month of Rabīʿ I (April 9–May 8, 669). He appointed Saʿīd b. al-ʿĀṣ as governor over al-Madīnah in the month of Rabīʿ II (May 9–June 6, 669)—it is also said, in the

month of Rabīʿ I in this year.[304] Altogether, Marwān was Muʿāwiyah's governor of al-Madīnah for eight years and two months. When Marwān was dismissed, ʿAbdallāh b. al-Ḥārith b. Nawfal was in charge of rendering judgment at al-Madīnah for him—that is what al-Wāqidī claims. When Saʿīd b. al-ʿĀṣ was put in charge, he dismissed ʿAbdallāh from that post and appointed Abū Salimah b. ʿAbd al-Raḥmān b. Awf as judge.

It was said that in this year the plague struck al-Kūfah. Al-Mughīrah b. Shuʿbah fled the plague, and when it lifted, he was asked, "Why don't you return to al-Kūfah?" So he went back and was stricken and died. It has also been said that al-Mughīrah died in the year 50(670/671). Muʿāwiyah added al-Kūfah to Ziyād's (territory). He was thus the first one to have al-Kūfah and al-Baṣrah combined (under his jurisdiction).

In this year Saʿīd b. al-ʿĀṣ led the people in the pilgrimage. The governors and officials during this year were the same as those during the previous year, except for the governor of al-Kūfah. There are differences regarding the date of al-Mughīrah's death, for some biographers said he perished in this year while others said it was in the following year.

---

304. According to Ibn Khayyāṭ, *Ta'rīkh*, I, 245, this happened in the year 48(668/9)

The Events of the Year 50

(January 29, 670-January 17, 671)

The raid of Busr b. Abī Arṭāt and Sufyān b. Awf al-Azdī in Byzantine territory occurred during this year. It was also said that the sea raid of Faḍālah b. ʿUbayd al-Anṣārī took place during this year.

The death of al-Mughīrah b. Shuʿbah occurred in this year according to al-Wāqidī and al-Madā'inī. (According to) Muḥammad b. ʿUmar—Muḥammad b. Mūsā al-Thaqafī—his father: Al-Mughīrah b. Shuʿbah was a tall man with an injured eye which had been wounded at Yarmūk.[305] He died in (the month of) Shaʿbān (August 24–September 21, 670), at the age of seventy. As for ʿAwānah, he said: According to what I was told by Hishām b. ʿUbayd,[306] al-Mughīrah perished in the year 51(671/672). Others said: No, he perished in the year 49(669/670).

I was told by ʿUmar b. Shabbah—ʿAlī b. Muḥammad: Ziyād was in charge of al-Baṣrah and its districts until this year. When al-Mughīrah b. Shuʿbah died at al-Kūfah while he was its

305. The decisive battle in the Muslim conquest of Syria was fought at Yarmūk, in northern Jordan, in Rajab 15 (August 636). See *EI*[1], s.v. al-Yarmūk.

306. C and Cairo read: Muḥammad.

governor, Muʿāwiyah wrote to Ziyād assigning him to be in charge of al-Kūfah and al-Baṣrah. He was the first one to have al-Kūfah and al-Baṣrah combined (under his jurisdiction). Ziyād appointed Samurah b. Jundab as his deputy over al-Baṣrah and set out for al-Kūfah. Ziyād would stay in al-Kūfah for six months and in al-Baṣrah for six months.

I was told by ʿUmar—ʿAlī—Maslamah b. Muḥārib: When al-Mughīrah died, Iraq was combined under Ziyād's jurisdiction, so he came to al-Kūfah, ascended the pulpit, praised and glorified God, and then said, "Indeed, when that matter came to me while I was at al-Bạrah, I wanted to set out for you with two thousand of the police force of al-Baṣrah. Then, when I remembered that you are people of truth, and that your truth often rejected the false, I came to you with my family. God be praised, Who removed from me what the people imposed and preserved for me what they lost . . . " until he finished the speech. When he was pelted with pebbles on the pulpit, he sat down until they ceased. Then he summoned some of his henchmen and commanded them to seize the gates of the mosque. He then said, "Let every man of you take the one sitting next to him, and do not say, 'I don't know who was sitting next to me.'" He then ordered a seat[307] to be put at the gate of the mosque for him, and summoned them, four at a time, to swear by God, "None of us threw pebbles at you." He freed whoever swore and arrested and set aside whoever did not swear until there were thirty men—it is also said, eighty. He then cut off their hands on the spot. Al-Shaʿbī said: By God, we never accused him of lying. Whenever he promised us good or evil, he carried it out. [88]

I was told by ʿUmar—ʿAlī—Salamah b. ʿUthmān—al-Shaʿbī: The first man Ziyād killed at al-Kūfah was Awfā b. Ḥiṣn. Ziyād had heard something about him, but when he sought him, he fled. When Ziyād inspected the people, Awfā marched past him. Ziyād asked, "Who is this?" When he was told that he was Awfā b. Ḥiṣn, Ziyād quoted, "His feet brought misery."[308] At that Awfā recited:

---

307. A *kursī* was a chair, throne, or judgment seat.
308. Maydānī, *Amthāl*, I, 21–22; tr. G. W. Freytag, *Arabum Proverbia* I, 25.

Indeed, Ziyād, Abū al-Mughīrah, does not
hurry, while the people have haste.

I feared you, by God, so know my oath,
fear of the serpents,[309] the attack of the vipers.

[89] You came when the land was confined, so there
was no refuge upon it for someone fearful.

Ziyād asked, "What is your opinion about ʿUthmān?" Awfā replied, "Husband of two daughters of the Messenger of God. I have not disowned him. That is my general opinion." Ziyād continued, "What, then, do you say about Muʿāwiyah?" Awfā answered, "Generous, forbearing." Ziyād then asked, "And what do you say about me?" Awfā responded, "I heard that you said in al-Baṣrah, 'I shall certainly seize the healthy for the sick and the one who comes for the one who turns away.'" Ziyād replied, "That's true." Awfā said, "You acted arbitrarily."[310] Ziyād retorted, "The braggart is nothing but an evil flute," and killed him. At that, ʿAbdallāh b. Hammām al-Salūlī said:

God thwarted the effort of Awfā b. Ḥiṣn,
when he became the sorcerer's chicken.

Destruction and misery led him to a lion
of a thicket and a deaf viper.

When Ziyād came to al-Kūfah, ʿUmārah b. ʿUqbah b. Abī Muʿayṭ came to him saying, "ʿAmr b. al-Ḥamiq is assembling some of the faction of Abū Turāb."[311] ʿAmr b. Ḥurayth asked him, "What leads you to report what you are not certain about and do not know what the result might be?" Ziyād then said "Both of you are wrong to talk with me about this openly,

---

This proverb is ascribed to al-Ḥārith b. Jabalah al-Ghassānī who said it to al-Ḥārith b. ʿAyyāf al-ʿAbdī who had satirized him, when the latter was brought captive to him. It is also ascribed to ʿUbayd b. al-Abraṣ who said it to al-Nuʿmān b. al-Mundhir.

309. *Al-ḥafāfīth*, pl. of *ḥufāth*: a large, mottled, red snake with a great head.

310. Lit. "You flailed about in the dark."

311. That is, "Father of Dust," an appellation of uncertain origin used of ʿAlī by his enemies. See E. Kohlberg, "Abū Turāb," 347–52.

while ʿAmr would refute what you say. Both of you go to ʿAmr b. al-Ḥamiq and say to him, "What is this group that you assemble? If anyone wants to speak with you, or you with him, do so in the mosque." ʿAmr b. al-Ḥamiq is also said to have been accused of that by Yazīd b. Ruwaym who told Ziyād, "ʿAmr has made both cities fester." At that, ʿAmr b. al-Ḥurayth remarked, "Yazīd has never been occupied with anything useful at any given time." Ziyād then told Yazīd b. Ruwaym, "As for you, you would have allowed ʿAmr b. al-Ḥamiq's blood to be shed; and as for ʿAmr [b. al-Ḥurayth], you would have spared his blood. Even if I knew that the marrow of his leg had liquified out of hatred for me, I would not be furious with him until he should rebel against me." Ziyād also made use of the *maq-* [90] *ṣūrah*[312] when the people of al-Kūfah pelted him with pebbles. When Ziyād set out from al-Baṣrah for al-Kūfah, he put Samurah b. Jundab in charge (of al-Baṣrah).

I was told by ʿUmar—Iṣḥāq b. Idrīs[313]—Muḥammad b. Sulaym: I asked Anas b. Sīrīn if Samurah b. Jundab had killed anyone. He replied, "Can those whom Samurah b. Jundab killed be counted? Ziyad made him deputy over al-Baṣrah and came to al-Kūfah. When he returned, Samurah had killed eight thousand people. Ziyād asked him, 'Aren't you afraid that you might have killed someone who was innocent?' Samurah replied, 'Even if I should kill as many more of them, I would not fear [it],' or words to that effect."

I was told by ʿUmar—Mūsā b. Ismāʿīl—Nūḥ b. Qays—Ashʿath al-Ḥuddānī—Abū Sawwār al-ʿAdawī: On one morning Samurah killed forty-seven men of my folk who had collected the Qur'ān.

I was told by ʿUmar—ʿAlī b. Muḥammad—Jaʿfar al-Sadafī—Awf: Samurah approached from al-Madīnah. When he was at the dwellings of the Banū Asad, a man went out from one of their alleys, and suddenly attacked the first cavalry. Someone among the folk then attacked the man, piercing him with a spear. The cavalry then advanced, and Samurah b. Jundab came upon the man as he lay wallowing in his blood. Sa-

312. See above, n. 257.
313. O reads: Uways.

murah asked, "Who is this?" and was told, "The first cavalry of the amīr struck him." Samurah remarked, "If you hear that we have ridden, avoid our spearheads."

I was told by 'Umar—Zuhayr b. Ḥarb—Wahb b. Jarīr—Ghassān b. Muḍar—Sa'īd b. Zayd: Qarīb and Zuḥḥāf rebelled while Ziyād was at al-Kūfah and Samurah at al-Baṣrah. We[314] went out by night and camped with the Banū Yashkur, who were seventy men—that was in Ramaḍān (September 22–October 21,
[91] 670). They then came to the Banū Ḍubay'ah, who were seventy men. As they went past one of their shaykhs called Ḥakkāk, he saw them and said, "Welcome to Abū al-Sha'thā.'"[315] They thought that the shaykh was Ibn Ḥiṣn,[316] so they killed him and dispersed among the places of worship belonging to the Azd. A group of them came to the plaza (*raḥbah*) of the Banū 'Alī, and another of the Mosque of al-Mu'ādil. At that, Sayf b. Wahb went forth against them with his friends and killed whomever came his way. Youths of the Banū 'Alī and of the Banū Rāsib also went forth against Qarīb and Zuḥḥāf, shooting arrows at them. Qarīb asked, "Is 'Abdallāh b. Aws al-Ṭāḥī among the folk?" while he was contending with him. Upon being told that he was, Qarīb exclaimed, "Onward, then, to the contest!" 'Abdallāh then killed him and brought (back) his head. Ziyād arrived from al-Kūfah, and began to rebuke him, saying, "O best of the Ṭāḥīs, if you had not succeeded against the folk, I would have removed you to the prison." Qarīb belonged to the Iyād and Zuḥḥāf to the Ṭayyi', and they were cousins. They were both the first ones to rebel after the people of al-Nahr. Ghassān said: I heard Sa'īd saying that Abū Bilāl said, "God did not bring Qarīb close.[317] I swear by God that I would rather fall from the sky than do what he did," (that is, act ruthlessly).[318]

I was told by 'Umar—Zuhayr—Wahb—his father: Ziyād treated the Ḥarūriyyah more harshly after Qarīb and Zuḥḥāf. He killed them and ordered Samurah to do the same. Ziyād would

314. Cairo: "they both," would seem to be the preferred reading.
315. Abū al-Sha'thā' means "one with matted or disheveled hair."
316. That is, the commander of Ziyād's police force.
317. Qarīb means "close" or "near."
318. According to Ibn al-Khayyāt, *Ta'rīkh*, I, 260–64, these events occurred in the year 53(672/3).

appoint Samurah deputy over al-Baṣrah whenever he went to al-Kūfah. So Samurah killed many of them. I was told by ʿUmar—Abū ʿUbaydah: At that time Ziyād spoke from the pulpit, "O people of al-Baṣrah, By God, take care of these for me or I shall certainly start with you. By God, if a single man of them escapes, you won't get one dirham of your stipends for the [entire] year." So the people rose up against them and killed them.

(According to) Muḥammad b. ʿUmar: In this year Muʿāwiyah [92]
ordered[319] that the pulpit of the Messenger of God be transported[320] to Syria. When it was moved, the sun was eclipsed so that the stars were seen plainly that day. When the people considered that to be very momentous, Muʿāwiyah said, "I didn't want to move it; rather, I feared that it would have become wormy, so I paid attention to it." Then he draped it that day. Muḥammad b. ʿUmar also mentioned that Khālid b. al-Qāsim told him that, according to Shuʿayb b. ʿAmr al-Umawī.

(I was told by) Muḥammad b. ʿUmar—Yaḥyā b. Saʿīd b. Dīnār—his father: Muʿāwiyah said, "Indeed, I thought that the pulpit and staff of the Messenger of God should not be left at al-Madīnah because [its people] were the enemies and murderers of the Commander of the Faithful, ʿUthmān," When Muʿāwiyah arrived, he looked for the staff, and Saʿd al-Qaraẓ had it. Abū Hurayrah and Jābir b. ʿAbdallāh then came to him, saying, "O Commander of the Faithful, we remind you of God, Almighty and Great. Do not do this. For it is not right for the pulpit of the Messenger of God to be removed from the place where he put it, nor for his staff to be removed to Syria. Would you remove the mosque!" At that, Muʿawiyah refrained and added six steps to the pulpit. As a result, today it has eight steps.[321] He also apologized to the people for what he did.

(According to) Muḥammad b. ʿUmar—Suwayd[322] b. ʿAbd al-Azīz—Isḥāq b. ʿAbdallāh b. Abī Farwah—Abān b. Ṣāliḥ—Qabīṣah b. Dhu'ayb: ʿAbd al-Malik[323] was concerned about the

---

319. O reads: "wanted to pull up the pulpit."
320. C reads: "and transport it."
321. See also Masʿūdī, *Murūj*, V, 66.
322. C reads: Mūsā.
323. ʿAbd al-Malik was Caliph from 65(685) until 86 (705). See *EI*², s.v. ʿAbd al-Malik b. Marwān.

pulpit. So Qabīṣah b. Dhu'ayb said to him, "I remind you of God, Almighty and Great, [warning] not to do this and not to transfer it. Indeed, when the Commander of the Faithful, Muʿāwiyah, moved it, the sun was eclipsed. The Messenger of God said, 'Whoever swears an oath upon my pulpit sinfully, his resting place shall be in the fire.'[324] You would remove it from al-Madīnah while it is part of the rights among the people at al-Madīnah." As a result, ʿAbd al-Malik refrained from that and
[93] abstained from mentioning it. When al-Walīd[325] was (ruler) and made the pilgrimage, he was interested in that, saying, "Tell me about it. I certainly think that I shall do [it]." Saʿīd b. al-Musayyib then sent to ʿUmar b. ʿAbd al-ʿAzīz,[326] saying, "Tell your master, 'Fear God, Almighty and Great, and don't be exposed to God, to whom be praise, nor to His wrath.'" When ʿUmar b. ʿAbd al-ʿAzīz spoke to him, al-Walīd refrained and abstained from mentioning it. When Sulaymān b. ʿAbd al-Malik[327] made the pilgrimage, ʿUmar b. ʿAbd al-ʿAzīz informed him about what al-Walīd had been interested in and the message Saʿīd b. al-Musayyib had sent to him. At that, Sulaymān remarked, "I did not like for that to be mentioned about ʿAbd al-Malik or about al-Walīd. This is arrogance, and is not for us or for this pulpit. We took over the world, and it is in our hands, and we want to support one of the symbols of Islām sent to it by transporting it to our presence. This is not righteous."

In this year Muʿāwiyah b. Ḥudayj was dismissed from Egypt and Ifrīqiyyah. Muʿāwiyah b. Abī Sufyān had sent ʿUqbah b. Nāfiʿ al-Fihrī to Ifrīqiyyah before he put Maslamah in charge of Egypt and Ifrīqiyyah. ʿUqbah conquered Ifrīqiyyah and laid out is (city of) Qayrawān.[328] Muḥammad b. ʿUmar claimed that its location, a thicket, was undesirable because of beasts of prey

---

324. This is a well-known hadīth. See Wensinck, *Handbook*, 198.

325. Al-Walīd was the son and successor of ʿAbd al-Malik as Caliph from 86(705) until 98(715) See EI^1, s.v. al-Walīd b. ʿAbd al-Malik.

326. ʿUmar b. ʿAbd al-ʿAzīz was the governor of al-Madīnah for his cousin, al-Walīd. He was Caliph from 99(717) until 101(720) See EI^1, s.v. ʿOmar b. ʿAbd al-ʿAzīz.

327. Sulaymān was Caliph from 98(715) until 99(717) See EI^2, s.v. Sulaimān b. ʿAbd al-Malik.

328. Qayrawān (Kairouan) is in central Tunisia, 156 km south of Tunis. See Ibn Khayyāṭ, *Ta'rīkh*, I, 247; and EI^2, s. v. al-Ḳayrawān.

and snakes and other kinds of animals. When God, Almighty and Great, summoned them, none of them remained but they all fled as the beasts of prey carried off their cubs. (According to) Muḥammad b. ʿUmar—Mūsā b. ʿAlī—his father: ʿUqbah b. Nāfiʿ announced, "Indeed when we settled they departed, blaming us, and went out fleeing from their dens."

I was told by al-Mufaḍḍil b. Faḍālah—Zayd b. Abī Ḥabīb—a man from the Egyptian army: We arrived with ʿUqbah b. Nāfiʿ who was the first person to lay out (the city). He divided it up [94] into dwellings and houses for the people, and built its mosque. We stayed with him until he was dismissed. He was the best of governors and the best commander.

Then in this year, Muʿāwiyah dismissed Muʿāwiyah b. Ḥudayj from Egypt and ʿUqbah b. Nāfiʿ from Ifrīqiyyah, and he put Maslamah b. Mukhallad in charge of all of Egypt and the West. He was the first one for whom the entire West, Egypt, Barqah, Ifrīqiyyah, and Ṭarābulus were combined. Maslamah b. Mukhallad put a mawlā of his called al-Muhājir in charge of Ifrīqiyyah, dismissed ʿUqbah b. Nāfiʿ, and removed him from affairs of government. Maslamah remained as governor over Egypt and the West, while Abū al-Muhājir was in charge of Ifrīqiyyah on his behalf, until Muʿāwiyah b. Abī Sufyān died.

In this year Abū Mūsā al-Ashʿarī died. It has also been said that the death of Abū Mūsā occurred in the year 52(672)

There is a difference of opinion about who led the people in the pilgrimage this year. Some people said Muʿāwiyah led them in pilgrimage. Others said his son Yazīd led them in the pilgrimage. In this year the governor of al-Madīnah was Saʿīd b. al-ʿĀṣ, while Ziyād was in charge of al-Baṣrah, al-Kūfah, the East, Sijistān, al-Sind, and al-Hind.

In this year Ziyād sought al-Farazdaq,[329] while the Banū Nahshal and Fuqaym incited (Ziyād) against him. As a result, al-Farazdaq fled from Ziyād to Saʿīd b. al-ʿĀṣ, who was then governor of al-Madīnah for Muʿāwiyah. He sought refuge with Saʿīd, and the latter granted him asylum.

329. Al-Farazdaq, "the lump of dough", was the famous poet, Hammām b. Ghālib who died ca. 110(728) or 112(730) See *EI*^{2}, s.v. al-Farazdaḳ.

Al-Farazdaq's Flight from Ziyād

I was told by ʿUmar b. Shabbah—Abū ʿUbaydah and Abū al-Ḥasan al-Madāʾinī and others: When al-Farazdaq satirized the Banū Nahshal and the Banū Fuqaym . . . Abū Zayd did not add to the chain of authorities (*isnād*) of his report more than I have mentioned. As for Muḥammad b. ʿAlī, he told me according to
[95] Muḥammad b. Saʿd[330]—Abū ʿUbaydah—Aʿyān b. Labaṭah b. al-Farazdaq—his father—his father: When I satirized al-Ashhab b. Rumaylah and al-Baʿīth they were both disgraced. The Banū Nahshal and the Banū Fuqaym incited Ziyād b. Abī Sufyān against me. Others claimed that Yazīd b. Masʿūd b. Khālid b. Mālik b. Ribʿī b. Salmā b. Jandal b. Nahshal also incited against him. Aʿyan said: Ziyād did not recognize (who al-Farazdaq was) until he was told, "The bedouin youth who clutched his coin,[331] and threw off his clothing."

(According to) Abū ʿUbaydah—Aʿyan b. Labaṭah—his father—his father: My father, Ghālib, sent me with his caravan and merchandise in order to sell it and purchase items for him and to buy clothing for his family. Upon arriving at al-Baṣrah, I sold the merchandise, took the money it brought, and put it inside my clothes, holding on to it. Then a man confronted me who seemed to me like a devil. When he remarked, "How often you check it," I responded, "And what prevents me?" He replied, "Now then, if it were someone else I knew, he would not keep it." At that, I asked, "And who is he?" He replied, "Ghālib b. Ṣaʿṣaʿah." So I summoned the people of the Mirbad,[332] and saying "Take it!" I scattered the money upon them. When someone said, "Cast off your robe, O son of Ghālib," I cast it off. When another said, "Cast off your shirt," I cast that off. Yet another said, "Cast off your turban." So I cast that off until I was left in underwear. But when they said, "Cast off your underwear," I replied, "I shall not cast it off and go naked. I am not insane." When the news reached Ziyād, he sent cavalry to the Mirbad to bring me to him. But a man of the Banū al-

---

330. O reads: Saʿdān.

331. The text reads: *waraqahu*; O reads: *ridfahu*, "his backside;" C reads: *rizqahu*, "his ration."

332. The Mirbad was an open space in al-Baṣrah used as a market-place.

Hujaym came on horseback, saying, "They are coming for you. To the rescue!" He mounted me behind him, and galloped off until we escaped. When the cavalry arrived, I had already left.

Ziyād then took my two uncles, Dhuhayl[333] and al-Zuḥḥāf, [96] the sons of Ṣaʿṣaʿah, who were registered in the *dīwān* for two thousand dirhams apiece. Since they were there, he imprisoned them. I sent word to them both, "If you wish, I would come to you." But they both replied, "Don't come near us. Indeed, this is Ziyād. What might he do to us, although we have not committed any crime?" They both stayed several days. Then some people interceded with Ziyād, saying, "These are two attentive and obedient shaykhs who have committed no crime except for what a bedouin youth belonging to the desert people did." At that, Ziyād released them, and they both said to me, "Inform us about your entire business for your father—provisions or clothing?" I then told them both everything. They bought it, and I went off to Ghālib, bringing everything with me. When I came to him, the news about me had already reached him. When he asked me, "How did you do?" I told him what had happened. He remarked, "Indeed you did well." And he rubbed my head.

At that time al-Farazdaq was not composing poetry, but he composed poetry afterwards. Ziyād thus harbored that (escapade) against him.

Then al-Aḥnaf b. Qays, Jāriyah b. Qudāmah of the Banū Rabīʿah b. Kaʿb b. Saʿd, al-Jawn b. Qatādah al-ʿAbshamī,[334] and al-Ḥutāt b. Yazīd Abū Munāzil one of the Banū Ḥuwayy[335] b. Sufyān b. Muhjāshiʿ travelled to visit Muʿāwiyah b. Alī Sufyān. He assigned each of them stipends of one hundred thousand dirhams, while he assigned al-Ḥutāt a stipend of seventy thousand. When they were on the road, they questioned each other and told about their stipends. Since al-Ḥutāt had received only seventy thousand, he returned to Muʿāwiyah. When the latter asked him, "What brought you back, O Abū Munāzil?" he re-

---

333. O reads: Zunbīl.

334. For al-Jawn b. Qatādah see Ibn al-Athīr, *Usd*, I, 312–13.

335. C reads: Jawn. For al-Ḥutāt b. Yazīd see Ibn al-Athīr, *Usd*, I, 379, which has a version of this account explaining that al-Aḥnaf and Jāriyah had been supporters of ʿAlī.

plied, "You have disgraced me among the Banū Tamīm. Is not my lineage sound? Am I not old? Am I not obeyed by my clan?" When Muʿāwiyah replied that he was, he asked, "Why then did
[97] you belittle me before the folk?" Muʿāwiyah explained. "Indeed I purchased their faith from the folk and entrusted you with your faith and your views about ʿUthmān b. ʿAffān"—al-Ḥutāt was an ʿUthmānī. At that he said, "Me, too; purchase my faith from me." So Muʿāwiyah ordered the full stipend of the folk for him. But al-Ḥutāt disparaged his stipend, so Muʿāwiyah withheld it. Al-Farazdaq then said about that:[336]

Both your father and my uncle, O Muʿāwiyah, bequeathed
an inheritance. So his relatives own the inheritance.[337]

Why did you take [338] the legacy of al-Ḥutāt,
while the liquidity of Ḥarb's legacy is frozen for you?

For if this matter had happened during the Jāhiliyyah,
You would have known whose auxiliary cavalry is insignificant.

And if it was during [the time of] faith [something] like this would be hateful to you.
We have our rightful possession,[339] or he choked on the water he drank.[340]

And if it happened when we were [there], while the hand was generous,
a sharp [sword] would determine its blow, penetrating you.

(Muḥammad b. ʿAlī recited: While there was abundance[341] in the palm of the hand.)

---

336. Other versions of this poem are in Boucher, *Divan*, III, 139; Bevan, *Nakā'iḍ*, 608–9; Iṣfahānī, *Aghānī*, XIX, 37; Ṣāwī, *Sharḥ*, 56–7. The first eight lines are quoted by Ibn al-Athīr, *Usd*, I, 379.

337. Boucher, *Divan* reads: "relatives are the first to inherit."

338. Boucher, *Divan* reads: "devour."

339. Boucher, *Divan* reads: "And if this matter happened in someone else's kingdom, you would fulfill it."

340. See Maydānī, *Amthāl*, II, 429; Freytag, *Proverbia*, II, 943: "He eats an elephant and chokes on an insect," said of someone who tries to avoid lying.

341. O reads: "something pleasant."

You were hurled at something, O Muʿāwiyah, before which
are huge chasms whose steepness is difficult,

While I did not give[342] half[343] from powerlessness
except yourself. Even if his squadrons were hostile to me,

Am I not the most respected of people with regard to relatives and clan? [98]
and more forbidding than they towards neighbors when his side is wronged?

And no [woman] bore after the Prophet and his family
the likes of me, a stallion among men resembling him.

My father is Ghālib, and the man is a confidant whose
descent is traced to Ṣaʿṣaʿah,[344] so who is there related to him?[345]

The courtyard of my house is beside the Pleiades,
and before it the full moon passing among its stars.[346]

My ancestors are stoney[347] mountains, as many as pebbles,
and my lineage is the lineage of generosity, so who would call it to account?

I am the son of one who gives life to the *waʾīd*[348] and a guarantor
against fate when its profits were difficult.

---

342. Boucher, *Divan* reads: "was not given."
343. That is, submission and obedience to the government. See Ṣāwī, *Sharḥ*, 57.
344. Bevan, *Naḳāʾiḍ*, 609 reads:

My forefather is Ghālib and the man
Ṣaʿṣaʿah who traces his descent to Dārim.

Dārim b. Mālik b. Ḥanẓalah was one of the main tribal divisions of Tamīm.
345. The previous four lines are in the *Naḳāʾiḍ* but not in the *Divan*.
346. This line occurs in the *Dīwān* after the following line as:
The courtyard of my house is spacious. . . .

347. Bevan, *Naḳāʾiḍ* reads: "lofty."
348. A *waʾīd* is an unwanted child condemned to be buried alive.

How many forefathers I have, O Muʿāwiyah, who are still
more illustrious;[349] what his side turns away competes with the wind.

The branches of the two Māliks[350] augmented him, and your father,
who was from ʿAbd al-Shams, does not resemble him.[351]

You see him as the blade of the sword shaking for generosity,
noble,[352] achieving glory, when his mustache sprouted,

Long of sword-belt, since he was,
Quṣayy and ʿAbd al-Shams are not among those who address him.[353]

[99] Muʿāwiyah then returned thirty thousand dirhams to the family of al-Ḥutāt, and that also made Ziyād angry with al-Farazdaq. When Nahshal and Fuqaym complained about al-Farazdaq, Ziyād's anger against him increased. But when he sought him, al-Farazdaq fled and came to ʿIsā b. Khuṣaylah b. Muʿattib b. Naṣr b. ʿIlāṭ b. Khālid al-Sulamī.

Ibn Saʿd said: Abū ʿUbaydah and Abū Mūsā al-Faḍl b. Mūsā b. Khuṣaylah told me: When Ziyād drove out al-Farazdaq, the latter came at night to my uncle, ʿIsā b. Khuṣaylah, saying, "O Abū Khuṣaylah, indeed this man has frightened me, and my friend and everyone in whom I was placing my hopes have rejected me. I have come to you to hide." Abū Khuṣaylah welcomed him, and al-Farazdaq stayed with him for three nights. Then al-Farazdaq told him, "It seems to me that I should go to Syria." Abū Khuṣaylah replied, "You are welcome to stay with me for as long as you like, and if you should depart, this Arḥabiyyah[354] she-camel is yours." So he rode off after a night, and

349. The text reads: *agharra*, lit. a horse with a blaze on its forehead, bright, esteemed.

350. The lineage of the Banū Dārim went back to Mālik b. Ḥanẓalah b. Mālik b. Zayd Manāt b. Tamīm.

351. Boucher, *Divan* reads: "is not on speaking terms with him."

352. Boucher, *Divan* reads: "generous."

353. This line is in the *Naḳāʾiḍ* but not in the *Divan*.

354. The Arḥabiyyah was a breed of fast she-camel named after the Banū Ar-

ʿIsā sent someone with him until he got beyond the houses. By morning he had gone more than a three-nights' journey. Al-Farazdaq said about that:[355]

Al-Bahzī bestowed[356] a mount[357] on me, no matter who disapproved
of the people, and the crimes of the criminal are feared.

And who, O ʿIsā, would blame his guest?
Your guest is well-treated, his food delicious.[358]

He said, "Know that she is an Arḥabiyyah [100]
and that she is at your disposal for your night journey.[359]

When morning came I put al-Mulqā and Ḥanbal[360] behind me.
She did not go forth until its darkness lifted [from] the star.[361]

She moves away from the people of al-Ḥufayr[362] as if she were
a male ostrich whose female ostriches compete during the darkness of night.

She saw Duwayyah[363] before her eyes and the dawn
appeared for her [leaving] from smooth peaked Ṣaʿl,[364]

ḥab branch of the Banū Hamdān, who owned camels famous for their speed, descended, according to legend, from a fantastic camel stallion that came once a year to mix with the tribe's herds. See Boucher, *Divan*, I, 233.

355. Other versions of this poem are in Boucher, *Divan*, III, 87; Bevan, *Naḳāʾiḍ*; II, 610; Iṣfahānī, *Aghānī*, XIX, 30–1; and Ṣāwī, *Sharḥ*, 763–4.

356. Bevan, *Naḳāʾiḍ*; Boucher, *Divan* read: "satisfied" or "protected."

357. Boucher, *Divan* reads: "all together."

358. This line is in the *Naḳāʾiḍ* but not in the *Divan*.

359. This is the second line in the *Divan*.

360. Ḥanbal was a marsh or meadow in the territory of the Banū Tamīm. See Yāqūt, *Muʿjam*, III, 350.

361. That is, until the star rose from its darkness. The *Naḳāʾiḍ* and the *Divan* have "the night" instead of "the star." This the eleventh line in the *Divan*.

362. Al-Ḥufayr was the first stop on the road from al-Baṣrah to Mecca. "She" is the riding camel. This is the eighth line in the *Divan*.

363. Bevan, *Naḳāʾiḍ*; Boucher, *Divan* read: Ruwayyah. The latter was a hill near Ḥanbal.

364. This is the twelfth line in the *Divan*.

As a sail which has the stream of her halter
on the Tigris [Dijlah] except [for] its nose and the corners of its mouth.[365]

When you went past al-Ghāriyyān,[366] then be safe,
and the ravines of Falj turned away behind me.

He also said:

The means of ʿIsā saved me from ruin,
and whoever's protector he is, is not alone.[367]

It is a long *qaṣīdah*.

When Ziyād heard that al-Farazdaq had left, he sent ʿAlī b. Zahdam, one of the Banū Nawlah[368] b. Fuqaym, in search of him. Aʿyan said: ʿAlī sought him in the house of a Christian
[101] woman called Bint Marrār of the Banū Qays b. Thaʿlabah who dwelt in Qaṣīmah Kāẓimah.[369] She pulled him out through a crack in her house and ʿAlī was unable to catch him. Al-Farazdaq said about that:[370]

I came to the daughter of al-Marrār, who took the opportunity to desire.
and the likes of me is not desired below stairs.[371]

---

365. Boucher, *Divan* reads:

As if a neck, her halter doubled on it,
from al-Sāj, if not her nose and its throats.

366. Bevan, *Naḳā'iḍ* reads: "When I passed beyond al-Ghāriyyān;" Boucher, *Divan* reads: "When al-Furayyān came before me." Al-Furayyān was a mountain in the territory of the Banū Asad between al-Nibāj and al-Nakrah. This is the thirteenth line in the *Divan*.

367. Ṣāwī, *Sharḥ* reads: "Al-Bahzī bestowed her on me, myself his ransom." This is also in Bevan, *Naḳā'iḍ*, 610.

368. Bevan, *Naḳā'iḍ* reads: Banū Maw'alah.

369. Bevan, *Naḳā'iḍ* reads: Quṣaybah. Qaṣīmah Kāzimah was on the Gulf coast below al-Baṣrah. A *qaṣīmah* is a tract of sand covered with small shrubs.

370. These lines are also in Bevan, *Naḳā'iḍ*, 611, and Boucher, *Divan*, 66.

371. Bevan, *Naḳā'iḍ*, 611 reads:

You refused the daughter of al-Marrār, who ripped up in order to desire,
And the likes of me is not desired behind the barn;

But my desire, if you wish our meeting[372] [is]
the vast expanse[373] of the deserts, not desire[374] for jungles.

She is said to have been Rabīʿah bt. al-Marrār b. Salāmah al-ʿIjlī, the mother of Abū al-Najm al-Rājiz.

(According to) Abū ʿUbaydah—Mismaʿ b. ʿAbd al-Mālik: Al-Farazdaq reached al-Rawḥā'[375] and settled among the Bakr b. Wā'il and was safe. He thus said, eulogizing them:[376]

When she compared whither to journey,[377] she did not find
for her rising up[378] [anyone] like the tribe of Bakr b. Wā'il,

More virtuous and more faithful towards an obligation which they contract,
when the top of the summits balanced the upper backs.[379]

It is a long *qaṣīdah*. He also eulogized them in other *qaṣīdahs*.

Al-Farazdaq would live in al-Kūfah when Ziyād lived in al-Baṣrah, and when Ziyād lived in al-Kūfah, al-Farazdaq would live in al-Baṣrah. Ziyād would live in al-Baṣrah for six months and in al-Kūfah for six months, When Ziyād learned about what al-Farazdaq did, he wrote to his official in charge of al-Kūfah, ʿAbd al-Raḥmān b. ʿUbayd, "Al-Farazdaq is a wild male [102]
beast grazing in the wastelands. When people come upon him, he becomes frightened and leaves them for other territory, where he pastures. So seek him until you seize him."

Boucher, *Divan*, 66 reads:

You came to the daughter of al-Marrār, who tears off her veil,
and the likes of me is not desired beneath the cushions [or trees].

372. Boucher, *Divan* reads: "my desire."
373. Boucher, *Divan* reads: "wide."
374. Bevan, *Naḳā'iḍ*; Boucher, *Divan* read: "hiding."
375. Al-Rawḥā' is said to be a place between al-Madīnah and Mecca. See Yāqūt, *Muʿjam*, II, 828–9.
376. These lines are also in Bevan, *Naḳā'iḍ*, 612, and Iṣfahānī, *Aghānī*, XIX, 31–2.
377. Bevan, *Naḳā'iḍ* reads: "She had been inclined between the departure."
378. Bevan, *Naḳā'iḍ* reads: "for her private parts."
379. Explained in Bevan, *Naḳā'iḍ*: "The humps became like the withers from drought and sparse pasture."

Al-Farazdaq said: I was sought most diligently so that those who used to shelter me began to turn me out of their homes. As a result, the land was restricted for me. While I had my head wrapped up in my garment upon the road, whoever came in search of me passed me by.

When it was night, I came to some of my uncles belonging to the Banū Ḍabbah while they were celebrating a wedding. I had not tasted food before that. When I said I came for their (wedding feast), I got some food. But while I was sitting, I noticed someone leading a horse, and the tip of a spear had gone through the doorway of the house and was entering where we were. My hosts went up to a reed wall, lifted it up, and I went out under it. Then they said, "We didn't see him." After they searched for a while, the searchers left. When it was morning my relatives came to me, saying, "Leave for the Ḥijāz, out of Ziyād's reach, so he won't seize you. For if he had seized you last night, you would have destroyed us." They collected the price of two female riding camels, and spoke for me to Muqāʿis, one of the Banū Taym Allāh b. Thaʿlabah who was a guide who conveyed merchants.

We then went out to Bāniqyā until we reached one of the inhabited fortresses. Since the gate was not opened for us, as it was a moonlit night, we threw down our saddlebags beside the wall. I asked, "O Muqāʿis, do you think that if Ziyād should send men after we reach al-ʿAtīq, that they would overpower us?" He replied, "Yes, they are watching for us, but they would not be going beyond al-ʿAtīq"—the latter was a defensive fortification (*khandaq*) which had belonged to the Persians.[380] I asked, "What do people say?" He replied, "They say, 'Give him
[103] a respite of a day and a night, then take him,' so set out." He added, "Indeed, I fear the lions." At that, I responded, "Lions are easier than Ziyād."

We then set out and left behind anything we saw, while a figure accompanied us without leaving us. I said, "O Muqāʿis, do

380. It was part of the Khandaq Sābūr. See Ṭabarī, *Taʾrīkh*, I, 2286; Ibn Rustah, *Aʿlāq*, 107–8; Bakrī, *Muʿjam*, 914; Yāqūt, *Muʿjam*, II, 476; Musil, *The Middle Euphrates*, 111, 347–8; Nyberg, "Die sassanidische Westgrenze," 318; Frye, "The Sasanian System of Walls for Defense." 8–11.

you see this figure? We leave behind everything else we pass, but indeed this figure has been keeping up with us since nightfall." He replied, "This is the lion." At that, it seemed to understand our conversation, and went forward until it lay down in the middle of the road. When we saw that, we halted and tied both forelegs of both our she-camels with two hobbles. I took my bow while Muqāʿis said, "O Thaʿlab! Do you know from whom we fled to you? From Ziyād." At that, it flicked pebbles with its tail so that the dust settled on us and on both of our she-camels. I asked, "Should I shoot at it?" And he replied, "Don't stir him up. When morning comes, he will leave." The lion then began to roar like thunder while Muqāʿis menaced it until daybreak. When the lion saw that (it was dawn), it turned away, and al-Farazdaq composed the following:[381]

I did not consider myself a coward after what
    I experienced at night beside the canals,

A lion, as if it were a camel [when it stands] on its paws
    strong clawed, firm[382] clawed,

When I heard it's roar, I burst into tears
    for myself, and said, "Whither shall I flee?"[383]

While I encouraged myself, and said, "Be steadfast,"
    and cinched up my clothing in the anxiety of the situation.

So you are easier to confront[384] than Ziyād,
    go to you! O render of journeys![385]

(According to) Ibn Saʿd—Abū ʿUbaydah—Aʿyan b. Labaṭah—his father—Shabath b. Ribʿī al-Riyāḥī: These verses were recited to Ziyād, and he seemed to take pity on al-Farazdaq, saying, "If he should come to me, I would grant him a guaran- [104]

381. These lines are also in Bevan, *Naḳā'iḍ*, 617.
382. The text reads: *mu'jadah*; O reads: *mūkhazah*, "stabbing."
383. Lit: "Where is my flight?"
384. Bevan, *Naḳā'iḍ* reads: "with us."
385. Bevan, *Naḳā'iḍ*: "render of travellers" is better.

teed safe-conduct and a stipend." When al-Farazdaq heard about that, he said:[386]

This heart recalled a memory about its longing,
remembered a longing that it will never forget.

It remembered Ẓamyā' whom it does not forget
even if nearly ten pilgrimages[387] have passed since having contact with her.

And there is no gazelle with her fawn in the lowlands, the lowlands of Tihāmah,
grazing on[388] *arāk*[389] in its luxurient[390] vegetation,[391]

Tan-skinned,[392] with dark-red[393] tear ducts,[394] she watches
over a fawn which she considers to be weak,[395]

Who fell into a snare in the valley[396] of Walwalān
so she struggled until they thought she would escape,[397]

Lovelier than Ẓamyā' on a day when she ventured,[398]
nor rain clouds whose thunder-head went away in the evening.

---

386. This poem is also in Bevan, *Naḳā'iḍ*, 617–18, and Boucher, *Divan*, 20–21.
387. That is, "years."
388. Bevan, *Naḳā'iḍ* reads: "watching out for."
389. *Arāk* is a spiny shrub on which camels graze and from which toothbrushes are made.
390. The text reads: *manābitihi*; C reads: *makhāzimihā*, "pasture;" Boucher, *Divan* reads: *makhārimihā*, "openings."
391. Boucher, *Divan* reads: "ravines."
392. *Al-udm*, when refering to deer, is a light brown, almost white color. See Ibn Manẓūr, *Lisān*, XII, 10–12. Boucher, *Divan* reads: "bending."
393. *Ḥawwā'* is the color of a lip between red and black. See Ibn Manẓūr, *Lisān*, XIV, 207.
394. Bevan, *Naḳā'iḍ* reads: *ḥawrā'*, "very black and very white eye."
395. The text reads: *fatrā*; C reads: *qaṭrā*, "stingy."
396. The text reads: *bi-wādī*; Bevan, *Naḳā'iḍ*; Boucher, *Divan* read: *bi'aʿlā*, "on the summit."
397. Bevan, *Naḳā'iḍ*, 618 reads: "you thought she would break."
398. Boucher, *Divan* reads: "when I encountered her."

How many protectors are around her with a bridle.[399]
while enemies of folk are vowing [to shed] my blood.

When they threatened me in the presence of Ẓamyā', such threats [105]
grieved her, and she said, "Don't abuse him."

Ziyād summons me for the stipend, but I would not
come to him as long as someone with a noble lineage distributes wealth.[400]

With Ziyād, if he wants their stipend,
are many men in whom poverty is seen,

Sitting before the gates, petitioners for a need
because of serious[401] needs or a new need.

When I feared that his stipend would be
black fetters or twisted brown whip-cords,

I reached a lean she-camel, emaciated
from travelling by night and traversing the desolate land.

She exhales in a wide open space from the hollow[402]
when the protruding ends of her ribs expand the girth.[403]

You see her when the day reaches noon as if
she seeks to outrace a camel stallion, or to steal a wager from him.

She wades when the echo rings out after slumber
of the early night, roaring, its dark[404] thickets.

---

399. The text reads: *fi-ṣarīmah*, which can also mean "in an isolated patch of sand."

400. This and several following lines are also in Ibn ʿAbd Rabbihi, *Iqd*, V, 320.

401. Bevan, *Naḳā'iḍ*; Boucher, *Divan*, 21 read: "somewhat old."

402. Bevan, *Naḳā'iḍ* reads: "the air."

403. A *dafr* is a strap made of plaited goat's hair used as a camel-saddle girth.

404. *Khuḍrā* refers to the darkness of long winter nights. This line is in the *Naḳā'iḍ* but not in the *Divan*.

[106] So, if she swerved aside [it was] obliquely, or a waterless desert
made her[405] hurry, you see the dusty cracks from it.

They gallop past reddish[406] pebbles as if
they crushed[407] coals thereby from every gravel bed.

How many a secret enemy has she gone past
in fear of him until she is a bridge for herself.[408]

One directs her to the desert who does not regard[409]
the son of Abū Sufyān as having nobility or an excuse.

Don't rush me, my two companions, for perhaps
I will reach the watering place before an early-flying[410] *kudrah*.[411]

In the bosom of the darkness of night, I set out
with a youth who was nodding his head, whose drowsiness had intoxicated him.

Drowsiness struck him on the head until he was as
one whose skull was wounded by rocks which left a crack in it.

From the journey and travelling all night,[412] you would think that[413]

---

405. Bevan, *Naḳā'iḍ* reads: "us."
406. Bevan, *Naḳā'iḍ* reads: "grayish."
407. Bevan, *Naḳā'iḍ* reads: "shattered."
408. Boucher, *Divan*, 21 reads:

On the back of a galloper as if its sides
were backs of hard tracts of soil appearing red.

409. Boucher, *Divan* reads: "Whom you do not regard as having."
410. *Ghādiyah* are birds that fly out in the morning or morning clouds. See Ibn Manẓūr, *Lisān*, XV, 118.
411. A *kudrah* is a swiftly-flying desert bird. This is the last line in the *Divan*.
412. Boucher, *Divan* reads: "journeying uninterruptedly."
413. Boucher, *Divan* reads: "until it was as though."

drowsiness gave him wine to drink in every stopping place.

We dragged along, and took care of him until it seemed as though
he saw the first rays of dawn, a troop of golden horsemen.

We proceeded and reached al-Madīnah while Saʿīd b. al-ʿĀṣ b. [107]
Umayyah was in charge of it. As he was in a funeral procession, I followed him and found him sitting while the corpse was being buried. I went up and stood before him, saying, "This is the place of refuge for a man who is not guilty of [shedding] blood or [stealing] property." Saʿīd replied, "I hereby grant you refuge if you have not been guilty of either." Then he asked, "Who are you?" I answered, "I am Hammām b. Ghālib b. Ṣaʿṣaʿah. I have praised the amīr, and if he saw fit to give me permission, I would let him hear it, so do so." At that Saʿīd said, "Let me have it." So I recited:[414]

By great-humped [camels] which please the guests as a well
and become heavy in their kneeling-places,

until I came to the end, and Marwān said:[415]

Sitting, they looked at Saʿīd.

I responded, "By God, indeed you are standing up, O Abū ʿAbd al-Malik."

Kaʿb b. Juʿayl also spoke up, "This, by God, is the dream that I saw last night." Saʿīd asked, "What did you see?" He replied, "I saw myself walking in one of the streets of al-Madīnah. All at once I was with Ibn Qitrah in a hole, and it seemed as though he wanted to get me, so I avoided him. Al-Ḥuṭay'ah[416] then rose up and split the space between myself and Ibn Qitrah

---

414. This line is from a *qaṣīdah* which is also in Bevan, *Naḳā'iḍ*, 619, and Boucher, *Divan*, 35.

415. Boucher, *Divan*, 37 reads: "Standing, they looked at Saʿīd." See also Bevan, *Naḳā'iḍ*, 619, and Iṣfahānī, *Aghānī*, XIX, 21.

416. Al-Ḥuṭay'ah, "the deformed," was the Arab poet Jarwal b. Aws (b. ca. 582) who appears to have been still alive when Saʿīd b. al-ʿĀṣ was governor of al-Madīnah. See *EI*², s.v. al-Ḥuṭay'a.

so that he went past me, saying, "Say what you want, for you know whoever has departed, while whoever has remained does not know you." Kaʿb told Saʿīd, "This, by God, refers to poetry which will not be explained from this day on."

Al-Farazdaq remained in al-Madīnah for a while and in Mecca for a while, and he said about that:[417]

Who would inform Ziyād about me?
ambling on, the courier [*barīd*] conveys the message,

That I have fled to Saʿīd,
and whoever Saʿīd defends is untouched.

[108] I fled to him from a wild lion
whose prey the [other] lions leave alone.

So, if you like, you were related to the Christians,
and, if you like, you were related to the Jews,

(It is also transmitted: And you and I were related to the Jews),

And, if you like, you were related to Fuqaym,
and you would be related to me and I would be related to the monkeys,

And more loathsome to me than they are the Banū Fuqaym,
but I will do what you want.

He also said:[418]

Threats came to me from Ziyād, so I did not sleep,
while a flood of agony [was] before me and the hill of the plains,

I thus spent the night as if I felt a Khaybariyyah fever
coursing through my veins or the poison of a snake.[419]

---

417. These lines are also in Bevan, *Naḳāʾiḍ*, 619; with variants, and in Iṣfahānī, *Aghānī*, XIX, 31.

418. These lines are also in Bevan, *Naḳāʾiḍ*, 20, and Boucher, *Divan*, 114.

419. *Al-arāqim* are snakes colored black and white. See Ibn Manẓūr, *Lisān*, XII, 249–50.

I wouldn't think that you would leave me alone, Ziyād son of Ḥarb,
and one with a grudge, I have shamed him not unjustly.

(ʿAmr also recited to me: And with the grudge you have shamed me not unjustly),

A *qaṣīdah* from me fought Iraq
hurling invectives, with sharp, piercing points,

Light on the mouths of narrators, heavy
on their opponent, settling in the seasons.[420]

It is a long (poem). Al-Farazdaq remained between Mecca and al-Madīnah until Ziyād perished.

In this year the death of al-Ḥakam b. ʿAmr al-Ghifārī occurred at Marw. This happened after he had returned from a raid against the people of the mountain of al-Ashall. [109]

Al-Ḥakam b. ʿAmr Raids al-Ashall

I was told by ʿUmar b. Shabbah—Ḥātim b. Qabīsah—Ghālib b. Sulaymān—ʿAbd al-Raḥmān b. Ṣubḥ: I was with al-Ḥakam b. ʿAmr in Khurāsān. Ziyād wrote to (Ibn) ʿAmr, "The weapons of the people of the mountain of al-Ashall are felts and their vessels are gold." So Ibn ʿAmr raided them until his force reached the middle (of the pass), whereupon the enemy took to the mountain trails and roads and surrounded him. At that he dispaired of the matter and put al-Muhallab[421] in charge of the war. Al-Muhallab continued to strive until he captured one of their leading men and said to him, "Choose whether I should kill you or whether you will get us out of this pass." The man then told him, "Light a fire in one of these roads, order the baggage brought up, and turn towards that road so the folk will think that you have already started to travel along it. At that, they will gather [there] for you and abandon the other roads.

420. The text reads: *mawāsim*, "seasons"; these were times of poetic competition.

421. Al-Muhallab b. Abī Ṣufrah al-Azdī (ca. 8–82[630–701/2]) became a famous Baṣran general. See *EI*¹, s.v. al-Muhallab b. Abī Ṣufra.

Then leave them for another, and they will not overtake you until you have left the pass." They did so, and escaped, taking great amounts of booty.

We were told by ʿUmar—ʿAlī b. Muḥammad: When al-Ḥakam b. ʿAmr returned from the mountain of al-Ashall he put al-Muhallab in charge of his rear guard. They travelled on narrow mountain roads, and the Turks resisted them, taking to the roads against them. On one of those mountain trails they found a man singing two verses from behind a wall:

[110] You are consoled by steadfastness and your good fortune. You don't see
an outstanding refuge other than the former nights,

As if my heart, from my memory of the refuge
and the people of refuge, has the feathers of a bird fluttering in it.

When he was brought to al-Ḥakam, the latter asked him about his circumstance. The man explained, "I competed with my cousin, so I left. I went upand down in the land until I settled in this country." Al-Ḥakam took him to Ziyād in Iraq. Al-Ḥakam escaped from (the pass) so that he reached Harāt, and then he returned to Marw.

I was told by ʿUmar—Ḥātim b. Qabīsah—Ghālib b. Sulaymān—ʿAbd al-Raḥmān b. Ṣubḥ: Ziyād wrote to al-Ḥakam, "By God, if you survive, I would certainly behead you!" That was because Ziyād had written to him when the news reached him about what booty he had taken, "Indeed the Commander of the Faithful has written to me to select gold, silver, and precious objects for him so don't move anything until you take that out." Al-Ḥakam had written back to him, "Now then, indeed, your letter arrived [in which] you mention that 'the Commander of the Faithful has written to me to select all [the] gold, silver, and precious objects for him, so don't move anything.' Indeed, the Book of God, Almighy and Great, is prior to the letter of the Commander of the Faithful. Indeed, by God, if the heavens and the earth were of one piece[422] a servant must fear

422. Qur'ān 21:30.

God, Almighty and Great. God, praise be to Him, Most High, gave him a way out." He also told the people to go and take their booty, so they did, while he had set aside the fifth. He divided that booty among them equally. Al-Ḥakam then said, "O God, if I have done what You consider good, then take me." [111]
Thus he died in Khurāsān at Marw. (According to) ʿUmar—ʿAlī b. Muḥammad: When al-Ḥakam was dying at Marw, he appointed Anas b. Abī Unās as his deputy—that was in this year.

The Events of the Year 51

(January 18, 671–January 7, 672)

Among the events during this year were the winter campaign of Faḍālah b. ʿUbayd against Byzantine territory, the summer raid of Busr b. Abī Arṭāt, and the execution of Ḥujr b. ʿAdī and his companions.

Ḥujr b. ʿAdī's Execution

Hishām b. Muḥammad—Abū Mikhnaf—al-Mujālid b. Saʿīd, al-Ṣaqʿab b. Zuhayr, Fuḍayl b. Khadīj, and al-Ḥusayn b. ʿUqbah al-Marādī have all told me some of this narrative, so their account was combined with what I transmitted of the narrative about Ḥujr b. ʿAdī al-Kindī and his companions: When Muʿāwiyah b. Abī Sufyān put al-Mughīrah b. Shuʿbah in charge of al-Kūfah in Jumādā 41 (September 2–October 30, 661), he summoned him. After praising and glorifying God, he said, "Now then, indeed a forbearing person has been admonished in the past.[423] Al-Mutalammis[424] has said:

---

423. See Freytag, *Proverbia*, I, 55–7.

424. Jarīr b. ʿAbd al-Masīḥ (or ʿAbd al-ʿUzzah) al-Mutalammis (d. ca. 569) was

A forbearing person has been admonished in the past,
and man was taught only in order to learn.

The wise might do what you want without instruction. Although I have wanted to advise you about many things, I left them alone, trusting in your discernment of what pleases me, what helps my regime and what sets my subjects [*raʿiyyah*] on [112]
the right path. I would continue to advise you about a quality of yours—do not refrain from abusing ʿAlī and criticizing him, nor from asking God's mercy upon ʿUthmān and His forgiveness for him. Continue to shame the companions of ʿAlī, keep them at a distance, and don't listen to them. Praise the faction of ʿUthmān, bring them near, and listen to them." At that al-Mughīrah responded, "I have experienced [others], and [they] have experienced me. Before working for you I worked for others. I do not mind rejection, nor promotion, nor demotion. After you have experienced [me], you will praise or blame [me]." Muʿāwiyah replied, "No, we shall praise if God wills."

(According to) Abū Mikhnaf—al-Ṣaqʿab b. Zuhayr—al-Shaʿbī: We never had a governor like him afterwards, even if previously there had been good officials.

Al-Mughīrah remained governor of al-Kūfah for Muʿāwiyah for seven years and (some) months. He was the best behaved and the most (strongly) in favor of well-being, in spite of the fact that he would not stop blaming ʿAlī for what had happened and for killing ʿUthmān. He continued to curse those who had killed the latter, while he called for mercy and forgiveness for ʿUthmān and vindication for his companions. When Ḥujr b. ʿAdī heard that, he used to say, "May God rebuke and curse you instead." Then he stood up and said, "Indeed, God, Almighty and Great, says, 'Be custodians in fairness, witnesses for God.'[425] I testify that the one you rebuke and condemn is more deserving of merit, and the one you vindicate and extol is more entitled to blame." Al-Mughīrah would then tell him, "O Ḥujr, your arrow was shot; now I am governor over you. O Ḥujr, woe unto you. Fear the regime. Fear its wrath and its power. Indeed [113]

a minor pre-Islamic poet from Baḥrayn. See ʿAbd al-Qādir al-Baghdādī, *Khizānat al-adab*, III, 73, Vollers, "Mutalammis," and Ziriklī, *al-Aʿlām*, II, 119.

425. Qur'ān 4:135.

the fury of the regime can destroy many of the likes of you." Then he would desist and forgive Ḥujr. He continued thus until, at the end of his governorship, al-Mughīrah arose and said what he used to say about ʿAlī and Muʿāwiyah, which was, "O God, have mercy on ʿUthmān b. ʿAffān and don't punish him, but reward him for his best work. For, indeed, he acted according to Your Book and the example [*sunnah*] of Your Prophet. He united our speech, and prevented our blood from being shed, and yet, he was wrongly killed. O God, have mercy also on his adherents, supporters, friends, and those who seek vengeance for him." He would also call for ʿUthmān's murderers (to be punished). At that, Ḥujr b. ʿAdī jumped up, and let out a scream at al-Mughīrah that everyone who was in the mosque and outside of it heard, saying, "You certainly do not understand what men burn for, because of your senility,[426] O man. Order our rations and stipends for us, for you have certainly withheld them from us, and that is not your right, and no one who preceded you has desired that. You have become passionate about blaming the Commander of the Faithful and praising the criminals." At that, more than two-thirds[427] of the people stood up with him saying, "By God. Ḥujr was right and honest. Order our rations and stipends for us, for this talk of yours doesn't do us any good, and it gives us nothing profitable." And they increased this kind of talk.

At that, al-Mughīrah descended (from the pulpit) and entered (the governor's residence). When his folk asked permission to attend him, he admitted them, and they said, "Why do you leave this man alone who makes this statement and whose insolence is so bold during your regime. Indeed, you acquire two faults thereby. The first is the degradation of your regime. The other is that if it should reach Muʿāwiyah, it would make him
[114] angry with you." ʿAbdallāh b. Abī ʿAqīl al-Thaqafī was the most severe of them (in) speaking to him about the matter of Ḥujr and its importance. Al-Mughīrah answered, "I have killed him. He will come to a governor after me, and will regard him like me and treat him in the same way as you see him treating

426. Iṣfahānī, *Aghānī*, XVI, 2: "What he burns for, or are you senile?"
427. O reads: "thirty of;" Iṣfahānī, *Aghānī*: "thirty men."

me. As a result, that governor will seize Ḥujr at once, and kill him in an evil way. Indeed my appointed time draws near, and my actions have become weak. I do not want to start the people of this city killing the best among themselves and shedding their blood. They are fortunate thereby, while I am miserable. Muʿāwiyah will grow strong in this world, while al-Mughīrah will be humbled on the Day of Resurrection. But, I shall receive those who are pleasing and forgive those who are displeasing. I shall praise the prudent and admonish the impudent until death should separate me from them. They will remember me if they should put officials to the test after me."[428]

(According to) Abū Mikhnaf—ʿUthmān b. ʿUqbah al-Kindī—a shaykh of the district who related this account: By God we put them to the test, and found him to be the best of them. He was the most commendable toward the innocent, the most forgiving toward those who were offensive, and the most receptive to excuses.

(According to) Hishām—ʿAwānah: Al-Mughīrah became governor of al-Kūfah in Jumādā 41(661/662), and he died this year. Al-Kūfah and al-Baṣrah were then combined for Ziyād b. Abī Sufyān. Ziyād advanced until he entered the citadel at al-Kūfah. Then he ascended the pulpit, and after he had praised and extolled God, he said, "Now then, indeed, we have been put to the test and we have tested. We have ruled and rulers have ruled us, and we have found that this matter would only be set right in the end by that which set it right at the beginning: tractable obedience, the same in secret as openly, when people are absent as when they are present, and [in] their hearts as [on] their tongues. We found that only flexibility without weakness and strength without violence would reform the people. As for myself, by God, I shall not undertake a matter with [115]
you unless I carry it out to its smallest detail. There is no lie to which God and the people are witness greater than the lie of an imām upon the pulpit." Then he mentioned ʿUthmān and his companions, and praised them, and mentioned his murderers, and cursed them. Ḥujr then got up and did as he had done to al-Mughīrah.

428. See Iṣfahānī, *Aghānī*, XVI, 4.

Whenever Ziyād would return to al-Baṣrah he would put ʿAmr b. al-Ḥurayth in charge of al-Kūfah.[429] When he had returned to al-Baṣrah, he heard that the partisans of ʿAlī had gathered to Ḥujr and had openly cursed and disavowed Muʿāwiyah, and that they had thrown pebbles at ʿAmr b. al-Ḥurayth. At that, he set out for al-Kūfah and, upon arriving there, he entered the citadel. Then he went out and ascended the pulpit wearing a robe of silk brocade and a green silk scarf, having parted his hair, while Ḥujr was sitting in the mosque surrounded by more of his companions than before. After Ziyād had praised and extolled God, he said, "Now then, injustice and transgression have fatal consequences. Indeed, these [people] gathered and did evil. They felt safe from me, so they took liberties with me. I swear by God, if you do not straighten out, I shall cure you with your [own] medicine." He continued "I shall have accomplished nothing if I don't protect the plaza of al-Kūfah from Ḥujr and make him an example for whoever should come after him. Woe unto your mother, O Ḥujr! You found a wolf for dinner." Then he recited:

> Tell Nuṣayḥah about the herdsman of her camels,
> that he found a wolf for dinner.[430]

Regarding the cause of the matter concerning Ḥujr, someone other than Awānah said that which I was told by ʿAlī b. Ḥasan—Muslim al-Jarmī—Makhlad b. al-Ḥasan—Hishām—Muḥammad b. Sīrīn:[431] Ziyād spoke one Friday,[432] and by pro-
[116] tracting the sermon he delayed the *ṣalāt* (worship). At that, Ḥujr b. ʿAdī said to him, "The *ṣalāt*!" But he continued speaking. Ḥujr then repeated, "The *ṣalāt*!" But he continued speaking. When Ḥujr was afraid the (proper time for) worship would be past, he took a fist-full of pebbles and stood up to worship,

429. C reads: "he stayed in al-Kūfah six months, then he put ʿAmr b. al-Ḥurayth in charge of it."

430. Lit: "dinner found a wolf for him." That is, he went out looking for dinner and chanced upon a wolf, so the wolf ate him, said of someone whose pursuit of his own needs leads him to destruction. See Maydānī, *Amthāl*, I, 329; Freytag, *Proverbia*, I, 599–600.

431. Muḥammad b. Sīrīn (34–110[654–728]) was an early Baṣran authority on ḥadīth. See Ibn Saʿd, *Ṭabaqāt*, VII, 140–50.

432. The text reads: *fī al-jumʿah*.

and the people stood up with him. When Ziyād saw that, he descended (from the pulpit) and led the people in worship. When he had finished, he wrote to Muʿāwiyah about the matter of Ḥujr and exaggerated it. Muʿāwiyah then wrote back to him, "Clamp him in irons, then deliver him to me." When Muʿāwiyah's letter arrived, and Ḥujr's folk wanted to protect him, Ḥujr said, "No, pay heed and obey instead."

When he had been clamped in irons, he was delivered to Muʿāwiyah. When Ḥujr entered the latter's presence, he said, "Peace be upon you, O Commander of the Faithful, and the mercy of God and His blessings." But Muʿāwiyah replied to him, "Commander of the Faithful! By God, I will not be addressed by you or consider speaking to you. Take him out and behead him." Upon being taken out from Muʿāwiyah's presence, Ḥujr said to those who were in charge of dealing with him, "Give me leave until I perform two prostrations." They replied, "Perform them." When he had performed two prostrations which he shortened, he said, "Lest you suppose that I am doing other than what I am, I would have liked for my prostrations to take longer than they did. These two prostrations are as good as any previous devotions." Then he told whomever of his folk attended him, "Don't undo the irons, and don't wash the blood off of me. I may meet Muʿāwiyah in the future on the street." Then he was brought forth, and his head was cut off.

(According to) Makhlad—Hishām: Whenever Muḥammad was asked about washing martyrs, he used to tell them the account of Ḥujr. Muḥammad said, When ʿA'ishah, the Mother of the Believers, met Muʿāwiyah (Makhlad said: I suppose he was in Mecca), she asked, "O Muʿāwiyah, where was your forbearance (*ḥilm*) towards Ḥujr? He replied, "[Someone] rightly-guided did not attend me on that occasion, O Mother of the Believers." Ibn Sīrīn said, "We heard that when his death was immanent he began to make a gurgling sound saying, "My day [117]
[of death] is long because of you, O Ḥujr."

(According to) Hishām—Abū Mikhnaf—Ismāʿīl b. Nuʿaym al-Namirī—Ḥusayn b. ʿAbdallāh al-Hamdānī: When I was in the police force of Ziyād, he said, "One of you hurry off to Ḥujr, and summon him." At that the commander of the police, who was Shaddād b. al-Haytham al-Hilālī, told me to go and summon him. When I came to him, saying, "Comply with the governor," his friends said, "Don't go to him or show respect." Upon returning to Ziyād and informing him, he ordered the commander of the police to send men with me, so he sent several men. We then came to Ḥujr, saying, "Comply with the governor." When they cursed and reviled us, we returned to Ziyād, and informed him about it. At that, Ziyād rushed to the notables of the Kūfans, saying, "O people of al-Kūfah, do you break with one hand while you console with the other? Your bodies are with me, while your affections are with this obsessed, stupid, crazy Ḥujr. By God, this comes from your plotting and your deceit. By God, demonstrate your innocence to me, or I shall bring against you folk by whom I shall bring about your downfall and your humiliation." At that, they rushed to Ziyād saying, "God forbid, may He be praised, that we have any other view in this situation than obedience to you and to the Commander of the Faithful. Command us to do whatever will satisfy you and demonstrate our obedience and our disagreement with Ḥujr." Ziyād replied, "Then let every one of you go to this group around Ḥujr and summon your brother, son, relative, and whoever of your clan obeys you, so that you make every one [of them that] you can stand up and leave him." They did this and made the majority of those (who were) with Ḥujr b. ʿAdī stand up.

When Ziyād saw that the majority of those with Ḥujr had stood up and left him, he told Shaddād b. al-Haytham al-Hilālī—it is also said, Haytham b. Shaddād—the commander of his police, "Hurry off to Ḥujr. If he complies with you[r request], bring him to me, and if not, order whoever is with you to pull out the clubs of the marketplace.[433] Then assault them with the clubs so that you may bring him to me, and beat whoever resists." Al-Hilālī then came to Ḥujr, saying, "Comply with the governor!" The friends of Ḥujr replied, "No, there

433. The text reads: *ʿumud*. Ziyād's guard (*ḥaras*) was armed with staffs or clubs. Since a payment was levied on the people of the marketplace to support the guard, they may have patrolled the marketplace with their clubs. The clubs were probably stored in a bin in the mosque. See Behrnauer, "Mémoire," 467; Ṭabarī, II, 79.

shall be no satisfaction.[434] We shall not comply with him." Al-Hilālī then told his men, "Seize the clubs of the marketplace." At that, they rushed to pull out the clubs, and advanced with them. ʿUmayr b. Yazīd al-Kindī of the Banū Hind—that is Abū al-ʿAmaraṭah—said, "Indeed, I am the only man among you who has a sword, and that will not be enough for you." Ḥujr asked, "What do you think?" ʿUmayr replied, "Get away from this place, and join your family. Your folk will defend you." As Ziyād stood watching them while he was upon the pulpit, the police came with clubs. One of the Ḥamrāʾ, called Bakr b. ʿUbayd, struck the head of ʿAmr b. al-Ḥamiq with a club, felling him. Abū Sufyān b. ʿUwaymir and ʿAjlān b. Rabīʿah, who both belonged to the Azd, came to him and carried him (off). They brought him to the house of a man who belonged to the Azd called ʿUbaydallāh b. Mālik. They concealed him there, and he stayed hidden until he left.[435]

(According to) Abū Mikhnaf—Yūsuf b. Yazīd—ʿAbdallāh b. ʿAwf[436] b. al-Aḥmar: When we left for the campaign of Bājumayrā, one year before the death of Muṣʿab (in 71[679]), I was accompanied by an Aḥmarī.[437] By God, I had not seen him since the day on which ʿAmr b. al-Ḥamiq was struck, and I did not think that I would recognize him if I saw him. When I saw him then, I supposed that he was Bakr. As we were still in view of the houses of al-Kūfah, I disliked asking him if he was the man [119]
who had struck ʿUmar b. al-Ḥamiq, lest he contradict me. As a result, I told him, "I have not seen you since the day on which you struck the head of ʿAmr b. al-Ḥamiq with the club in the mosque; I recognize you now." He answered me, "You have not lost your eyesight. How strong your vision is. That was the Devil's matter. Indeed, I had heard that it was a righteous matter, and I have regretted that blow, so I ask God's forgiveness." At that, I said to him, "Don't you think, by God, that you and I should not part until I hit you a blow on your head like that

434. Lit: "no comfort for an eye."
435. See the account in Iṣfahānī, *Aghānī*, XVI, 3–4.
436. Iṣfahānī, *Aghānī*: ʿUbaydallāh b. ʿAwn.
437. O reads: "that blow," but see Iṣfahānī, *Aghānī*, XVI, 4. An Aḥmarī was one of the Ḥamrāʾ, a group of Iranian soldiers settled at al-Kūfah.

which you struck ʿAmr b. al-Ḥamiq, [so that] either I die or you die?" He then adjured and implored me by God, but I refused him and summoned a young servant of mine called Rashīd, one of the captives from Iṣbahān, who had his firm spear with him. When I took it from Rashīd, I attacked Bakr with it. He then dismounted from his animal, and I caught him when both of his feet were level with the ground. I grazed the top of his head with the spear so that he fell on his face. I then went on my way, and left him. He recovered afterwards, and I met him two more times. Each time he would say, "God is between you and me." And I would reply, "God, Almighty and Great, is between you and ʿAmr b. al-Ḥamiq."

Then he resumed the previous account: When Bakr struck ʿAmr that blow and those two men carried him off, the friends of Ḥujr withdrew to the gates of the Kindah. A man of Ḥudhām who was in the police was striking a man called ʿAbdallāh b. Khalīfah al-Ṭāʾī with a club. He struck him a blow and knocked him down, saying extemporaneously:

She knew on the day of tumult, my friend,
that I, whenever my troop flees,

[120] And its enemies multiply or diminish,
that I am lethal on the morning it started.

The hand of ʿĀʾidh b. Ḥamalah al-Tamīmī was also struck and his eyetooth was broken, so he said:

If they break my eyetooth and the bone of my forearm,
Indeed, I have the force of experience,
And the strife of the battling hero.

Wresting a club from one of the police, he fought with it, protecting Ḥujr and his friends until they left the front of the gates of the Kindah. Ḥujr's mule had been (left) standing, and Abū al-ʿAmarraṭah brought her to him, saying, "They are all bastards except you. By God, I certainly think that you have killed yourself and killed us with you." Ḥujr then put his foot in the stirrup, but he was unable to mount, so Abū al-ʿAmarraṭah lifted him onto his mule. Abū al-ʿAmarraṭah then rushed to his own horse, and had just mounted when Yazīd b. Ṭarīf, who had a slight limp, reached him. He struck Abū al-ʿAmarraṭah with his club on the thigh, and Abū al-ʿAmarraṭah drew this sword and struck the head of Yazīd b. Ṭarīf with it so that he fell on his face. He recovered afterwards, and ʿAbdallāh b. Hammām al-Salūlī says about him:

I blame the son of baseness, except for you, openly,
to a hero, courageous and unyielding,

Returning the blow of the armored ones with his sword,
on the top of the head when there is dismay, other than base,

To a horseman of both attacking [sides] the day you both met, [121]
at Ṣiffīn, a sire, the best offspring of sires.

I considered[438] fighting with Ibn Barṣā al-Ḥitār[439]
as you fought with Zayd on the Day of Dār Ḥakīm.

That sword was the first one which was employed to strike at al-Kūfah in the disputes among the people.

Ḥujr and Abū al-ʿAmarraṭah proceeded until they both reached Ḥujr's residence. Many of his supporters gathered to Ḥujr, and Qays b. Qahdān al-Kindī went forth on his donkey, setting out for the assemblies of the Kindah, saying:

O folk of Ḥujr, resist and contend
on behalf of your brother for a while, so fight.

Let Ḥujr not be abandoned by you.
Is there not among you a lancer and an archer,

And an armored horseman, and infantryman,
and swordsman who does not quit?

But many of the Kindah did not join Ḥujr, and Ziyād said, while he was on the pulpit, "Let the Hamdān, Tamīm, Hawāzin, the sons of Aʿṣur, the Madhḥij, Asad, and the Ghaṭafān rise

438. Cairo reads: "You considered."
439. Lit: "circle of the rump."

up and come to the cemetery of the Kindah. Whoever gathers there is to proceed to Ḥujr and bring him to me." Then, since he disliked to dispatch a troop of the Muḍar together with a troop of the people of al-Yaman, because discord and disagreement might occur between them, and fanaticism might ruin
[122] their relationship, he said, "Let the Tamīm, Hawāzin, the sons of Aʿṣur, the Asad, and the Ghaṭafān stay, and let the Madhḥij and Hamdān proceed to the cemetery of the Kindah. Then let them go to Ḥujr and bring him to me. Let the rest of the people of the Yaman go and halt at the cemetery of the Ṣā'idiyyīn, and [then] proceed to their companion, and bring him to me." At that, the Azd, Bajīlah, Kathʿam, Anṣār,[440] Khuzāʿah, and Quḍāʿah went out and halted at the cemetery of the Ṣāʿidiyyīn. The Ḥaḍramawt did not go out with the people of the Yaman because of their position among the Kindah. They disliked having to go out in pursuit of Ḥujr, because the Ḥaḍramawt traditionally called upon the Kindah for support (in war).[441]

(According to) Abū Mikhnaf—Yaḥyā b. Saʿīd b. Mikhnaf—Muḥammad b. Mikhnaf: indeed I was with the people of the Yaman in the cemetery of the Ṣā'idiyyīn when the leaders of the people of the Yaman assembled deliberating about the matter of Ḥujr. ʿAbd al-Raḥmān b. Mikhnaf told them, "I offer you advice. If you should accept it, I would hope that you would be safe from blame and offense. I think you should delay a little, for soon youths of the Hamdān and Madhḥij will save you the trouble of what you dislike doing, namely the misdeed of your folk concerning your companion." They agreed on that. As a result, by God, it was only when, and certainly not until, we learned that the Madhḥij and Hamdān had entered and taken every one they found of the Banū Jabalah,[442] that the people of the Yaman marched past along the sides of the houses of the Kindah as an excuse. When Ziyād heard about that, he praised the Madhḥij and Hamdān, and blamed the rest of the people of the Yaman.

---

440. The Anṣār, "Helpers," were Muslims from al-Madīnah who had settled in al-Kūfah.

441. See above, n. 277.

442. Iṣfahānī, *Aghānī* reads: "among the Banū Bajīlah." That is, those who were friends of Ḥujr.

When Ḥujr reached his house, and saw how few of his folk were with him and heard that the Madhḥij and Hamdān had [123] halted at the cemetery of the Kindah and the rest of the people of the Yaman at the cemetery of the Ṣā'idiyyīn, he said to his companions, "Depart, for by God, you won't be able to deal with those of your folk who have gathered against you. I don't want to subject you to destruction." As they were about to depart, the lead cavalry of the Madhḥij and Hamdān caught them. So ʿUmayr b. Yazīd, Qays b. Yazīd, ʿUbaydah b. ʿAmr al-Baddī, ʿAbd al-Raḥmān b. Muḥriz al-Ṭumaḥī, and Qays b. Shimr engaged them in battle. The cavalry fought against him[443] for a while, inflicting wounds. Qays b. Yazīd was captured while the rest of (Ḥujr's) folk escaped. At that, Ḥujr told them, "Scatter! Don't fight! I shall take to one of the side streets, then take a road near the Banū Ḥūt."[444] He went off until he reached the house of one of their men called Sulaym b. Yazīd. Ḥujr entered Sulaym's house, while (Ziyād's) folk came seeking him until they reached that house. At that, Sulaym b. Yazīd took his sword, and was about to go out to them, while his daughters wept. So Ḥujr asked him, "What do you intend?" Sulaym replied, "I want, by God, to ask them to leave you. If they do so, [fine]; and if not, I shall protect you, fighting them with this sword of mine as long as its blade is firm in my hand." Ḥujr told him, "You are no bastard. Then what a miserable thing I will have brought upon your daughters." Sulaym answered, "Indeed, by God, they will only be safe and provided for with the Living [One], Who does not die. I shall never exchange shame for anything, and you shall not go out of my house as a prisoner while I am alive and possess my sword-blade. If I am killed protecting you, then you should do what seems good to you." Ḥujr asked, "Is there no wall in this house of yours which I could break through or an opening I could get out through? Perhaps God, Almighty and Great, will save me from them and save you as well. If [Ziyād's] folk do not capture me in your house, they will not harm you." Sulaym replied, "Yes, here is an opening which will get you out to [124]

443. C and Iṣfahānī, *Aghānī* read: "against them."
444. The manuscripts and Cairo and Iṣfahānī, *Aghānī* read: Banū Ḥarb.

the houses of the Banū al-ʿAnbar and to others of your folk."

He then went out, past the Banū Dhul, who told him, "[Ziyād's] folk have already gone by in search of you, following your tracks." He told them, "I am fleeing from them." He then went out, with their youths showing him the way. They took him through the alleys until he reached the Nakhaʿ. At that point he told them, "Depart, may God have mercy upon you." At that, they left him, and he came to the house of ʿAbdallāh b. al-Ḥārith, the brother of al-Ashtar, and entered it. As soon as he came in, ʿAbdallāh threw down the cushions, rolled out the carpets, and received him joyfully with good cheer. Then he learned that the police were asking about him among the Nakhaʿ. That was because a black slave girl called Admā' met them and asked, "Whom do you seek?" When they answered that they were seeking Ḥujr, she responded, "There he is. I saw him among the Nakhaʿ." At that, they went off towards the Nakhaʿ. Ḥujr then left the home of ʿAbdallāh in disguise, and ʿAbdallāh b. al-Ḥārith rode with him at night until he came to the house of Rabīʿah b. Nājid al-Azdī, among the Azd, where he stayed for a day and a night.

When they were unable to capture Ḥujr, Ziyād summoned Muḥammad b. al-Ashʿath, and told him, "O Abū Maythā', by God, either bring Ḥujr to me or I shall chop down every single palm tree of yours and demolish every single house. Then you will not be safe from me until I cut you to pieces." He answered, "Grant me a respite so that I may look for him." Ziyād replied, "I grant you a respite for three days. If you bring him,
[125] [fine]; if not, consider yourself doomed." Muḥammad was taken out red faced, and pushed roughly towards the prison. At that, Ḥujr b. Yazīd al-Kindī said to Ziyād, "Let me vouch for him, and release him to search for his companion. If he were freed, his faculties would be more adequate to capture him than if he were imprisoned." Ziyād asked, "Will you vouch for him?" He replied that he would and Ziyād declared, "However, by God, if he escapes from you, I shall certainly make you visit death, even if you are honored by me now." Ḥujr b. Yazīd answered, "Indeed, he will not do it, so release him." Then Ḥujr b. Yazīd interceded with him for Qays b. Yazīd, who had been brought to Ziyād as a prisoner. Ziyād told them, "Don't worry

about Qays. We have known his views about ʿUthmān and his bravery at the Battle of Ṣiffīn with the Commander of the Faithful." Then he sent for Qays. When he was brought to him, Ziyād told him, "Indeed, I knew that you did not fight along with Ḥujr because you shared his views, but you fought along with him out of solidarity. I have forgiven you for it because of what I know about your good views and the excellence of your bravery, but I will not leave you alone until you bring me your brother, ʿUmayr." Qays answered, "I will bring him to you, if God wills." Ziyād said, "Then give me someone who will vouch for him along with yourself." Qays replied, "This Ḥujr b. Yazīd will vouch for him along with me." Ḥujr b. Yazīd said, "Yes, I vouch for him on condition that you grant him security for his property and his blood." Ziyād replied, "You have that." Then they both hurried off and brought ʿUmayr in his wounded condition. Ziyād ordered for him to be weighed down with iron. Then the men took ʿUmayr and lifted him until, when he was waist-high, they threw him down so he fell on the ground. Then they lifted him up again and threw him down. They did that with him several times. At that, Ḥujr b. Yazīd got up and asked Ziyād "Did you not guarantee his property and his blood? May God reform you." Ziyād replied, "Of course, I guaranteed his property and his blood, and I am not shedding his blood or taking his property." Ḥujr b. Yazīd retorted, "May God reform you, he is almost cured to death by it." Ḥujr b. Yazīd drew near to ʿUmayr while those people of the Yaman [126] who were with him rose up, drew near ʿUmayr, and spoke to him. Ziyād then asked, "Do you vouch to me for him, so that whenever he commits a misdeed, you will bring him to me?" They said that they would and Ziyād asked, "Do you also vouch to [pay] me blood money for the blows at the place of worship?"[445] When they replied, "We vouch for it," Ziyād let ʿUmayr go.

Ḥujr b. ʿAdī stayed in the residence of Rabīʿah b. Nājid al-Azdī for a day and a night. Then Ḥujr sent a youth of his called Rashīd, belonging to the people of Iṣbahān, to Muḥammad b. al-Ashʿath (saying), "I have heard what this stubborn tyrant did

445. C reads: "against the Muslims."

to you. Don't be alarmed at all by him. I will come out to you. Gather a group of your folk, then enter Ziyād's presence and ask him to grant me a guarantee of safe-conduct in order to send me to Muʿāwiyah so he may see what he thinks of me." Ibn al-Ashʿath then went out to Ḥujr b. Yazīd, Jarīr b. ʿAbdallāh, and ʿAbdallāh b. al-Ḥārith, the brother of al-Ashtar, and brought them. They entered Ziyād's presence, interceded with him, and beseeched him to grant Ḥujr a guarantee of safe-conduct in order to send him to Muʿāwiyah so the latter could see what he thought of him. When Ziyād did so, they sent Ḥujr's messenger back to him informing him that they had gotten what he had asked for, and commanding him to come. When he came and entered Ziyād's presence, Ziyād said, "Welcome to you Abū ʿAbd al-Raḥmān, war in the time of war, and war while the people have made peace. 'A many-colored dog harms its own family.' "[446] Ḥujr replied, "I did not renounce obedience or withdraw from any community. Indeed I am on my allegiance." Ziyād answered, "How wrong, O Ḥujr. You break with one hand and nurse with the other. When God gives you an opportunity, you want us to overlook it. Not at all, by God." Ḥujr asked, "Didn't you grant me a guarantee of safe-conduct so that I should come to Muʿāwiyah and he could see what he thinks of me?" Ziyād replied, "Yes, we have done so. Take him off to the prison." When Ḥujr had been sent out of his presence, Ziyād remarked, "However, by God, if there were no
[127] guarantee of safe-conduct, he would not depart without spilling his own heartsblood."[447] (According to) Hishām b. ʿUrwah—ʿAwānah: Ziyād remarked, "By God, I certainly intend to snip the thread of his neck."

(According to) Hishām b. Muḥammad—Abū Mikhnaf, and al-Mujālid b. Saʿīd—al-Shaʿbī, and Zakariyyāʾ b. Abī Zāʾidah—Abū Iṣḥāq: When Ḥujr was sent out of Ziyād's presence, he shouted at the top of his voice, "O God, I am on my allegiance. I don't revoke it or call for its revocation. Listen to God and the

446. Maydānī, *Amthāl*, II, 14–15; Freytag, *Proverbia*, II, 89–90. Such a dog, by barking at others, gives its masters away, so they perish and the dog with them.

447. Iṣfahānī, *Aghānī*, XVI, 4 reads: "without casting down his sinews."

people." He was wearing a cloak with a hood (*burnus*) on a cold morning. He was thus imprisoned for ten nights while Ziyād's only labor was to seek the leaders of Ḥujr's companions.

At that, ʿAmr b. al-Ḥamiq and Rifāʿat b. Shaddād left and halted at al-Madāʾin. Then they departed until they came to the territory of Mosul. They came to a mountain and hid there. When the official of that subdistrict (*rustāq*), who was a man belonging to the Hamdān called ʿAbdallāh b. Abī Baltaʿah, heard that two men had hidden in the mountainside, he suspected their circumstances. He set out for them with cavalry and local people towards the mountain. When he reached them, they both went out. As far as ʿAmr b. al-Ḥamiq is concerned, he was sick and his belly was billious[448] so he could not resist. But as for Rifāʿat b. Shaddād, he was young and strong, and jumped on his race horse. Rifāʿat asked ʿAmr, "Shall I fight on your behalf?" ʿAmr replied, "It would be of no use to me for you to fight. Save yourself if you can." When Rifāʿat attacked them, they parted for him, and he went out, his horse bolting with him, while the cavalry went off in pursuit of him. As ʿAmr was a good shot, he began to shoot every horseman who overtook him, injuring or wounding him. So they turned away from him. When ʿAmr b. al-Ḥamiq was taken, they asked him, "Who are you?" He replied, "One who, if you leave him alone, would be peaceful to you, and if you fight him would harm [128]
you." Thus they asked him, but he refused to tell them. Ibn Abī Baltaʿah then sent him to the governor of Mosul, who was ʿAbd al-Raḥmān b. ʿAbdallāh b. ʿUthmān al-Thaqafī. When the latter saw ʿAmr b. al-Ḥamiq, he recognized him, and wrote to Muʿāwiyah with his information. Muʿāwiyah wrote back, "ʿAmr claimed that he stabbed ʿUthmān b. ʿAffān nine times with a dagger that he had with him, so stab him nine times just as he stabbed ʿUthmān." At that, ʿAmr was taken out and stabbed nine times, and he died from the first or second blow.

(According to) Abū Mikhnaf—al-Mujālid—al-Shaʿbī, and Zakariyyāʾ b. Abī Zāʾidah—Isḥāq: When Ziyād sent in search of the companions of Ḥujr, they began to flee from him, and he

448. The text reads: *saqā*, to be full of yellow water which collects in the stomach from illness.

seized whomever of them he was able. He sent the commander of the police, who was Shaddād b. al-Haytham, to Qabīṣah b. Ḍubayʿah b. Ḥarmalah al-ʿAbsī. When Qabīṣah summoned his folk and took his sword, Ribʿī b. Ḥirāsh b. Jahsh al-ʿAbsī and a few men belonging to his folk came to him. When he wanted to fight, the commander of the police said to him, "You are secure for your blood and your property, so why would you kill yourself?" His friends then said to him, "You have been granted security, so why do you kill yourself and us with you?" He replied, "Woe unto you! Indeed, by God, if I fall into the hands of this bastard son of the whore[449] I will never be released from him unless he kills me." They answered, "By no means," so he put his hand in theirs and they brought him to Ziyād. When they had entered his presence, Ziyād said, "By the tribe of ʿAbs, you are respected by me for the faith. However, by God, I shall certainly make an occupation for you instead of in-
[129] citing riots and attacking governors." Qabīṣah said, "I only came to you under a guarantee of safe-conduct." Ziyād ordered, "Take him off to the prison."

Qays b. ʿUbād al-Shaybānī also came to Ziyād telling him, "There is a man among us belonging to the Banū Hammām called Ṣayfī b. Fasīl, one of the leaders of Ḥujr's companions. He is the most violent of people against you." When Ziyād had him brought to him, he said to Ṣayfī, "O Enemy of God, what do you say about Abū Turāb?" Ṣayfī replied, "I do not know Abū Turāb." Ziyād asked, "What will make you recognize him?" Ṣayfī answered, "I do not know him." Ziyād asked, "Don't you know ʿAlī b. Abī Ṭālib?" When Ṣayfī replied that he did, Ziyād responded, "That is Abū Turāb." Ṣayfī rejoined, "Certainly not! He is Abū al-Ḥasan and al-Ḥusayn." At that, the commander of the police said to him, "The amīr says to you that he is Abū Turāb, and you say 'no'?" Ṣayfī responded, "If the amīr lied, do you want me to lie and give false testimony as he did?" Ziyād told him, "This also is added to your crime. Bring me the stick!" It was brought and Ziyād asked, "What do you say?"[450] Ṣayfī answered, "The best words that I

449. That is, Ziyād.
450. Iṣfahānī, *Aghānī*, adds: "about ʿAlī."

was saying about one of God's servants [I say about the Commander][451] of the Faithful." Ziyād commanded, "Beat his shoulder with the staff until he hugs the ground." So Ṣayfī was beaten until he stayed on the ground. Then Ziyād said, "Stop beating him. What do you say about ʿAlī?" Ṣayfī replied, "By God, if you slice me up with razors and knives, I would only say what you heard me say." Ziyād said, "Curse him or I shall certainly behead you." Ṣayfī retorted, "Then you have already cut it off, by God. And if you refuse to do anything except cut it off, I will be satisfied with God and you will be wretched." Ziyād commanded, "Push him by his neck," and added, "Load him with iron, and cast him into prison."

Then he sent for ʿAbdallāh b. Khalīfah al-Ṭāʾī who had been present with Ḥujr and had fought (Ziyād's men) fiercely. Ziyād sent Bukayr b. Ḥumrān al-Aḥmarī, who was an assistant of the officials, for him with some of his companions. When they proceeded in search of him, and found him in the Mosque of ʿAdī [130]
b. Ḥātim, they took him out. But ʿAbdallāh was formidable. When they wanted to leave with him, he resisted, struggling and fighting with them. So they bashed him, and threw stones at him until he fell down. At that, Maythāʾ, his sister, called out, "O kinfolk of Ṭayyiʾ! Do you betray Ibn Khalīfah with your tongue and your spearhead?"[452] When al-Aḥmarī heard her summons, he was afraid that the Ṭayyiʾ would gather and that he would perish. So he fled, and the women of Ṭayyiʾ went out and brought ʿAbdallāh into a house. Al-Aḥmarī hurried off until he came to Ziyād, saying, "Indeed, the Ṭayyiʾ gathered against me, and I could not withstand them, so I have returned to you." Ziyād then sent for ʿAdī,[453] as he was in the mosque, and had him arrested, saying, "Bring him to me." ʿAdī had been informed about ʿAbdallāh's story, so he asked, "How shall I bring you a man whom the folk have killed?" Ziyād replied, "Bring [him] to me so I may see that they have killed him." ʿAdī then made an excuse, saying, "I don't know where he is or

451. Bracketed words added from Isfahānī, *Aghānī*.

452. The account up to this point is also in Iṣfahānī, *Aghānī*, XVI, 7 with variants.

453. ʿAdī b. Ḥātim al-Ṭāʾī was the leader of the Ṭayyiʾ at al-Kūfah.

what he has done." At that, Ziyād imprisoned him, and everyone in the city belonging to the Yaman and the Rabīʿah and the Muḍar concerned themselves with ʿAdī. They came to Ziyād, and interceded with him on ʿAdī's behalf. Meanwhile, ʿAbdallāh was taken out and hidden with the Buḥtur.[454] He then sent word to ʿAdī, "If you wish me to come out so that I would put my hand in yours, I will do so." At that, ʿAdī sent word back to him, "By God, if you were right under my feet, I would not lift them from you." Ziyād then summoned ʿAdī, telling him, "Indeed, I shall release you on condition that you undertake to expel ʿAbdallāh from al-Kūfah for me and lead him to the mountains." ʿAdī replied that he would, returned, and sent word to ʿAbdallāh b. Khalīfah, "Leave, and if his anger subsides, I shall speak with him about you so that you may return if God wills." Thus ʿAbdallāh left for the mountains.

Ziyād was also brought Karīm b. ʿAfīf al-Khathʿamī, so he asked, "What is your name?" He answered, "I am Karīm b. ʿAfīf." Ziyād responded, "Alas for you or woe unto you! How good is your name and the name of your father,[455] and how evil
[131] is your action and your view." ʿAfīf answered, "However, by God, you have only known my view for a short time." Ziyād then sent for the companions of Ḥujr until he had collected twelve men of them in the prison.

Ziyād then summoned the leaders of the fourths,[456] saying, "Testify against Ḥujr about what he did to you." At that time the leaders of the fourths were ʿAmr b. Ḥurayth in charge of the fourth of the people of al-Madīnah, Khālid b. ʿUrfuṭah in charge of the fourth of the Tamīm and the Hamdān, Qays b. al-Walīd b. ʿAbd Shams b. al-Mughīrah in charge of the fourth of the Rabīʿah and the Kindah, and Abū Burdah b. Abū Mūsā in charge of the Madhḥij and the Asad. There four testified that Ḥujr had gathered crowds about him, openly abused the Caliph, and called for war against the Commander of the Faithful. They also swore that he claimed that matters would only be set right

454. The Buḥtur were a clan of the Ṭayyiʾ. See Ibn Manẓūr, *Lisān*, IV, 47.
455. Karīm means "noble" or "generous"; ʿAfīf means "decent."
456. The fourths were divisions of the Kūfan army created by Ziyād but were unrelated to the districts in the city as is often claimed.

by the family of Abū Ṭālib, that he attacked the city and drove out the official of the Commander of the Faithful, excused Abū Turāb openly and asked God's mercy on him, and disavowed Abū Turāb's enemy and the people who fought him. They also testified that those persons who associated with him were the leaders of his companions and had views and concerns similar to his. Then Ziyād ordered them to leave. Qays b. al-Walīd returned to him afterwards, saying, "I heard that when they had been escorted out, they reconsidered." At that, Ziyād sent to the Kunāsah[457] and, having purchased stubborn camels, he fastened litters upon them. Then he carried those leaders upon the camels in the public plaza from daybreak until evening, declaring, "Whoever wishes, let him reconsider." But none of them stirred.

When Ziyād had examined the testimony of the witnesses, he said, "I do not consider this testimony to be conclusive, and I would like for there to be more than four witnesses." (According to) Abū Mikhnaf and al-Ḥārith b. Ḥusayrah—Abū al-Kanūd, that is ʿAbd al-Raḥmān b. ʿUbayd, and Abū Mikhnaf —ʿAbd al-Raḥmān b. Jundab, and Sulaymān b. Abī Rāshid— [132]
Abū al-Kanūd, these were the names of the witnesses: In the name of God, the Compassionate, the Merciful, this is what Abū Burdah b. Abī Mūsā testified against him before God, Lord of both worlds. He testified that Ḥujr b. ʿAdī refused obedience, withdrew from the community, cursed the Caliph, called for war and civil discord, and gathered crowds about himself, summoning them to violate the oath of allegience (*bayʿah*) and depose the Commander of the Faithful, Muʿāwiyah. In the baldest way, he also disbelieved in God, Almighty and Great. Ziyād then said, "Give similar testimony. By God, I shall certainly endeavor to cut the thread of the necks of treacherous fools." At that the leaders of the fourths gave similar testimony to that of Abū Burdah, and there were four of them.

Ziyād then summoned the people, saying, "Give similar testimony to that of the leaders of the fourths." When he read the document to them, the first person to stand up was ʿUnāq b.

457. The Kunāsah (rubbish heap) was the location of a camel-market in al-Kūfah.

Shuraḥbīl b. Abī Dahm al-Taymī of the Taym Allāh b. Thaʿlabah, saying, "Include my name." At that, Ziyād said, "Start with the names of Quraysh, then write the name of ʿUnāq among the witnesses, and whoever else we and the Commander of the Faithful recognize as having sincere advice and integrity." Iṣḥāq b. Ṭalḥah b. ʿUbaydallāh then testified, and Mūsā b. Ṭalḥah, Ismāʿīl b. Ṭalḥah b. ʿUbaydallāh, al-Mundhir b. al-Zubayr, ʿUmārah b. ʿUqbah b. Abī Muʿayṭ, ʿAbd al-Raḥmān b. Hannād, ʿUmar b. Saʿd b. Abī Waqqāṣ, ʿĀmir b. Masʿūd b. Umayyah b. Khalaf, Muḥriz b. Jāriyah b. Rabīʿah b. ʿAbd
[133] al-ʿUzzā b. ʿAbd Shams, ʿUbaydallāh b. Muslim b. Shuʿbah al-Ḥaḍramī, ʿUnāq b. Shuraḥbīl b. Abī Dahm, Wāʾil b. Ḥujr al-Ḥaḍramī, Kathīr b. Shihāb b. Ḥuṣayn al-Hārithī, Qaṭan b. ʿAbdallāh b. Ḥuṣayn, al-Sarī b. Waqqāṣ al-Ḥārithi—who wrote his testimony while he was absent on duty—al-Sāʾib b. al-Aqraʿ al-Thaqafī, Shabīb b. Ribʿī, ʿAbdallāh b. Abī ʿAqīl al-Thaqafī, Maṣqalah b. Hubayrah al-Shaybānī, al-Qaʿqāʿ b. Shawr al-Dhuhlī, and Shaddād b. al-Mundhir b. al-Ḥārith b. Waʿlah al-Dhuhlī, who used to be called Ibn Buzayʿah. Ziyād said, "This one does not have a father to whom he is related. Omit him from the witnesses." Ziyād was then told that Shaddād was the brother of al-Ḥudayn and the son of al-Mundhir. Ziyād ordered for him to be put down with his father's name, and he was. Shaddād heard about it and said, "Woe unto me for the son of the adulteress![458] Wasn't his mother better known than his father? By God, he is only related to his mother, Sumayyah." Ḥajjār b. Abjar al-ʿIjlī (was also among the witnesses). The Rabīʿah became angry with these witnesses among the Rabīʿah who testified, and they told them, "You testified against our friends and allies." They answered, "We were only among the people, and many people from among their own folk testified against them." In addition (the witnesses included) Labīd b. ʿUṭārid al-Tamīmī, Muḥammad b. ʿUmayr b. ʿUṭārid al-Tamīmī, Suwayd b. ʿAbd al-Raḥmān al-Tamīmī from the Banū Saʿd, Asmāʾ b. Khārijah al-Fazārī, who used to apologize for his participation, Shāmir b. Dhī al-Jawshan al-ʿĀmirī, Shaddād and Marwān the two sons of al-Haytham the Hilālīs, Miḥṣan b. Thaʿlabah from

458. That is, Ziyād.

among the allies of Quraysh, al-Haytham b. al-Aswad al-Nakha'ī, who used to apologize to them, 'Abd al-Raḥmān b. Qays al-Asadī, al-Ḥārith and Shaddād the two sons of al-Azma' [134] the Hamdānīs, then the Wādi'īs, Kurayb b. Salmah b. Yazīd al-Ju'fī, 'Abd al-Raḥmān b. Abī Sabrah al-Ju'fī, Zaḥr b. Qays al-Ju'fī, Qudāmah b. al-'Ajlān al-Azdī, 'Azrah b. 'Azrah al-Aḥmasī. Ziyād also summoned al-Mukhtār b. Abī 'Ubayd and 'Urwah b. al-Mughīrah b. Shu'bah to testify against Ḥujr, but they were evasive. (The list also included) 'Umar b. Qays Dhū al-Liḥyah and Hānī b. Abī Hayyah, the two Wādi'īs.

Thus seventy men testified against Ḥujr. Ziyād then said, "Eliminate everyone except those who have been known for [their] lineage and uprightness in their faith." They did so until they had reached this number. The testimony of 'Abdallāh b. al-Ḥajjāj al-Taghlibi[459] was eliminated. The testimony of these witnesses was recorded on a scroll, then Ziyād presented it to Wā'il b. Ḥujr al-Ḥaḍramī and Kathīr b. Shihāb al-Ḥārithī. He sent them both to the prisoners, ordering them both to take them out. Shurayḥ b. al-Ḥārith, the judge, and Shurayḥ b. Hāni' al-Ḥārithi were also recorded among the witnesses. As far as Shurayḥ the judge is concerned, he said, "Ziyād asked me about Ḥujr, and I told him that he would fast and worship at night." As far as Shurayḥ b. Hāni' al-Ḥārithī is concerned, he used to say, "I was not a witness. I had heard that my testimony had been recorded, so I said it was a lie and rebuked [Ziyād]."

Wā'il b. Ḥujr and Kathīr b. Shihāb came and brought out the folk in the evening, and the commander of the police accompanied them until he took them out of al-Kūfah. When they reached the cemetery of 'Arzam, Qabīṣah b. Dubay'ah al-'Absī looked at his house, which was in the (district of the) cemetery of 'Arzam, and there were his daughters looking down. Qabīṣah asked Wā'il and Kathīr, "Allow me to counsel my family." They did so. When he drew near them, as they were weeping, he said nothing to them for a while. Then he told them to be silent, so they were. He then said, "Fear God, Almighty and [135] Great, and be steadfast, for I hope for one of two happy endings

459. Cairo reads: al-Tha'labī.

from my Lord in this destination of mine: either martyrdom which is happiness, or coming back to you in good health. Indeed, the One Who has been providing for you and suffices me for your provisions is God, Most High, Who is alive and does not die. I hope that He will not neglect you, and that He will preserve me along with you." Then he departed, passing by his folk. When his folk began to pray to God for his well-being, he said, "That makes no difference to me. The destruction of my folk is more serious than my circumstance"—meaning, "since they aren't helping me." He was hoping that they would rescue him.

(According to) Abū Mikhnaf—al-Naṣr b. Ṣāliḥ al-ʿAbsī—ʿUbaydallāh b. al-Ḥurr al-Juʿfi: By God, I was standing at the door of al-Sarī b. Abī Waqqāṣ when they went past with Ḥujr and his friends. I asked, "Are there not ten groups to rescue these, nor five?" At that, he began to lament, and none of the people answered me. They took them away and brought them to the Gharīyūn where Shurayḥ b. Ḥāni' caught up with them with a letter. He told Kathīr, "Deliver this letter of mine to the Commander of the Faithful." Kathīr asked, "What is in it?" Shurayḥ replied, "Don't ask me. It contains something I need." At that, Kathīr refused, saying, "I don't want to bring the Commander of the Faithful a letter the contents of which I do not know. Perhaps it might not be agreeable to him." Shurayḥ then brought it to Wā'il b. Ḥujr, who accepted it from him. Then they took them away until they brought them to Marj ʿAdhrā', which was twelve miles from Damascus.[460]

Those Whom Ziyād Sent to Muʿāwiyah

[136] Ḥujr b. ʿAdī b. Jabalah al-Kindī, al-Arqam b. ʿAbdallāh al-Kindī from the Banū al-Arqam, Sharīk b. Shaddād al-Ḥaḍramī, Ṣayfī b. Fasīl, Qabīṣah b. Ḍubayʿah b. Ḥarmalah al-ʿAbsī, Karīm b. ʿAfīf al-Khathʿamī from the Banū ʿĀmir b. Shahrān (then from Quḥāfah), ʿĀṣim b. ʿĀwf al-Bajalī, Warqā' b. Sumayy al-Bajalī, Kidām b. Ḥayyān and ʿAbd al-Raḥmān b. Ḥassān both of the ʿAnazah from the Banū Humaym, Muḥriz b. Shihāb al-Tamīmī

460. See Yāqūt, *Muʿjam*, IV, 488.

from the Banū Minqar, and ʿAbdallāh b. Ḥawīyah al-Saʿdī from the Banū Tamīm.

They took them away until they halted at Marj ʿAdhrāʾ, where they were imprisoned. Then Ziyād sent two other men after them escorted by ʿĀmir b. al-Aswad al-ʿIjlī—ʿUtbah b. al-Akhnas, from the Banū Saʿd b. Bakr b. Hawāzin, and Saʿd b. Nimrān al-Hamdānī (then al-Nāʿiṭī). Thus there were fourteen men. Muʿāwiyah then sent to Wāʾil b. Ḥujr and Kathīr b. Shihāb, admitted them both, opened up their letter, and read it to the Syrians. It said:

> In the name of God, the Compassionate and Merciful. To the Servant of God, Muʿāwiyah, the Commander of the Faithful, from Ziyād b. Abī Sufyān. Now then, indeed God blessed the Commander of the Faithful well, deceived his enemies for him, and saved him the trouble of one who wronged him. Indeed, oppressors belonging to this Turābiyyah, Sabāʾiyyah, whose leader is Ḥujr b. ʿAdī, opposed the Commander of the Faithful, withdrew from the community of Muslims, and declared war on us. God has made us victorious over them, and enabled us to deal with them.
> I summoned the best people of the city, their notables and [137]
> those among them possessed of maturity and faith. They testified against them concerning what they believed and did. I have sent them to the Commander of the Faithful, and have written the [names of] the upright witnesses of the people of the city, and the best of them, at the bottom of this letter of mine.

When he had read the letter and the testimony of the witnesses against them, Muʾāwiyah asked, "What do you think about this group whose own folk testify against them with what you heard?" Yazīd b. Asad al-Bajalī told him, "I think that you should disperse them among the villages of Syria, so it would save you the trouble of dealing with their sedition." Wāʾil b. Ḥujr also presented the letter of Shurayḥ b. Hāniʾ to Muʿāwiyah, so he read it. It said:

> In the name of God, the Compassionate and Merciful. To the Servant of God, Muʿāwiyah, Commander of the

> Faithful, from Shurayḥ b. Hāni'. Now then, I have heard that Ziyād wrote to you concerning my testimony against Ḥujr b. ʿAdī, and indeed my testimony about Ḥujr b. ʿAdī is that he is among those who perform the *ṣalāt*, give charity [*ẓakāt*], always perform the rites of pilgrimage [*ḥajj*] and the ʿ*umrah*[461] annually, command good and forbid evil, and [is among those] whose blood and property are forbidden. So kill him if you like, and let him alone if you like.

Muʿāwiyah read Surayḥ's letter to Wā'il b. Ḥujr and Kathīr, and then said, "I only saw this after he had removed himself from your testimony." The folk were thus imprisoned at Marj ʿAdhrā' while Muʿāwiyah wrote to Ziyād:

> Now then, I have understood what you related accurately about the matter of Ḥujr and his companions and the testimony against him from your side. I have examined it, and sometimes I thought killing them would be better than leaving them alone, and sometimes I thought granting them pardon would be better than killing them. So Goodby.

At that, Ziyād wrote back to him by means of Yazīd b. Ḥujayyah b. Rabīʿah al-Taymī:

> Now then, I have read your letter and understood your views about Ḥujr and his companions. I was astonished at your doubt about the matter concerning them, since those who are more knowledgeable about them have testified against them with what you have heard. If you have any desire for this city, do not send Ḥujr and his companions back to me.

[138] Yazīd b. Ḥujayyah advanced until he went past the prisoners at ʿAdhrā', saying, "O you! By God, I don't see your acquittal, and I have brought a letter calling for slaughter. Instruct me then to do whatever you like, whatever you think would be of advantage to you. I will do it for you and say it." At that, Ḥujr

---

461. The ʿ*umrah*, or minor pilgrimage consists of the rites near the Kaʿbah, which were customarily performed as a separate ritual during the month of Rajab. See *EI*[1], s. v. ʿUmra.

said, "Tell Mu'āwiyah that we preserve our allegience. We don't seek to abrogate it, and we will not abrogate it. On the contrary, enemies and untrustworthy people testified against us." When Yazīd brought the letter to Mu'āwiyah, he read it. Yazīd also told him of Ḥujr's speech. Mu'āwiyah then remarked, "Ziyād is more reliable than Ḥujr as far as we are concerned." At that, 'Abd al-Raḥmān b. 'Umar b. Umm al-Ḥakam al-Thaqafī—it is also said, 'Uthmān b. 'Umayr al-Thaqafī—said, "Scrap it! Scrap it!" And Mu'āwiyah responded to him, "Don't encourage reconcilation!" The Syrians went out without understanding what Mu'āwiyah and 'Abd al-Raḥmān had said.[462] Coming to al-Nu'mān b. Bashīr, they told him what Ibn Umm al-Ḥakam had said. Al-Nu'mān explained, "They are as good as dead."

'Āmir b. al-Aswad al-'Ijlī, who was at 'Adhrā', approached desiring to inform Mu'āwiyah about the two (additional) men whom Ziyād had sent. As he turned to leave, Ḥujr b. 'Adī stood up before him, shackled with chains, saying, "O 'Āmir, listen to me. Tell Mu'āwiyah that my blood is forbidden to him, and inform him that we were given a guarantee of safe-conduct and that we have become reconciled to him. Tell him also to fear God and examine our case." When 'Āmir repeated similar words back to him, Ḥujr repeated it to him several times, while the latter would repeat it back. 'Āmir then said, "I have understood you, you have repeated [it] many times." Ḥujr responded, "I did not speak dishonorably, while he blames me.[463] Indeed, by God, you will be preferred and rewarded, while Ḥujr will be brought and killed. I shall not blame you if you find my speech burdensome. Take your leave." At that, he seemed to be ashamed and remonstrated, "No, by God, that was not my meaning. I shall certainly give notice and make the effort." He [139]
seemed to assume that he would do it, while Ḥujr refused to believe him.

'Āmir entered Mu'āwiyah's presence, and informed him about the matter of the two men. Yazīd b. Asad al-Bajalī rose

462. 'Abd al-Raḥmān was probably telling Mu'āwiyah to tear up Ziyād's letter.

463. Cairo reads: "does he blame me?"

saying, "O Commander of the Faithful, give me my two cousins." Jarīr b. ʿAbdallāh had written about them, "Two men belonging to my folk from the people of the community, men of sound views. An untrustworthy slanderer libeled them to Ziyād, so he sent them both in the group of Kūfans whom he sent to the Commander of the Faithful. They are among those who do not undertake any innovation in Islam nor do wrong to the Caliph." That was to their advantage with the Commander of the Faithful. When Yazīd asked about them, Muʿāwiyah remembered the letter of Jarīr, so he said, "Your cousin, Jarīr, has written to me about them both, praising them charitably, and he deserves to have his word trusted and his sincere advice accepted. you have asked me about your cousins, so you may have them both." Wā'il b. Ḥujr also asked for al-Arqam, so Muʿāwiyah let him go. Abū al-Aʿwar al-Sulamī asked for ʿUtbah b. al-Akhnas, so Muʿāwiyah gave him to him. Ḥumrah b. Mālik al-Hamdānī asked for Saʿd b. Nimrān al-Hamdānī, so Muʿāwiyah gave him to him. Ḥabīb b. Maslamah also interceded with him for Ibn Ḥawīyah, so Muʿāwiyah released him.

At that, Mālik b. Hubayrah al-Sakūnī rose addressing Muʿāwiyah, "O Commander of the Faithful, leave my cousin, Ḥujr, to me." But Muʿāwiyah answered, "Indeed, your cousin, Ḥujr, is the leader of the folk, and I fear that if I release him he would corrupt my city for me. Tomorrow we must send you and your friends off to him in Iraq." So Mālik told him, "By God, you were not just to me, O Muʿāwiyah. I fought your cousin along with you. I faced them in a battle like that of Ṣiffīn until your
[140] side was victorious, your heel raised up, and you did not fear misfortunes. Then I asked you for my cousin, and you assaulted me and read into what I said things that are of no advantage to me. You were afraid of what you alleged the consequences of the misfortunes [would be]." Then he left and sat at home.

Muʿāwiyah then sent Hudbah b. Fiyyād al-Quḍāʿī of the Banū Salāmān b. Saʿd, al-Ḥusayn b. ʿAbdallāh al-Kilābī, and Abū Sharīf al-Baddī, and they brought the prisoners in the evening. When al-Khathʿamī saw al-Aʿwar, he said, "Half of us will be killed and half saved." Saʿd b. Nimrān said, "O God, make me one of those who are saved, as long as You are satisified with me." ʿAbd al-Raḥmān b. Ḥassān al-ʿAnazī said, "O God, make me one of those whose disgrace honors You, as long as you are satisfied with me. How often I presented myself for killing. God thus has willed what He desired."

The messenger of Muʿāwiyah then came to them with orders to release six and to kill eight, telling them, "We have been ordered to let you disavow ʿAlī and curse him. If you do so, we shall release you; and if you refuse, we shall kill you. The Commander of the Faithful also declares that he has been allowed to shed your blood by the testimony of the people of your city against you, although he has refrained from that. So renounce this man, and we shall release you." They replied, "O God, we shall not do that." He then ordered for their graves to be dug, and their shrouds to be brought. They spent the entire night worshipping, so, when morning came, Muʿāwiyah's men said, "Hey you! We saw you last night prolonging worship and doing it well, so inform us of what you have to say about ʿUthmān." They replied, "He was the first who deviated in judgment and acted wrongly." At that, Muʿāwiyah's men declared, "The Commander of the Faithful knew you better." They then stood up in front of the prisoners saying, "Denounce this [141] man!" They replied, "We vindicate him instead, and denounce whoever denounces him." At that, every man took one of them in order to kill him. When Qabīṣah b. Ḍubayʿah fell into the hands of Abū Sharīfah al-Baddī, he told the latter, "The [former] hatred has been changed to peace between my folk and your folk, so let someone else kill me." So Abū Sharīfah answered him, "Kinship helped you," and took al-Ḥaḍramī and killed him, while al-Quḍāʿī killed Qabīṣah b. Ḍubayʿah.

Then Ḥujr told them, "Leave me alone so I may perform ablutions." They told him to do so. When he finished, he told them, "Leave me alone so I can make two prostrations. I certainly swear to God that I have never performed ablutions without making two prostrations." They told him to worship, and he did so. Then he stopped, saying, "By God, I never worshipped more quickly than this, and if you think that I have no anxiety about death, I would have liked to prolong it." Then he added, "O God, we appeal to You for help against our community, since the Kūfans have testified against us, and since the

Syrians are killing us. However, by God, if you killed me here, I would be the first Muslim horseman to perish in this valley, and the first Muslim man at whom its dogs barked." When al-Aʿwar Hudbah b. Fiyāḍ strode to him with his sword, Ḥujr's sinews trembled, and al-Aʿwar declared, "Certainly not! You claimed that you were not anxious about death. I will leave you, so renounce your companions." But Ḥujr replied, "Why shouldn't I be anxious, since I see a grave dug, a shroud spread out, and a sword unsheathed. By God, if I were anxious about killing I would not say that which angers the Lord." At that, al-Aʿwar killed him, and they began to kill them one by one until they had killed six.

ʿAbd al-Raḥmān b. Ḥassān al-ʿAnazī and Karīm b. ʿAfīf al-Khathʿamī then said, "Send us to the Commander of the Faith-
[142] ful, and we shall say what he does about this man." When they sent to Muʿāwiyah informing him of their statement, he sent word back to them, "Bring both of them to me." When they had entered his presence, al-Khathʿamī exclaimed, "God! God! O Muʿāwiyah, indeed, you will be transported from this transitory abode to the eternal abode hereafter, then questioned about what you hoped to gain by killing us and why you shed our blood." Muʿāwiyah inquired, "What do you say about ʿAlī?" He replied, "I say what you do about him," adding, "Shall I renounce the faith of ʿAlī who used to worship God along with it?" He then fell silent, and Muʿāwiyah did not want to answer him. Shāmir b. ʿAbdallāh of the Banū Quḥāfah got up, asking, "O Commander of the Faithful, give me my cousin." Muʿāwiyah replied, "You have him, except I am going to imprison him for a month." Shāmir would send word to Muʿāwiyah every two days and intercede with him, and the latter told him, "Indeed, I would think you were precious for Iraq if the likes of you were among them." Then Shāmir brought him up again, so Muʿāwiyah said, "We have commuted your cousin's sentence for you." He then summoned al-Khathʿamī and released him on condition that he would not enter al-Kūfah as long as he was ruler. Muʿāwiyah then said, "Choose whichever Arab land you would prefer for me to send you to." Al-Khathʿamī chose Mosul. He used to say, "If Muʿāwiyah

should die, I would come to the city." But he died a month before Mu'āwiyah.

Then Mu'āwiyah turned to 'Abd al-Raḥmān al-'Anazī, and asked him, "O brother of the Rabī'ah, what do you say about 'Alī?" He replied, "Let me alone, and don't question me. That would be better for you." Mu'āwiyah rejoined, "By God, I shall not leave you alone until you tell me about him." 'Abd al-Raḥmān declared, "I testify that he was one of those who frequently remember God, order what is right, stand up for justice, and forgive the people." Mu'āwiyah continued, "What then do you say about 'Uthmān?" He replied, "He was the first to open the gate of injustice and lock the gates of righteousness." Mu'āwiyah declared, "You have condemned yourself." 'Abd al-Raḥmān answered, "No, I have killed you instead." None of the Rabī'ah in the valley would speak when Shāmir al- [143]
Khath'amī talked about Karīm b. 'Afīf al-Khath'amī, and none of Shāmir's folk would speak to him about Karīm. Mu'āwiyah then sent 'Abd al-Raḥmān to Ziyād, and wrote to him, "Now then, indeed, this al-'Anazī is the worst one you sent, so give him the punishment he deserves, and kill him in the worst way." When he was brought to Ziyād, Ziyād sent him to Quss al-Nāṭif, and he was buried alive there.

When al-'Anazī and al-Khath'amī were transported to Mu'āwiyah, al-'Anazī had said to Ḥujr, "O Ḥujr, may God not take you away. What an excellent brother of Islam you are." Meanwhile al-Khath'amī said, "Don't be distant, and don't be deprived, for you have commanded good and forbidden evil." Then they were taken away, while Ḥujr followed them with his eyes, saying, "Sufficient for death was a cutter of the rope of relationships." 'Utbah b. al-Akhnas and Sa'd b. Nimrān were taken away a few days after Ḥujr and released.

Ḥujr's Companions Who Were Killed

Ḥujr b. 'Adī, Sharīk b. Shaddād al-Ḥaḍramī, Ṣayfī b. Fasīl al-Shaybānī, Qabīṣah b. Ḍubay'ah al-'Absī, Muḥriz b. Shihāb al-Sa'dī, then al-Minqarī, Kidām b. Hayyān al-'Anazī, 'Abd al-Raḥmān b. Ḥassān al-'Anazī whom he sent to Ziyād so he was buried alive at Quss al-Nāṭif. Thus there were seven who were killed, enshrouded, and prayed over. It is alleged that when al-Ḥasan heard about the killing of Ḥujr and his companions, he inquired, "Did they pray over them, bury them, and make them face towards the *qiblah*?"[464] Upon being told that they had, he remarked, "They were defeated by them, by the Lord of the Kaʿbah."

Ḥujr's Companions Who Were Saved

[144] Karīm b. ʿAfīf al-Khathʿamī, ʿAbdallāh b. Ḥawīyah al-Tamīmī, ʿAṣim b. ʿAwf al-Bajalī, Warqāʾ Sumayyah al-Bajalī, al-Arqam b. ʿAbdallāh al-Kindī, ʿUtbah b. al-Akhnas of the Banū Saʿd b. Bakr, and Saʿd b. Nimrān al-Hamdānī. There were seven of them.

When Muʿāwiyah had refused to release Ḥujr to Mālik b. Hubayrah al-Sakūnī—many of Mālik's folk of the Kindah and al-Sakūn, and many people of the Yaman, had gathered to him—he said, "By God, we can do without Muʿāwiyah more than Muʿāwiyah can do without us. We would find a replacement for him among his folk, while he would not find a replacement for us among the people. Set out for his man, and free him." At that, they proceeded to travel, certain that Ḥujr and his companions were at ʿAdhrāʾ and that they had not been killed. Thus their killers met them, having just left there. When they saw Mālik among the people, the killers supposed, however, that he had brought them to rescue Ḥujr from them. Mālik asked, "Why are you coming?" and was told, "The prisoners repented, and we have come to inform Muʿāwiyah." Mālik did not answer them, and proceeded towards ʿAdhrāʾ. When someone who came from there met him, he informed Mālik that the prisoners had been killed. At that, Mālik said, "Bring the folk to me." The cavalry followed Mālik and his men, and, outdistancing them, they entered Muʿāwiyah's presence. When they told him the news—what Mālik b. Hubayrah and the people who were with him had come for—Muʿāwiyah told them, "Be

464. See above, n. 110.

silent! Rather it is a passion that he feels in himself, and is about to die down."

Mālik returned, settling in his residence, and he did not come to Mu'āwiyah. Mu'āwiyah sent to him, but he refused to come. When night came, Mu'āwiyah sent one hundred thousand dirhams to Mālik, saying to him, "The Commander of the Faithful is prevented from allowing you to intercede with him about your cousin except [out of] sympathy for you and your friends, lest they resume another war for you. If Ḥujr b. 'Adī [145] had survived, I fear that he would have caused you and your friends to go to him, and that would have been an affliction for the Muslims which would be more serious than killing Ḥujr." So Mālik accepted it and was in good spirits; coming to Mu'āwiyah on the following day, he entered the latter's presence with throngs of his folk, and Mu'āwiyah was pleased with him.

(According to) Abū Mikhnaf—'Abd al-Mālik b. Nawfal b. Masāḥiq: 'Ā'ishah sent 'Abd al-Raḥmān b. al-Ḥārith b. Hishām to Mu'āwiyah concerning Ḥujr and his friends. Upon arriving after Mu'āwiyah had killed them, 'Abd al-Raḥmān asked him, "Where did the forbearance of Abū Sufyān disappear from you?" Mu'āwiyah replied, "It vanished from me when mild people like you among my folk abandoned me, and Ibn Sumayyah[465] convinced me, so I acquiesced."

(According to)Abū Mikhnaf—'Abd al-Malik b. Nawfal—'Ā'ishah: If changing matters would not have made them worse than before, we would have done differently with regard to the killing of Ḥujr. By God, I used to know him as a Muslim who performed the pilgrimage and the *'umrah*.[466]

(According to) Abū Mikhnaf—'Abd al-Mālik b. Nawfal —Abū Sa'īd[467] al-Maqburī: When Mu'āwiyah made the pilgrimage, he passed by 'Ā'ishah, so he asked permission to enter her presence, and she admitted him. When he sat down, she asked him, "O Mu'āwiyah, do you trust me not to conceal from you one who would kill you?" He replied, "I have entered a safe

465. That is, Ziyād. As Mu'āwiyah is not likely to have used the derogatory "Ibn Sumayyah," this account appears to be tendentious.

466. See above, n. 461.

467. Cairo reads: Sa'īd. He was Sa'īd b. Abī Sa'īd.

house." She went on, "O Muʿāwiyah, don't you fear God because of the killing of Ḥujr and his companions?" He answered, "It was not I who killed them, rather those who testified against them killed them."

(According to) Abū Mikhnaf—Zakariyyā' b. Zā'idah—Abū Isḥāq: I was around people who were saying, "The first disgrace in al-Kūfah was the death of al-Ḥasan b. ʿAlī, the killing of Ḥujr b. ʿAdī, and the false claim of Ziyād to affinity [with the family of Abū Sufyān]." Abū Mikhnaf (said): It was claimed that at his
[146] death, Muʿāwiyah said, "My day was three times as long because of Ibn Adbar," that is, Ḥujr.

(According to) Abū Mikhnaf—al-Ṣaqʿab b. Zuhayr—al-Ḥasan: Muʿāwiyah had four flaws, and any one of them would have been a serious offense: (his) appointment of troublemakers for this community so that he stole its rule without consultation with its members, while there was a remnant of the Companions and possessors of virtue among them; his appointment of his son as his successor after him, a drunkard (and) a winebibber who wears silk and plays ṭunbūrs;[468] his allegation about Ziyād, while the Messenger of God has said, "The child belongs to the bed, and the adulterer should be stoned;"[469] and his killing of Ḥujr. Woe unto him twice for Ḥujr and his companions."

Hind bt. Zayd b. Makhramah al-Anṣārī said, while she was escorting (the funeral procession), mourning Ḥujr:[470]

Rise, O shining moon!
Look! Do you see Ḥujr departing,

Departing to Muʿāwiyah son of Ḥarb,
to be killed by him, as the amīr claimed?

---

468. A *ṭunbūr* was a long-necked, stringed instrument with a small sound chest. See *EI*¹, Supp., s.v. Ṭunbūr.

469. This ḥadīth is often cited with regard to Muʿāwiyah's recognition of Ziyād as the illegitimate son of Abū Sufyān and Sumayyah. See Ibn ʿAbd Rabbihi, *ʿIqd*, V, 5; Lichtenstadter, "From Particularism to Unity," 225; Pellat, *Jāḥiz*, 84.

470. These lines are also in Iṣfahānī, *Aghānī*, XVI, 10; and Masʿūdī, *Murūj*, V, 15.

The tyrants sported their power after Ḥujr,
and al-Khawarnaq and al-Sadīr were pleasant for them,[471]

While the lands became barren,
as though clouds full of rain do not revive them.

O Ḥujr, Ḥujr of the Banū ʿAdī,
may safety and happiness receive you.

I fear for you what destroyed ʿAdī,[472]
while an old man is roaring in Damascus.

He thinks killing the best is all right for him,
who has a wazīr from the worst people.

If only Ḥujr had died a [natural] death,
and had not been slaughtered like camels are slaughtered.

If he should perish then every leader of folk
of the world will come to destruction.

Al-Kindiyyah said, lamenting Ḥujr—it is also said that the Anṣārī woman was the one to say this:

The tears of my eye are continuous rain that falls [147]
weeping for Ḥujr unstinting.[473]

If the bow were upon his captivity,
al-Aʿwar would not impose the sword on him.

The poet also said, inciting the Banū Hind of the Banū Shaybān against Qays b. ʿUbād, when he slandered Ṣayfī b. Fasīl:

---

471. Al-Khawarnaq and al-Sadīr were famous pre-Islamic palaces in the neighborhood of al-Ḥīrah. Al-Khawarnaq was about one mile east of modern Najaf. See Yāqūt, *Muʿjam*, II, 490–94, III, 59–61; *EI*², s. v. al-Khawarnaḳ.

472. Iṣfahānī, *Aghānī* reads: "I fear for you the assault of the family of Ḥarb."

473. The text reads: *mā tuqtiru*; Cairo reads: *mā tafturu*, "unabating."

Ibn Fasīl appealed, "O for Murrah!" an appeal,
and the tip of the sword encountered the palm of a hand and a wrist.

So incite the Banū Hind whenever you encounter them,
and address Ghiyāth and his son saying,

"Let Qutaylah weep for the Banū Hind, just as
the wife of Ṣayfī wept while she arranged a funeral."

This Ghiyāth is Ibn ʿImrān b. Murrah b. al-Ḥārith b. Dubb b. Murrah b. Dhūl b. Shaybān who was a noble, while Qutaylah was the sister of Qays b. ʿUbād. The latter lived until he fought alongside Ibn al-Ashʿath in battle. Ḥawshab then told al-Ḥajjāj b. Yūsuf, "There is among us a man who is a leader of seditions and risings against the government. There was never a sedition in Iraq without his being eagerly involved in it. He is a Turābī who curses ʿUthmān. He has rebelled with Ibn al-Ashʿath and participated with him in all his battles. He incited the people until, when God destroyed them, he came and sat in his house." When al-Ḥajjāj sent for him and beheaded him, the sons of his father said to the family of Ḥawshab, "But you certainly slandered us." And they replied, "You certainly slandered our friend instead."

[148] Abū Mikhnaf (said): ʿAbdallāh b. Khalīfah al-Ṭāʾī had accompanied Ḥujr b. ʿAdī. When Ziyād sought ʿAbdallāh, he dropped out of sight. Ziyād then sent the police for him, who at that time were people of the Ḥamrāʾ, and they arrested him. At that, his sister, al-Nawār, went out saying, "O kinfolk of Ṭayyīʾ! Do you surrender your spearheads and your tongue? ʿAbdallāh b. Khalīfah!" The Ṭāʾīs then assaulted the police, struck them, and snatched ʿAbdallāh b. Khalīfah from them. When the police returned to Ziyād and informed him, the latter fell upon ʿAdī b. Ḥātim while he was in the mosque, saying, "Bring me ʿAbdallāh b. Khalīfah." ʿAdī asked, "What's the matter with him?" When Ziyād told him, he said, "This is something that happened in a tribal district I do not know." Ziyād demanded, "By God, bring him to me." ʿAdī retorted, "No, by God, I shall never bring him to you. I brought you my cousin whom you

killed. By God, if he were beneath my feet, I would not lift them off of him." At that, Ziyād ordered ʿAdī to the prison.

Every Yamanī or Rabaʿī in al-Kūfah then came to Ziyād and interceded with him, saying, "You do this to ʿAdī b. Ḥātim, a Companion of the Messenger of God." Ziyād replied, "I would release him under one condition." They asked, "What is it?" He said, "That his cousin should leave me and not enter al-Kūfah as long as I have authority here." When ʿAdī was informed of that, he agreed and sent for ʿAbdallāh b. Khalīfah, saying, "O my nephew, indeed this [man] has been insistent in your case, and has refused everything except your exile from your city as long as he has authority. So get to the two mountains."[474] At that, ʿAbdallāh b. Khalīfah left and began to write to ʿAdī, and ʿAdī began to encourage him, so ʿAbdallāh wrote to him:

I remembered Laylā and youths in the afternoon
and the memory of childhood is a torment for one who remembers.

Youth passes away, so I missed its hardship
and, O, what passion you had in it, after it fled away.

Then cease remembrance of youth and its loss [149]
and its remnants[475] when it parts from you, and desist.

And weep for friends when they have all gone,
while they do not find a source except the spring of death.

Their fates summoned them and he whose day approached
of the people, so know that it would not be postponed.

Those were my adherents and refuge
the day when I face[476] one whose burning is memorable.

And I did not desire after them as a diversion,
anything worldly, nor to have my life prolonged.

---

474. That is, Mts. Ajah and Salmah of the Jabal Ṭāʾī in northern Arabia.
475. The text reads: *āsārahu*; Cairo reads: *āthārahu*, "its vestiges."
476. The text reads: *ulfī*; C reads: *alqā*, "encounter."

I say, "By God, I shall not forget to remember them
for all time, unless I die and am buried."

Peace upon the people of ʿAdhrā', redoubled
from God, and let the cumulus clouds give to drink,

And Ḥujr receive in them mercy from God,
For Ḥujr has pleased God and is excused.

And may incessant torrents and perpetual rain continue
upon the grave of Ḥujr until he is summoned to be assembled.

So, O Ḥujr, who will bleed the throats of the horses,[477]
and of the aggressive king whenever he acts unjustly,

[150] And who will preach the truth after you, speaking,
about piety, and who, if injustice was mentioned, changed it?

So what a good brother of Islam you were! And I
wish for you to be granted immortality and to be delighted.

You used to give the sword its due in the war,
and acknowledge good and disavow evil.

O our two brothers of Humaym, you were both protected,
and prepared easily for good works, so receive the good news!

O my two Kindifī brothers, receive the good news!
for you were both kept alive in order to be told good news.

O brothers of Ḥaḍramawt and Ghālib
and Shaybān, you met an easy reckoning.

477. That is, lead them into battle.

You were fortunate, and I did not hear [anything] more proper than your
dispute at the time of great death, or more steadfast.

I shall weep for all of you as long as a star shines and the dove
coos and rustles in the depth of both valleys.

So I said, not being unjust, "O Gawth son of Ṭayy'i,
when I was afraid that I would be made to go among you,

Did you have the opportunity and not defend your brother? [151]
while he defended himself until he leaned over, then collapsed.

You separated from me, and I was left deserted,
as if I were a stranger squeezed with hands.

Who do you have like me at every attack?
and who do you have like me when courage appears?

And who do you have like me when war starts,
while the one who risks his life was active in it and girded?"

So here am I, whose dwelling is in the mountains of Ṭayyi',
exiled, and if God willed, He could change it.

My enemy exiled me unjustly from the place to which I migrated,
and I was content with what God willed and decreed.

My folk surrendered me for no crime,
as if they were not my folk and kinsmen.

If I were accustomed to a dwelling in the mountains of Ṭayyi',
and it was a dwelling for a short while and a presence,

I would not be afraid that I would be considered a foreigner.
may God revile whoever reviles Him, and multiply it.

[152] May God revile the Ḥaḍrami foe, Wā'il
and may they suffer annihilation from the abundant spearheads.

And may the folk suffer destruction who took sides
against us and told a shocking lie.

So folk, do not put me with Gawth son of Ṭayyi',
because their fate made them miserable and was changed.

I don't attack them on a caparisoned [horse] and I don't scatter
dust upon them at Kuwayfah.[478]

Say to my friend, if you set out heading eastwards,
Jadīlah and the two communities, Maʿn and Buḥtur,

And Nabhān and al-Afnā' from the root of Ṭayyi',
"Am I not a strong possessor of wealth among you?

Do you not remember the battle-day of ʿUdhayb, when my strongest oath
before you was that I would never be seen turning back?

And my attack against Mihrān, while the group was undefended,
and my killing of the heroic, death-defying armband wearer?

[153] And on the day the battle of Jalūlā' occurred, I was not blamed,
and the victories of the battle-day Nihāwand andTustar.

And you forget about me on the battle-day of the water hole, while the lances
were broken in their shoulders at Ṣiffīn.

May his Lord punish ʿAdī b. Ḥātim for me,
for my rejection and my disappointment, an ample punishment.

478. "Little Kūfah" was a place near Baziqiyā in central Iraq. See Ibn Manẓūr, *Lisān*, IX, 312; Yāqūt, *Muʿjam*, IV, 331.

Do you forget my reckless bravery, O son of Ḥātim?
In the evening your aggressiveness did not help you against Ḥidhmir.[479]

I defended you against the folk until they weakened;
I was the most grim, the strongest adversary.

They fled and did not stay where I was, as if
they considered me a lion lurking in the reed thicket.

I assisted you when [those] near withdrew and [those] distant fled, and I was made to achieve victory single-handed.

So my repayment [is] that I am deprived among you,
imprisoned, and that I am disgraced and captured.

How many promises I have from you that you will return to me,
but [even] a fox cannot escape the appointed time with regard to me."

Then I began to tend the old she-camel for a while, and sometimes [154]
I would summon to drink, if the shepherds summoned to drink.

As if I have not ridden a racehorse for a raid,
and have not left the armored opponent thrown to the ground,

And I have not opposed attacking cavalry with the sword,
when he who retreats goes backwards, then pulls back and forth,

And I have not spurred on the racer right after the troop,
heading for the heights of Sijās[480] and Abhar,

479. Cairo reads: "Ḥizmir."
480. Sijās is the territory between Hamadhān and Abhar.

And I have not frightened the deer from me in an attack,
like the watering-place for the she-camel,[481] then I descend victorious,

And I have not been seen among the cavalry that thrusts at each other with lances,
at Qazwīn[482] or Sharwīn,[483] nor have raided Kundur.[484]

And that [was] a time the praiseworthiness of which has departed from me,
and what was known about it became unknown for me.

So my folk would not stay away, even if I were absent,
and were lost among them and hidden,

And [there is] no good in the world and life after them,
even though I were distant of abode, held back from them.

[155] But ʿAbdallāh b. Khalīfah died in the two mountains before Ziyād did.

ʿUbaydah al-Kindī, then al-Baddī, said, reproaching Muḥammad b. al-Ashʿath for his abandonment of Ḥujr:

You surrendered your uncle, you did not fight in front of him
in fear, and, but for you, he would have been unassailable.

You killed an envoy of the family of Muḥammad,
and you stripped off his swords and armor.

If you were from Asad, you would understand my nobility,
and consider the family of al-Hubāb to be an intercessor for me.

---

481. *Al-ablam* is a she-camel that has not yet had a child. See Ibn Manẓūr, *Lisān*, XII, 54.

482. Qazwīn is a town and its district northwest of al-Rayy (Tehrān) and south of Gīlān. See *EI²*, s.v. Ḳazwīn.

483. The Jibāl Sharwīn is on the western border of Ṭabaristān, next to Gīlān. See Yāqūt, *Muʿjam*, III, 283–84.

484. There was a village called Kundur near Qazwīn. See Yāqūt, *Muʿjam*, IV, 309.

In this year Ziyād sent al-Rabīʿ b. Ziyād al-Ḥārithī as governor of Khurāsān after the death of al-Ḥakam b. ʿAmr al-Ghifārī. Al-Ḥakam had appointed Anas b. Abī Unās to succeed him in his jurisdiction aftter his death. This Anas was the one who led the prayer over al-Ḥakam when he died. Al-Ḥakam was buried in the house of Khālid b. ʿAbdallāh, the brother of Khulayd b. ʿAbdallāh al-Ḥanafī. Al-Ḥakam had written to Ziyād about his appointment of Anas, so Ziyād dismissed Anas and put Khulayd b. ʿAbdallāh al-Hanafī in his place. I was told by ʿUmar —ʿAlī b. Muḥammad: When Ziyād dismissed Anas and put Khulayd b. ʿAbdallāh al-Ḥanafī in his place, Anas said:

Who will tell Ziyād about me?
ambling on, the courier [*barīd*] trots with it.

Do you dismiss me and nourish Khulayd?
Ḥanīfah has found what it wants.

Help yourselves to the Yamāmah[485] and cultivate it, [156]
for the first and last of you are slaves.[486]

Ziyād put Khulayd in charge for a month, then dismissed him and put Rabīʿ b. Ziyād al-Ḥārithī in charge of Khurāsān at the beginning of this year. The people moved with their families to Khurāsān and settled there. Then Ziyād dismissed al-Rabīʿ.

I was told by ʿUmar—ʿAlī—Maslamah b. Muḥārib and ʿAbd al-Raḥmān b. Abān al-Qurashī: Al-Rabīʿ reached Khurāsān and conquered Balkh peacefully, since they had closed it after al-Aḥnaf b. Qays made peace with them. He also conquered Quhistān[487] by force. There were Turks[488] in its districts, so he killed (some of) them and put (the others) to flight. One of them

485. The Yamāmah is the region in central Arabia from which the Banū Ḥanīfah had come. See *EI*[1], s.v. al-Yamāma.

486. The Banū Ḥanīfah were farmers in the Yamāmah, but Muʿāwiyah is said to have confiscated land near al-Qaṭāʾi in the Yamāmah which he had cultivated by four thousand slaves. See Ibn al-Athīr, *Kāmil*, IV, 201.

487. Quhistān is the mountainous region south of Nishāpūr in central Iran. See *EI*[2], s.v. Ḳūhistān.

488. These "Turks" were probably Hephthalites from Bādghīs, Harāt, and Pūshang. See M. A. Shaban, *Abbāsid Revolution*, 32; and *EI*[2], s. v. Hayāṭila.

who survived was Nīzak Ṭarkhān,[489] whom Qutaybah b. Muslim[490] killed when he was governor. I was told by ʿUmar—ʿAlī: Al-Rabīʿ campaigned and crossed the river [491] accompanied by his servant, Farrūkh, and his slave-girl, Sharīfah. He plundered and returned safely, whereupon he set Farrūkh free. Al-Ḥakam b. ʿAmr had crossed the river before him during his governorship, but did not conquer (anything).

I was told by ʿUmar—ʿAlī b. Muḥammad: The first Muslim to drink from the river was a mawlā of al-Ḥakam who scooped (it out)with his shield. Then he handed (it) to al-Ḥakam, so he drank, made his ablutions, and performed two prostrations beyond the river. He was the first of the people who did that; then he returned.

In this year Yazīd b. Muʿāwiyah led the people in the pilgrimage. Aḥmad b. Thābit told me that according to whoever recounted it according to Isḥāq b. ʿĪsā according to Maʿshar, while al-Wāqidī said likewise. The governor over al-Madīnah during this year was Saʿīd b. al-ʿAṣ, while Ziyād was in charge of al-Kūfah, al-Baṣrah and all of the eastern territory, and Shurayḥ was in charge of rendering judgment at al-Kūfah While ʿUmayr b. Yathribī was in charge of rendering judgment at al-Baṣrah.

---

489. Nīzak Ṭarkhān was the Hephthalite ruler of Bādghīs. See Shaban, *Abbāsid Revolution*, 65

490. Qutaybah b. Muslim (49–96[669/70–715]) was a Muslim general engaged in the conquest of Central Asia as governor of Khurāsān for al-Walīd from 86(705) until 96(715) He killed Nīzak Ṭarkhān after a revolt in 91(709). See Shaban, *Abbāsid Revolution*, 67; *EI*², s. v. Ḳutaiba b. Muslim.

491. The "river" is the Oxus or Jayḥūn, the modern Amū Daryā. See *EI*², s. v. Amū Daryā.

The Events of the Year [157]

52

(January 8, 672–December 26, 672)

Al-Wāqidī claimed that the raid of Sufyān b. ʿAwf al-Azdī occurred during this year, as well as his winter campaign in Byzantine territory. He also claimed that Sufyān died there and appointed ʿAbdallāh b. Masʿadah al-Fazārī as his successor. Others have said that in this year Busr b. Abī Arṭāt led the people in the winter campaign in Byzantine territory, and that he was accompanied by Sufyān b. ʿAwf al-Azdī. They also said that Muḥammad b. ʿAbdallāh al-Thaqafī led the summer raid in this year.

Saʿīd b. al-ʿĀṣ led the people in the pilgrimage in this year according to Abū Maʿshar, al-Wāqidī and others. The officials of the provincial capitals during this year were the same as in the previous year.

The Events of the Year 53

(December 27, 672–December 15, 673)

Among the events that happened during this year was the winter campaign of ʿAbd al-Raḥmān b. Umm al-Ḥakam al-Thaqafī in Byzantine territory.

During this year Rhodes,[492] an island in the sea, was conquered. Junādah b. Abī Umayyah al-Azdī conquered it, and, according to Muḥammad b. ʿUmar, the Muslims settled there, cultivated it, and acquired wealth there. Cattle grazed about, so when evening came, they brought them into the fortress. They also had a lookout who would warn them about anyone at sea who wanted to surprise them. Thus they would be on guard against them. They were most difficult for the Byzantines, so the latter blockaded them by sea and cut off their ships. Muʿāwiyah used to lavish provisions and stipends on them, and the enemy used to be afraid of them. When Muʿāwiyah died, Yazīd b. Muʿāwiyah brought them back.

The death of Ziyād b. Sumayyah also occurred in this year. [1
I was told by ʿUmar—Zuhayr—Wahīb—his father—Muḥammad b. Isḥāq—Muḥammad b. al-Zubayr—Fīl, the mawlā of Zi-

492. See *EI*[1], s. v. Rhodes; Kūfī, *Futūḥ*, II, 126.

yād: Ziyād ruled Iraq for five years, then he died in this year. I was told by ʿUmar—ʿAlī b. Muḥammad: When Ziyād descended upon Iraq, he lasted until the year 53, then he died at al-Kūfah in the month of Ramaḍān (August 20–September 18, 673), while his deputy in charge of al-Baṣrah was Samurah b. Jundab.

How Ziyād b. Sumayyah Perished

I was told by ʿAbdallāh b. Aḥmad al-Marwazī—his father—Sulaymān—ʿAbdallāh b. al-Mubārik—ʿAbdallāh b. Shawdhab—Kathīr b. Ziyād: Ziyād wrote to Muʿāwiyah, "Indeed, I have seized Iraq with my left hand while my right hand is empty." So Muʿāwiyah added al-ʿArūḍ to him, which is the Yamāmah and what is adjacent to it. At that, Ibn ʿUmar prayed against him, so Ziyād caught the plague and died. When he heard the news, Ibn ʿUmar said, "Off with you, Ibn Sumayyah, for this world does not remain for you, and you did not attain the other [world]."

I was told by ʿUmar—ʿAlī: Ziyād wrote to Muʿāwiyah, "I have seized Iraq for you with my left hand while my right hand is empty, so fill it with the Ḥijāz." He sent al-Haytham b. al-Asad al-Nakhaʿī with that (message), and Muʿwiyah wrote his pact for Ziyād with al-Haytham. When the people of the Ḥijāz heard that, a group of them came to ʿAbdallāh b. ʿUmar b. al-Khaṭṭāb relating that to him. He said, "Pray to God for Him to spare you his trouble." He then faced the *qiblah* with them and prayed with them. The plague then broke out on Ziyād's [159]
finger, and he sent to Shurayḥ, who was his judge (*qāḍī*), saying, "You see what happened to me. I was advised to have it cut off, so counsel me." Shurayḥ then advised him, "I fear that there will be scars on your hand and suffering in your heart, and that the appointed time will approach anyway. You would thus meet God, Almighty and Great, mutilated while you had cut off your hand out of aversion to meeting Him. The alternative is that there might be improvement after a while, and since you had cut off your hand, you would live mutilated and be a reproach for your son." At that, Ziyād gave up the idea, and Shurayḥ left. When the latter was asked about it, he in-

formed them of what he had advised Ziyād. At that, they rebuked him, asking, "Why didn't you advise him to cut it off?" He replied, "The Messenger of God said, "The advisor is entrusted."

I was told by ʿAbdallāh b. Aḥmad al-Marwazī—his father—Sulaymān—ʿAbdallāh: I heard someone who related that Ziyād sent to Shurayḥ asking his advice about cutting off his hand. Shurayḥ replied, "Don't do it. If you should live, you would be mutilated, and if you perish, you would have sinned against yourself." Ziyād remarked, "I sleep with the plague in one blanket," so he decided to do it. But when he saw the fire and the cauterizing instrument, he became anxious and refrained from doing it.

I was told by ʿUmar—ʿAbd al-Malik b. Qurayb al-Aṣmaʿī—Ibn Abī Ziyād: When death attended Ziyād, his son told him, "O my father, I have prepared sixty garments in which I shall wrap you." Ziyād replied, "O my son, better clothing than this has drawn near your father," or "mourning goes quickly." Thus he died and was buried at al-Thuwayyah beside al-Kūfah.[493] He had dispatched Yazīd towards the Ḥijāz as its governor. So Miskīn b. Dārim said;[494]

[160] I saw the "increase"[495] of Islām disappear
publicly when Ziyād took leave of us.

Al-Farazdaq said to Miskīn, and he did not satirize Ziyād until after the latter had died:

O Miskīn, God makes your eye weep, however
its tears flowed in error, so they descended.

You weep for an unbelieving man from a family of Maysān,[496]
like Kisrā in his place or Qayṣar.[497]

---

493. See also Masʿūdī, *Murūj*, V, 66–69. According to Dīnawarī, *Akhbār al-Ṭiwāl*, 239; Ziyād was buried in the cemetery of the Quraysh at al-Kūfah.

494. The following lines are also in the *Diwān* of al-Farazdaq. See Boucher, *Divan*, 48–9; Iṣfahānī, *Aghānī*, XVIII, 67; XIX, 28, 32; and Yāqūt, *Muʿjam*, IV, 715.

495. "Ziyād" means "increase."

496. Maysān was the district along the lower Tigris River above al-Baṣrah. See *EI*², s.v. Maysān. However, Ziyād's mother, Sumayyah, is said to have

I say to him when the announcement of his death comes to me,
rather him than a dusty gazelle in an isolated patch of sand.[498]

Miskīn then answered him, saying:

O man who does not speak out,
nor lead the folk unless he opposed me!

Bring me then a paternal uncle like mine or a father
like mine or a true maternal uncle like mine,

Like ʿAmr b. ʿAmr or a father like Zurārah,
or al-Bishr, on all sides I descended from the hills.

I continue to have things like spears and a swimmer,
and a camel[499] after night journeys from my dependents.

So this for days of defense, this
for my transportation, and this instrument for my departure.

Al-Farazdaq replied: [161]

Tell Ziyād when you come across his place of destruction,
that the female dove has flown from the sanctuary,

Flew and the front feathers of her wing continued to be ascribed to her,
until she called for help to the rivers and the reeds.

I was told by ʿAbdallāh b. Aḥmad—his father—Sulaymān—ʿAbdallāh—Jarīr b. Ḥāzim—Jarīr b. Yazīd: When I saw Ziyād,

---

been a native of Zandaward in the neighboring district of Kaskar and to have belonged to the dihqān of al-Ubullah. See Balādhurī, *Ansāb*, I, 489.

497. Kisrā was the Sasanian emperior, Qayṣar the Byzantine emperor. See *EI*², s.v. Ḳayṣar, Kisrā.

498. A *sarīmah* is a bridle or an isolated patch of sand. See Ibn Manẓūr, *Lisān*, XII, 339; Bevan, *Naḳā'iḍ*, III, 438.

499. A *khaṭārah* is a camel that puts its tail between its legs when it walks. See Ibn Manẓūr, *Lisān*, IV, 250.

he was red-faced, having a squint in his right eye, with a white triangular beard, wearing a patched shirt (*qamīs*), while he was on a female mule whose rein he had loosened.[500]

The death of al-Rabīʿ b. Ziyād al-Ḥārithī, who was the governor of Khurāsān for Ziyād, also occurred in this year.

How al-Rabīʿ b. Ziyād al-Ḥārithī Died

I was told by ʿUmar—ʿAlī b. Muḥammad: Al-Rabīʿ b. Ziyād was governor of Khurāsān for two years and several months and died in the year in which Ziyād died. He had appointed his son ʿAbdallāh b. al-Rabīʿ as his successor. The latter was governor for two months and then he died. Al-Rabīʿ's letter of appointment from Ziyād reached Khurāsān after he had been buried. ʿAbdallāh b. al-Rabīʿ appointed Khulayd b. ʿAbdallāh al-Ḥanafī as his successor over Khurāsān.

(According to) ʿAlī—Muḥammad b. al-Faḍl—his father: I heard that al-Rabīʿ b. Ziyād mentioned Ḥujr b. ʿAdī one day in Khurāsān, saying, "Arabs will continue to be killed in captivity
[162] after him. If they had risen up at Ḥujr's death, no man of them would be killed in captivity, but they acquiesced, so they became despised." Al-Rabīʿ remained for a week after saying that. Then he went out in white clothing on Friday, saying, "O people, I have become tired of life, and I am offering a prayer." They responded, "Amen." Then he raised his hand after worship, saying, "O God, if I have done good in Your sight, then take me to You at once." And the people said, "Amen!" He then went out, and collapsed before his clothing went out of sight. He was carried to his house, and appointing his son, ʿAbdallāh, as his successor, he died that very day. Then his son died, after appointing Khulayd b. ʿAbdallāh al-Ḥanafī as his successor. Ziyād then confirmed Khulayd and died himself while Khulayd was in charge of Khurāsān.

Ziyād perished, having appointed ʿAbdallāh b. Khālid b. Asīd over al-Kūfah. Muʿāwiyah then confirmed Samurah as gover nor of al-Baṣrah for eighteen months. (According to) ʿUmar—

500. According to Ibn Qutaybah, *Maʿārif*, 346, the rope had been folded on the mule's neck underneath the bridle rein.

Ja'far b. Sulaymān al-Ḍuba'ī: Mu'āwiyah confirmed Samurah (as governor) for six months after Ziyād. Then he dismissed him. At that, Samurah exclaimed, "God curse Mu'āwiyah! If I obeyed God as I obeyed Mu'āwiyah, He would never punish me.

I was told by 'Umar—Mūsā b. Ismā'īl—Sulaymān b. Muslim al-'Ijlī—his father: I passed by the mosque, while a man came to Samurah and brought his wealth as *zakāt*.[501] Then that man entered and began to worship in the mosque. Another man came and beheaded him, so his head was in the mosque and his body nearby. Abū Bakrah passed by and said, "God, praise Him, says, 'Whoever was purified has prospered, remembered the name of his Lord, and worshipped.'"[502] My father said: I witnessed that. Samurah did not die until a severe frost took him; [163]
he thus died an evil death. I witnessed him bringing many people, and setting them before him. He would ask each man, "What is your faith?" The man would reply, "I testify that there is only one single God Who has no partner, and that Muḥammad is His servant and His messenger, and that I am not one of the Ḥarūriyyah." He would then be brought out and beheaded, until there were more than twenty.

In this year Sa'īd b. al-'Āṣ led the people in the pilgrimage according to Abū Ma'shar, al-Wāqidī, and others. The governor of al-Madīnah during this year was Sa'īd b. al-'Āṣ, while 'Abdallāh b. Khālid b. Asīd b. al-'Āṣ governed al-Kūfah after the death of Ziyād. Samurah b. Jundab governed al-Baṣrah after the death of Ziyād, and Khulayd b. 'Abdallāh al-Ḥanafī governed Khurāsān.

---

501. *Zakāt* is the Islamic obligation to purify oneself through charity. See *EI*[1], s.v. Zakāt, and for a variant of this account see Ibn Abī al-Ḥadīd, *Sharh Nahj al-balāghah*, IV, 77.

502. Qur'ān 87: 14–15.

The Events of the Year 54

(December 16, 673–December 5, 674)

The winter campaign of Muḥammad b. Mālik in Byzantine territory took place during this year, as well as the summer campaign of Maʿn b. Yazīd al-Sulamī.

The conquest by Junādah b. Abī Umayyah of an island in the sea near Constantinople called Arwād also took place during this year, as al-Wāqidī claimed. Muḥammad b. ʿUmar related that the Muslims stayed there for a while—it is said, seven years—while Mujāhid b. Jabr was there. Tubayʿ, the son of Kaʿb's wife, said, "Do you see this step [*darajah*]? When it is removed, [word of] our homecoming will arrive." A strong wind then arose and blew away the step, and someone who announced Muʿāwiyah's death arrived, as well as Yazīd's letter about coming home. At this, we returned. The island was uninhabited and ruined after that, and the Byzantines were safe.

[164] During this year Muʿāwiyah also dismissed Saʿīd b. al-ʿĀṣ from al-Madīnah and appointed Marwān b. al-Ḥakam governor over it.

Why Muʿāwiyah Dismissed Saʿīd and Appointed Marwān as Governor over al-Madīnah

I was told by ʿUmar—ʿAlī b. Muḥammad—Juwayriyyah b. Asmāʾ—his shaykhs: Muʿāwiyah used to incite Marwān and Saʿīd b. al-ʿĀṣ against each other. He wrote to Saʿīd b. al-ʿĀṣ while the latter was in charge of al-Madīnah, "Demolish the house of Marwān." But Saʿīd did not demolish it, so Muʿāwiyah sent another letter to him about demolishing it. But he did not do it, whereupon Muʿāwiyah dismissed him and made Marwān governor. As far as Muḥammad b. ʿUmar is concerned, he related that Muʿāwiyah wrote to Saʿīd b. al-ʿĀṣ ordering him to seize all the property of Marwān and make it government property, and to seize Fadak[503] from Marwān—Muʿāwiyah had granted it to Marwān. At that, Saʿīd b. al-ʿĀṣ wrote back to him, saying, "He is a close relative." Muʿāwiyah then wrote to him for the second time ordering him to sequester Marwān's property. But Saʿīd b. al-ʿĀṣ refused and took both letters and placed them with a slave-girl. When Saʿīd b. al-ʿĀṣ was dismissed from al-Madīnah and Marwān became its governor, Muʿāwiyah wrote to Marwān b. al-Ḥakam ordering him to seize the property of Saʿīd b. al-ʿĀṣ in the Ḥijāz, sending the letter to him with (Marwān's) son ʿAbd al-Malik. Marwān told him, "If it were anything but a letter from the Commander of the Faithful, I would reject it." At that, Saʿīd b. al-ʿĀṣ called for both letters in which Muʿāwiyah had written to him about the property of Marwān, and in which he had ordered him to seize Marwān's property. Saʿīd took them to Marwān, who remarked, "Saʿīd was more attached to us than we were to him," and desisted from seizing Saʿīd's property. Saʿīd b. al-ʿĀṣ also wrote to Muʿāwiyah, "[I am] astonished at how the Commander of the Faithful treated us concerning our kinship, so that we would bear a grudge against each other. The Com- [165]
mander of the Faithful in spite of his prudence, steadfastness against those evils he abhors, and forgiveness, has introduced estrangement and enmity between us, while our descendents will possess that as an inheritance. By God, if we were not sons

---

503. Fadak was a small agricultural town in the northern Ḥijāz. See *EI*², s.v. Fadak.

of a single uncle, God would not have united us with him out of support for the wronged Caliph.[504] There was truth for us in the congruence of our speeech so that we would pay attention to that and in which we obtained good." At that, Muʿāwiyah wrote back to him disavowing that, and saying that, for Saʿīd's sake, he would return to the best (behavior) that Saʿīd knew about him.

The account now returns to that of ʿUmar—ʿAlī b. Muḥammad: When Muʿāwiyah appointed Marwān governor, he wrote to him, "Demolish the house of Saʿīd." When Marwān (started to) carry out the deed and rode to demolish it, Saʿīd asked him, "O Abū ʿAbd al-Malik, are you going to demolish my house?" Marwan replied, "Yes, the Commander of the Faithful wrote to me, and if he wrote about demolishing my [own] house, I would do it." Saʿīd remarked, "I would not do so." Marwān responded, "Certainly, by God, if he wrote to you, you would demolish it." Saʿīd retorted, "Certainly not, Abū ʿAbd al-Malik." Then he told his servant, "Go off and bring me Muʿāwiyah's letter." The servant then brought Muʿāwiyah's letter to Saʿīd b. al-ʿĀṣ about demolishing the house of Marwān b. al-Ḥakam. Marwān remarked, "He wrote to you, O Abū ʿUthmān, about demolishing my house, but you didn't demolish [it], and did not inform me." Saʿīd replied, "I did not demolish your house, yet I am not ensured against you. Muʿāwiyah wanted to incite us against each other." At that, Marwān exclaimed, "May my father and mother be your ransom! By God, you have more plumage[505] than we and offspring." Marwān returned without demolishing Saʿīd's house.

I was told by ʿUmar—ʿAlī—Abū Muḥammad b. Dhakwān al-Qurashī: Saʿīd b. al-ʿĀṣ came to Muʿāwiyah, who asked him, "O Abū ʿUthmān, how did you leave Abū ʿAbd al-Malik?" Saʿīd replied, "I left him taking control of your work and carrying
[166] out your command." Muʿāwiyah remarked, "Indeed he is like the owner of a loaf of bread which was baked enough so he ate it." Saʿīd responded, "Certainly not, by God, O Commander of the Faithful, indeed he is with the people. The whip is not used

---

504. That is, ʿUthmān.

505. The text reads: *rīshan*; C reads: *nasaban*, "lineage."

on them, and the sword is not allowed for them. They exchange like the impact of arrows, an arrow for you and an arrow against you."[506] Mu'āwiyah asked, "What separated you from him?" Sa'īd replied, "He was afraid of me for his dignity, and I feared him for mine." Mu'āwiyah asked, "So why is he obliged to you?" Sa'īd answered, "I pleased him when absent, and I pleased him when present." Mu'āwiyah remarked, you left us, O Abū 'Uthmān, in these trifles." Sa'īd responded, "Yes, O Commander of the Faithful. I assumed the burden, sufficed for the determination, and was close. If you called, I would answer, and if you left, I would remove."

Mu'āwiyah also dismissed Samurah b. Jundab from al-Baṣrah in this year and appointed 'Abdallāh b. 'Amr b. Ghaylān as governor there. I was told by 'Umar—'Alī b. Muḥammad: Mu'āwiyah dismissed Samurah and made 'Abdallāh b. 'Amr b. Ghaylān governor. He confirmed him in his post for six months, and 'Abdallāh b. 'Amr put 'Abdallāh b. Ḥiṣn in charge of his police.

In this year Mu'āwiyah also made 'Ubaydallāh b. Ziyād governor of Khurāsān.

How 'Ubaydallāh b. Ziyād Became Governor of Khurāsān

I was told by 'Umar—'Alī b. Muḥammad—Salamah b. Muḥārib and Muḥammad b. Abān al-Qurashī: After Ziyād died, 'Ubaydallāh visited Mu'āwiyah, who asked him, "Whom did my brother appoint as his deputy at al-Kūfah?" He replied, "'Abdallāh b. Khālid b. Asīd." Mu'āwiyah went on, "And whom did he put in charge of al-Baṣrah?" 'Ubaydallāh answered, "Samurah b. Jundab al-Fazārī." Mu'āwiyah then told him, "If your father had appointed you to a position, I would do so as well." At that, 'Ubaydallāh responded, "I implore you by [167]
God, lest someone shall say to me after you, 'If your father and your uncle had made you a governor, I would make you a governor.'"

When Mu'āwiyah wanted to make someone belonging to the

---

506. See Freytag, *Proverbia*, III, 238.

Banū Ḥarb a governor, he would make him governor of al-Ṭā'if. If he saw that he performed well and was not astonished at him, he would add the governorship of Mecca to his first position. If he governed well and ably looked after his responsibilities, Muʿāwiyah would combine al-Madīnah with both of his other positions. Thus, when a man was put in charge of al-Ṭā'if, it used to be said, "He is with Abū Jād."[507] Then when Muʿāwiyah put him in charge of Mecca, it was said, "He is with the Qur'ān." And when he put him in charge of al-Madīnah, it was said, "He has been skillful."

When ʿUbaydallāh said what he did, Muʿāwiyah put him in charge of Khurāsān. Then, when he had made him governor, he told him, "I have given trust to you as I do to my officials. Now then, I enjoin you by the ties of kinship, because of your special status with me, not to sell a lot for a little, and restrain yourself, and fulfill any agreement you make with an enemy, so you will reduce the burden for you[rself] and for me from you. Open your door to the people; thus you will have information from them. You and they are equal. When you decide on a matter, express it openly to the people, and no one will expect anything or make demands on you, while you will be able to carry [it] out. When you encounter your enemies, and they defeat you at the border of the territory, do not let them defeat you in its interior. If your companions need you to assist them personally, do so.

I was told by ʿUmar—ʿAlī—ʿAlī b. Mujāhid—Ibn Isḥāq: Muʿāwiyah appointed ʿUbaydallāh b. Ziyād as governor, saying, "Seize the sword if it does not cut." He also told him, "Fear God, and don't prefer anything to that, for there is compensa-
[168] tion in fearing Him. It preserves [you] from lowering your own reputation. If you make a promise, keep it; don't sell a lot for a little; and don't announce something until you have completely understood it['s consequences]. Once it has been announced, don't let it return to harm you. When you encounter your enemies, let those who are with you be more numerous. Swear to [your subjects] upon the Book of God; don't tempt anyone with that to which he has no right; and don't make

507. Lit. "the father of improvement", that is, at the beginning of his career.

anyone feel hopeless regarding his rights." Then 'Ubaydallāh took leave of him.

I was told by 'Umar—'Alī—Maslamah: 'Ubaydallāh set out from Syria for Khurāsān at the end of the year 53 (673) when he was twenty-five years old, sending Aslam b. Zur'ah al-Kilābī to Khurāsān in advance. He left Syria accompanied by al-Ja'd b. Qays al-Namarī who recited verses (*rajaz*) before him in an elegy for Ziyād.

On another occasion, 'Umar reported in his book which he entitled *The Book of Information About the People of al-Baṣrah*:[508] I was told by Abū al-Ḥasan al-Madā'inī that when Mu'āwiyah appointed 'Ubaydallāh b. Ziyād over Khurāsān, the latter went out wearing a turban—he was handsome—while al-Ja'd b. Qays recited an elegy for Ziyād to him:

Continue to rebuke me, my critic,
about what removed my blessing before today.

The benefactor has departed and the permanent protection,

And [having] grace, many sheep,[509] a huge fortune, many camels[510]

And the livestock walking after sleep.

If only all of the excellent [horses] with the folk [169]

Were given poison to drink a while before today,

With four [days] elapsing from the month of fasting.[511]

From it also is:

Tuesday which has past,

508. *Kitāb akhbār ahl al-Baṣrah.*

509. *Mu'aththal,* from *'aththala,* "to have many sheep." See I. Mustafa, et al., *Mu'jam,* I, 99.

510. *Al-ḥawm* is a herd of approximately one thousand camels. See Ibn Manẓūr, *Lisān,* XII, 62.

511. That is, the month of Ramaḍān.

A day on which the King decreed what He decreed:

The death of a righteous, glorifying [man], sturdy of strength.

Giving to Jaʿd was hot in him and blazed.

Ziyād was a mountain with difficult peaks,

Astute, if you looked for faults, he refused.

If Ziyād had survived, I would hope that God would not

Remove him.

ʿUbaydallāh wept that day until his turban fell off of his head.

ʿUbaydallāh reached Khurāsān, then he crossed the river to the mountain of Bukhārā on camels, He was thus the first to reach the Bukārāns by crossing the mountain with an army. He conquered Rāmīthan and Baykand,[512] both of which belong to Bukhārā, and reached the Bukhārāns from there. (According to) ʿAlī—al-Ḥasan b. Rashīd—his paternal uncle: ʿUbaydallāh b. Ziyād encountered Turks at Bukhārā. Qabj Khatun, their king's wife, was with the king. When God defeated them, the Turks urged her to put on her slippers. She put on one of them, while the other was left behind. The Muslims acquired the stocking which was worth two hundred thousand dirhams.

[170] I was told by ʿAlī—Muḥammad b. Ḥafṣ—ʿUbaydallāh b. Ziyād b. Maʿmar—ʿUbādah b. Ḥiṣn: I did not see anyone more courageous than ʿUbaydallāh b. Ziyād. An army of Turks encountered us in Khurāsān, and I saw him fighting. He charged them, penetrated their ranks, and disappeared from sight. Then he raised his pennon dripping with blood.

(According to) ʿAlī—Maslamah: There were two thousand Bukhārans, whom ʿUbaydallāh b. Ziyād brought to al-Baṣrah.

---

512. Rāmīthan/Rāmitīn and Baykand/Paykand were towns two *farsakhs* (twelve km) apart in the Bukhārā oasis. See the account of this campaign in Balādhurī, *Futūḥ*, 410. Rāmīthan was considered to be the old city of Bukhārā, while Baykand was a large commercial center, five *farsakhs* (thirty km) from Bukhārā. See W. Barthold, *Turkestan*, 116–18.

All of them were excellent archers.[513] Maslamah (said): The army of the Turks at Bukhārā was one of the numerous armies of Khurāsān. We were also told by ʿAlī—al-Hudhalī: There were five armies in Khurāsān, four of which al-Aḥnaf b. Qays encountered—(one) which encountered him between Quhistān and Abrashahr,[514] and the three which he met at the Marghāb.[515] The fifth army was that of Qārin which ʿAbdallāh b. Khāzim scattered.[516] (According to) ʿAlī—Maslamah: ʿUbaydallāh b. Ziyād stayed in Khurāsān for two years.

Marwān b. al-Ḥakam led the people in the pilgrimage in this year.

I was told by Aḥmad b. Thābit—someone—Isḥāq b. ʿĪsā—Abū Maʿshar, while al-Wāqidī and others said likewise: Marwān b. al-Ḥakam was in charge of al-Madīnah in this year, while ʿAbdallāh b. Khālid b. Asīd was in charge of al-Kūfah—some of them said al-Ḍahhāk b. Qays was in charge there—and ʿAbdallāh b. ʿAmr b. Ghaylān was in charge of al-Baṣrah.

---

513. See Balādhurī, *Futūḥ*, 376, 410–11; Yaʿqūbī, *Taʾrīkh*, II, 237; and Yāqūt, *Muʿjam*, I, 522. However Ziyād himself is said to have built a street in al-Baṣrah for four thousand Bukhārans (Ibn al-Faqīh, *Buldān*, 191) and to have employed them in his police force at al-Kūfah (Ibn Saʿd, *Ṭabaqāt*, VI, 152).

514. Abrashahr is the Arabicized form of Aparshahr, the late Sasanian name of the city of Nīshāpūr (Naysābūr), the district capital of western Khurāsān. See *EI*², s. v. Abarshahr.

515. The Marghāb is the Murghāb River in Eastern Khurāsān, on which the city of Marw was located. See *EI*¹, Supp., s.v. Merw al-Shāhidhān.

516. This was in Quhistān in 33(653) See Shaban, *Abbāsid Revolution*, 26.

The Events of the Year 55

(December 6, 674–November 24, 675)

[171] Among the events that happened during this year was the winter campaign of Sufyān b. ʿAwf al-Azdī in Byzantine territory. That is what al-Wāqidī said. However, some said the one who led the winter campaign in Byzantine territory in this year was ʿAmr b. Muḥriz; and others said the one who led the winter campaign there was ʿAbdallāh b. Qays al-Fazārī. Still others said that it was Mālik b. ʿAbdallāh.

During this year Muʿāwiyah dismissed ʿAbdallāh b. ʿAmr b. Ghaylān from al-Baṣrah and put ʿUbaydallāh b. Ziyād in charge.

Why Muʿāwiyah Dismissed ʿAbdallāh b. ʿAmr b. Ghaylān and Appointed ʿUbaydallāh over al-Baṣrah

I was told by ʿUmar—al-Walīd b. Hishām and ʿAlī b. Muḥammad (they each differed in some of the narrative): When ʿAbdallāh b. ʿAmr b. Ghaylān spoke from the pulpit of al-Baṣrah, one of the Banū Ḍabbah threw rocks at him. (According to) ʿUmar

—Abū al-Hasan: He was called Jubayr b. al-Ḍaḥḥāk, one of the Banū Ḍirār. When ʿAlī ordered the man's hand to be cut off, the latter said:

Attentive obedience and submission
are good and more forgiving for the Banū Tamīm.

The Banū Ḍabbah then came to him, saying, "Our companion inflicted what he suffered upon himself, and the amīr has carried out his punishment. We are not assured that, should the report about him reach the Commander of the Faithful, he would not order personal or group punishment. If the amīr sees fit to write a letter for us, one of us will take it to the Commander of the Faithful to inform him that the amīr cut off his hand merely out of suspicion and without clear evidence." So [172]
ʿAbdallāh wrote to Muʿāwiyah for them afterwards, and they held onto the letter until the beginning of the year arrived. Abū al-Hasan (said): Less than six months later the Ḍabbīs headed for Muʿāwiyah and visited him, saying, "O Commander of the Faithful, he dismembered our companion unjustly, and this is his letter to you." Muʿāwiyah read the letter and remarked, "As far as retaliation against my officials is concerned, it is not allowed, and there is no way against him, but if you should wish, I would pay your companion blood money." They replied, "Then do so." Muʿāwiyah then paid him blood money from the treasury, dismissed ʿAbdallāh, and told them, "Choose whom you would like for me to put in charge of your province." They replied, "Let the Commander of the Faithful choose for us." Since he knew the opinion held by the people of al-Baṣrah about Ibn ʿĀmir, he asked, "How would you like Ibn ʿĀmir, for he is someone about whose distinction, decency, and purity you have known?" They answered, "The Commander of the Faithful knows best." He began to repeat that to them in order to sound them out; then he said, "I have put my nephew, ʿUbaydallāh b. Ziyād, in charge of you."

(According to) ʿUmar—ʿAlī b. Muḥammad: In this year Muʿāwiyah dismissed ʿAbdallāh b. ʿAmr and put ʿUbaydallāh b. Ziyād in charge of al-Baṣrah, and he put ʿUbaydallāh Aslam b. Zurʿah in charge of Khurāsān. The latter did not raid or conquer any territory there. ʿUbaydallāh put ʿAbdallāh b. Ḥiṣn in charge of his police force and Zurārah b. Awfā in charge of rendering judgment, then he dismissed him and put Ibn Udhaynah al-ʿAbdī in charge of rendering judgment.

In this year Muʿāwiyah also dismissed ʿAbdallāh b. Khālid b. Asīd from al-Kūfah and put al-Ḍaḥḥāk b. Qays al-Fihrī in charge there.[517]

In this year Marwān b. al-Ḥakam led the people in the pilgrimage. I was told that by Aḥmad b. Thābit—Iṣḥāq b. ʿĪsā—Abū Maʿshar.

517. According to Ibn Khayyāṭ, *Taʾrīkh*, I, 265, this was in year 54(673/4).

The Events of the Year

56 [173]

(November 25, 675–November 13, 676)

Among these events was the winter campaign of Junādah b. Abī Umayyah in Byzantine territory. ʿAbd al-Raḥmān b. Masʿūd is also said to have led this campaign. Yazīd b. Shajarah al-Rahāwī is also said to have raided by sea while ʿIyād b. al-Ḥārith did so by land.

Al-Walīd b. ʿUtbah b. Abī Sufyān led the people in the pilgrimage according to the account I was told by Aḥmad b. Thābit—someone—Iṣḥāq b. ʿĪsā—Abū Maʿshar.

During this year Muʿāwiyah performed the minor pilgrimage (*ʿumrah*) during Rajab (May 20–June 18, 676).

During this year Muʿāwiyah summoned the people to acknowledge his son, Yazīd, as his successor, and made him heir apparent (*walī al-ʿahd*).[518]

Why Muʿāwiyah Made His Son, Yazīd, Heir Apparent

I was told by al-Ḥārith—ʿAlī b. Muḥammad—Abū Ismāʿīl-al-Hamdānī and ʿAlī b. Mujāhid—al-Shaʿbī: Al-Mughīrah came to

518. Lit: "possessor of a pact."

Muʿāwiyah, and gave him his resignation, while complaining of weakness. Muʿāwiyah relieved him and wanted to appoint Saʿīd b. al-ʿĀṣ. Al-Mughīrah's secretary heard of that, so he came to Saʿīd b. al-ʿĀṣ and informed him of this while a Kūfan called Rabīʿah or al-Rabīʿ of the Khuzāʿah was with him. The latter then came to al-Mughīrah, saying, "O Mughīrah, I certainly think that the Commander of the Faithful disliked you. I saw Ibn Khunays, your secretary, with Saʿīd b. al-ʿĀṣ informing him that the Commander of the Faithful would put him in charge of al-Kūfah." Al-Mughīrah responded, "Does he not say as al-Aʿshā said;

[174] Or was your master absent so you suffered a need?
and perhaps your master will return with backing.

Go slowly! I will go to Yazīd." Al-Mughīrah then went to see Yazīd, and proposed the acknowledgement to him. When Yazīd conveyed that to his father, Muʿāwiyah reappointed al-Mughīrah to al-Kūfah, ordering him to work for Yazīd's acknowledgement. Al-Mughīrah then departed for al-Kūfah, and his secretary, Ibn Khunays, came to him, saying, "By God, I did not deceive you nor betray you nor did I dislike your government, but I owed Saʿīd a favor, and I was grateful to him for it." Al-Mughīrah was pleased with him and took him back into his chancery. Al-Mughīrah also worked for Yazīd's acknowledgement, and sent an envoy to Muʿāwiyah about it.

I was told by al-Ḥārith—ʿAlī—Maslamah: When Muʿāwiyah wanted to acknowledge Yazīd (as his successor) he wrote to Ziyād, asking him for advice. Ziyād then sent for ʿUbayd b. Kaʿb al-Numayrī, saying, "Everyone who asks advice has trust, and every secret has a place to put it. Indeed people have devised for them two qualities—revealing secrets and giving out advice to people who do not deserve it. The only repository for secrets is one of two men—an otherworldly man who hopes for a reward and a man of this world who has self-respect and discernment which preserves his esteem. I have experienced them both from you, therefore I have praised that on your behalf. I have summoned you about a matter which I hesitate to put in writing. Indeed the Commander of the Faithful has written to me claiming that he has decided to acknowledge Yazīd [as his successor]. However, his is afraid of the people's disapproval. He hopes for their agreement, and asks my advice. Support for Islam and its security is important, while Yazīd is easy-going and neglectful, given his devotion to hunting. So meet the Commander of the Faithful, acting on my behalf, and inform him about Yazīd's actions. Tell him, 'Go slowly in this matter, [175] for it would be more appropriate in order to accomplish what you want. Don't hurry, because attainment with delay is better than haste without success.' "[519]

'Ubayd answered him, "There is an alternative." Ziyād asked, "What is it?" 'Ubayd advised, "Don't disparage Mu'āwiyah's view to him, and don't make him hate his son. I shall meet with Yazīd in secret, informing him on your behalf that the Commander of the Faithful has written to you asking your advice about Yazid's acknowledgement [as successor], and that you fear the disapproval of the people because of flaws which they hold against him. I shall also tell him that you think he should abandon the behavior that is held against him, so that the Commander of the Faithful's argument before the people would be strengthened. What you desire will be easy. Thus you will have prepared Yazīd and satisfied the Commander of the Faithful, as well as having avoided what you fear regarding the community." At that, Ziyād replied, "You have hit the nail on the head.[520] Depart with God's blessing. If you are successful, it will not be disavowed; and if you are mistaken, [it will] not be deception. I do not consider you to be one who makes mistakes, if God wills." 'Ubayd responded, "You say what you think, and God determines in secret what He knows." He then came to Yazīd and conferred with him (about) that, while Ziyād wrote to Mu'āwiyah urging him to be cautious and not to hurry. Mu'āwiyah accepted that, and Yazīd refrained from doing much of what he used to do. Then 'Ubayd came back to Ziyād, and the latter gave him a land-grant.

I was told by al-Ḥārith—'Alī: When Ziyād died, Mu'āwiyah called for a document about appointing Yazīd as his successor and read it to the people. In the event of his death, Yazīd would

519. The text reads: *fawt*; C reads: *mawt*, "death."
520. Lit. "You have hit the matter with its stone."

be heir apparent. He was able to get the people to acknowledge Yazīd except for five persons.[521]

I was told by Yaʿqūb b. Ibrahīm—Ismāʿīl b. Ibrāhīm—Ibn
[176] ʿAwn—a man at Nakhlah:[522] The people acknowledged Yazīd b. Muʿāwiyah except for al-Ḥusayn b. ʿAlī, Ibn ʿUmar, Ibn al-Zubayr, ʿAbd al-Raḥmān b. Abī Bakr, and Ibn ʿAbbās. So when Muʿāwiyah came (to al-Madīnah) he sent for al-Ḥusayn b. ʿAlī, saying, "O cousin, the people have been able to acknowledge Yazīd except for five persons of the Quraysh whom you lead. O cousin, what is your purpose in disagreeing?" He replied, "Do I lead them?" Muʿāwiyah replied that he did. Al-Ḥusayn said, "So send for them, and if they acknowledge [Yazīd], I would be one of them, and if not, don't be rushing me into something." Muʿāwiyah asked, "And would you do so?" When al-Ḥusayn replied that he would, Muʿāwiyah then obliged him not to inform anyone about their conversation. Although that was difficult for him, al-Ḥusayn granted that, and then left. Ibn al-Zubayr had a man wait for al-Ḥusayn in the street, who said, "Your brother, Ibn al-Zubayr asks you, 'What happened?'" He continued thus with al-Ḥusayn until he got something out of him. Then, after (meeting with) al-Ḥusayn, Muʿāwiyah sent for Ibn al-Zubayr, saying to him, "The people have been able to do this except for five persons of the Quraysh. You lead them, O cousin, so what is your purpose in disagreeing?" Ibn al-Zubayr asked, "Do I lead them?" When Muʿāwiyah replied that he did, Ibn al-Zubayr said, "So send for them, and if they acknowledge, I would be one of them, and if not, don't be rushing me into something." Muʿāwiyah asked, "And would you do so?" When he replied that he would, Muʿāwiyah obliged him not to inform anyone of their conversation. He replied, "O Commander of the Faithful, we are in the sanctuary of God, Almighty and Great, and the pact of God, praise Him, is serious." So he refused him and left. Then, after Ibn al-Zubayr, Muʿāwiyah sent for Ibn ʿUmar and spoke with him in

---

521. According to Ibn Khayyāt, *Taʾrīkh*, I, 248, Muʿāwiyah had the Syrians acknowledge Yazīd in the year 50(670/71).

522. This place is either Nakhlat Muḥmūd, the first stopping-place on the way from Mecca to al-Ṣādir, or Nakhlah al-Yamāniyyah, the valley south of Mecca where the Battle of Ḥunayn was fought. See Yāqūt, *Muʿjam*, IV, 769.

words that were softer than those he had used with his companion, saying, "Indeed, I fear that I would leave the community of Muḥammad after me like sheep without a shepherd. It has been possible for the people to do this except for five persons of Quraysh, whom you lead. So what is your purpose in disagreeing?" Ibn 'Umar replied, "What would you think about [177] something that will avoid censure and spare blood while you achieve your purpose thereby?" Mu'āwiyah replied, "I would like that." Ibn 'Umar said, "Set up your throne publicly, then I will come and acknowledge you on condition that I will enter after you into whatever the community shall agree upon. For, by God, if the community should agree upon an Abyssinian slave after you, I would do the same." Mu'āwiyah asked, "And would you do so?" He answered that he would. Then he left, and arriving at his home, he shut his door. People began to come but he would not admit them. Mu'āwiyah then sent for 'Abd al-Raḥmān b. Abī Bakr saying, "O Ibn Abī Bakr, by what hand or foot do you come to disobey me?" He replied, "I hope that it would be good for me." Mu'āwiyah responded, "By God, I intended to kill you." He answered, "If you do so, may God cause a curse to follow you in this world for it and make you enter the fire in the next [world] for it." The man at Nakhlah did not mention Ibn 'Abbās.[523]

Marwān b. al-Ḥakam was the governor of al-Madīnah during this year, while al-Ḍaḥḥāk b. Qays was in charge of al-Kūfah, 'Ubaydallāh b. Ziyād was in charge of al-Baṣrah, and Sa'īd b. 'Uthmān was in charge of Khurāsān.

The reason why Sa'īd was governor of Khurāsān is in the account which I was told by 'Umar—'Alī—Muḥammad b. Ḥafṣ: When Sa'īd b. 'Uthmān asked Mu'āwiyah to make him governor of Khurāsān, the latter replied, "'Ubaydallāh b. Ziyād is there." Sa'īd then asked, "Did not my father make you and raise you until you achieved through his effort the utmost point which he was not able to attain nor seek to surpass? But you were not grateful for his favor nor requited him for his benefits. You put this one (that is Yazīd b. Mu'āwiyah) ahead of me

523. According to Ibn Khayyāṭ, *Ta'rīkh*, I, 252–57, these events occurred in year 51(671/2)

and acknowledged him. By God, I am better than he with respect to father, mother, and self." Muʿāwiyah replied, "As far
[178] as your father's favor is concerned, I am obliged to repay him. It was out of gratitude for that that I sought revenge for his blood until matters ran their course, and I will not blame myself for rallying my forces. Regarding the superiority of your father over Yazīd's, your father, by God, was better than I and closer to the Messenger of God. Concerning the superiority of your mother over Yazīd's, it is not denied. A woman from Quraysh is better than a woman from the Kalb. As for your superiority over him, by God, I want the Ghūṭah[524] to be filled by men like you for Yazīd." At that, Yazīd told Muʿāwiyah, "O Commander of the Faithful, he is your paternal cousin, and you are the most worthy to consider his case. He censured me to you, so censure him." Muʿāwiyah then put Saʿīd in charge of the military affairs of Khurāsān and Isḥāq b. Ṭalḥah in charge of collecting taxes there. This Isḥāq was a maternal cousin of Muʿāwiyah, and his mother was Umm Abān bt. ʿUtbah b. Rabīʿah. When he reached al-Rayy, Isḥāq b. Ṭalḥah died, so Saʿīd was put in charge of both the taxes and military affairs of Khurāsān.

I was told by ʿUmar—ʿAlī—Maslamah: Saʿīd left for Khurāsān accompanied by Aws b. Thaʿlabah al-Taymī, the master of Qaṣr Aws, Ṭalḥah b. ʿAbdallāh b. Khalaf al-Khuzāʿī, al-Muhallab b. Abī Ṣufrah, and Rabīʿah b. ʿIsl, one of the Banū ʿAmr b. Yarbūʿ. There were bedouin folk barring the road against pilgrims in the depth of a defile. Saʿīd was told, "Here are folk barring the road against pilgrims, and they fear to take to the road lest you take them out with you. Saʿīd then took out some folk of the Banū Tamīm, among whom was Mālik b. al-Rayb al-Māzinī, along with youths who were with him.[525] Concerning them the poet declaimed:[526]

---

524. The Ghūṭah is the fertile cultivated region around Damascus irrigated by the Baradā River. See *EI*², s.v. al-Ghūṭa.

525. For additional details according to Abū ʿUbaydah and Abū al-Ḥasan al-Madāʾinī, see ʿAbd al-Qādir al-Baghdādī, *Khizānat al-adab*, II, 210; Kūfī, *Futūḥ*, IV, 187–99.

526. See Iṣfahānī, *Aghānī*, XIX, 163; Ibn Qutaybah, *Shuʿarāʾ*, 270.

God save you from al-Qasīm,[527] [179]

And from Abū Ḥardabah[528] the evil,

And from Ghuwayth[529] the cutpurse,

And Mālik and his poisoned sword.

(According to) ʿAlī—Maslamah: Saʿīd b. ʿUthmān arrived and crossed the river to Samarqand.[530] The people of the Ṣughd[531] came out against him, and they fought each other all day until nightfall, then they disengaged without further fighting.[532] At that, Mālik b. al-Rayb said, criticizing Saʿīd:

You continued to tremble on the Battle-day of the Ṣughd, standing
out of cowardice until I feared that you had become a Christian,

And there was not in ʿUthmān anything I knew,
except his offspring in his group when he turned back.

If it was not for the Banū Ḥarb, your blood would be sprinkled
inside broken and one-eyed vermin.

When the next day came, Saʿīd b. ʿUthmān went out to them and the Ṣughd resisted him. He fought them, routed them, and beseiged them in their city. Then they made peace with him and gave him fifty youths, the sons of their grandees, to be held

---

527. Al Qaṣīm is a region of the Najd in central Arabia.

528. Abū Ḥardabah was a member of the Banū Athālah b. Māzin. See Iṣfahānī, *Aghānī*, XIX, 163.

529. Ghuwayth was a member of the Banū Kaʿb b. Mālik b. Ḥanẓalah. See Iṣfahānī, *Aghānī*, XIX, 163.

530. Samarqand, on the Zarafshān River in Central Asia, was the main city of Ṣoghdia. See Le Strange, *Lands*, 463–65; Barthold, *Turkestan*, 83–93.

531. The Ṣughd were the Ṣoghdians who inhabited the region along the Zarafshān River in Central Asia, ancient Sogdiana. Le Strange, *Lands*, 460–73; Barthold, *Turkestan*, index: Soghdiana.

532. For this campaign see Balādhuirī, *Futūḥ*, 411.

as hostages by him. He then crossed (again) and stayed at al-Tirmidh.[533] He did not keep (his agreement) with them and brought the hostage youths with him to al-Madīnah.[534]

Saʿīd b. ʿUthmān arrived in Khurāsān while Aslam b. Zurʿah al-Kilābī was there on behalf of ʿUbaydallāh b. Ziyād. Aslam b.
[180] Zurʿah continued to live there until ʿUbaydallāh b. Ziyād wrote to him about entrusting Khurāsān to him for a second time. When the letter of ʿUbaydallāh reached Aslam, he knocked at night for Saʿīd b. ʿUthmān. At that, a slave girl of Saʿīd's gave birth to a boy prematurely. Saʿīd would say, "I shall certainly kill a man of the Banū Ḥarb [in retaliation] for him." Saʿīd came to Muʿāwiyah, complaining to him about Aslam, and the Qaysiyyah became angry. When Hamām b. Qabīsah al-Namarī entered and Muʿāwiyah noticed that his eyes were reddened, he said, "O Hamām, both your eyes are reddened." Hamām replied, "On the Battle-day of Ṣiffīn they were even redder." That distressed Muʿāwiyah, and when Saʿīd saw that, he held back from Aslam. Aslam b. Zurʿah thus remained in charge of Khurāsān as governor for ʿUbaydallāh b. Ziyād for two years.

---

533. Al-Tirmidh was the most important town in the district of Saghāniyān, north of the upper Oxus River between its confluence with the Wakhsh and Surkhān rivers. Le Strange, *Lands*, 440–41; Barthold, *Turkestan*, 75.

534. According to Balādhurī, *Futūḥ*, 411, Saʿīd took fifteen, forty or eighty noble youths hostage at Bukhārā. When he forced them into agricultural slavery at al-Madīnah, they are said to have killed him and committed mass suicide. See Balādhurī, *Ansāb*, V, 117–19; Narshakhī, *Tārikh-i Bukhārā*, translated by R. Frye as *The History of Bukhārā*, 40–41.

The Events of the Year 57

(November 14, 676–November 2, 677)

The winter campaign of ʿAbdallāh b. Qays in Byzantine territory occurred during this year.

According to al-Wāqidī, Marwān was dismissed from al-Madīnah in Dhū al-Qaʿdah 57 (September 5–October 4, 677). According to someone else, Marwān governed al-Madīnah during this year. Al-Wāqidī said: When Muʿāwiya dismissed Marwān, he appointed al-Walīd b. ʿUtbah b. Abī Sufyān over al-Madīnah. Abū Maʿshar's account is similar to that of al-Wāqidī. I was told that account by Aḥmad b. Thābit al-Rāzī—someone—Isḥāq b. ʿĪsā.

The governor in charge of al-Kūfah during this year was al-Ḍaḥḥāk b. Qays, while ʿUbaydallāh b. Ziyād was in charge of al-Baṣrah and Saʿīd b. ʿUthmān b. ʿAffān was in charge of Khurāsān.

The Events of the Year 58

(November 3, 677–October 23, 678)

[181] According to Abū Maʿshar, Muʿāwiyah dismissed Marwān from al-Madīnah in Dhū al-Qaʿdah (August 25–September 24, 678), and made Walīd b. ʿUtbah b. Abī Sufyān governor over it. I was told that by Aḥmad b. Thābit—someone—Iṣhāq b. ʿĪsā.

During this year Mālik b. ʿAbdallāh al-Khathʿamī raided Byzantine territory.

In this year Yazīd b. Shajarah was killed at sea according to al-Wāqidī. ʿAmr b. Yazīd al-Juhanī (said): It was Yazīd who led the winter campaign in Byzantine territory. It was also said: The one who raided by sea in this year was Junādah b. Abī Umayyah.

Al-Walīd b. ʿUtbah b. Abī Sufyān led the people in the pilgrimage this year. I was told a similar account by Aḥmad b. Thābit—someone—Isḥāq b. ʿĪsā—Abū Maʿshar. Al-Wāqidī and others said likewise.

In this year Muʿāwiyah put ʿAbd al-Raḥmān b. ʿAbdallāh b. ʿUthmān b. Rabīʿah al-Thaqafī in charge of al-Kūfah. He was the son of Umm al-Ḥakam, the sister of Muʿāwiyah b. Abī Sufyān. Muʿāwiyah had previously dismissed al-Ḍaḥḥāk b. Qays from it.[535] During ʿAbd al-Raḥmān's term of office in this year a group of the Khārijites rebelled who previously had recognized al-Mustawrid b. ʿUllifah and whom al-Mughīrah b. Shuʿbah had held in the prison. Al-Mughīrah had defeated them and put them in the prison. Then, when al-Mughīrah died, they left the prison.

(According to) Hāshim b. Muḥammad—Abū Mikhnaf—ʿAbd al-Raḥmān b. Jundab—ʿAbdallāh b. ʿUtbah al-Ghanawī: Ḥayyān b. Ẓabyān al-Sulamī gathered his companions about him. After praising and extolling God, he addressed them, "Now then, indeed God, Almighty and Great, decreed the *jihād* for us. Among us there are those whose term has been decided, those who still wait, and those [who are] righteous victors by their superiority. Whoever among us still waits will be one of [182]
our predecessors, the ones deciding their term, performing good deeds first. Whoever among you desires God and His reward, let him follow the way of his companions and his brothers. God will grant him the reward of this world and the better reward of the other world, and God is with those who are good."

Muʿādh b. Juwayn al-Ṭāʾī said, "O people of Islām, by God, if we knew that when we gave up *jihād* against oppressors and the rejection of injustice, we would have some excuse with God for doing so, abandoning it would be easier for us and lighter than undertaking it. But, since we were created with hearts and ears, we knew and were convinced that there will be no excuse for us until we reject oppression and change injustice by *jihād* against the oppressors." Then he continued, "Extend your hand and we shall acknowledge you." So Muʿādh and the folk acknowledged Ḥayyān b. Ẓabyān, striking him on the hand. That was during the governorship of ʿAbd al-Raḥmān b. ʿAbdallāh b. ʿUthmān al-Thaqafī who was the son of Umm al-Ḥakam, while Zāʾidah b. Qudāmah al-Thaqafī was in charge of the police.

Then, several days after that, the folk assembled at the residence of Muʿādh b. Juwayn b. Ḥuṣayn al-Ṭāʾī. Ḥayyān b. Ẓabyān addressed them, "Servants of God, advise[me] with your

535. According to Ibn Khayyāṭ, *Taʾrīkh*, I, 269, this was in the year 57(676/7).

opinion. Where do you instruct me to go." Muʿādh told him, "I think you should set out with us to Ḥulwān so that we can settle there, for it is a district between the plain and the mountain and between the city and the frontier—that is the frontier of al-Rayy. Thus, whoever shares our view among the people of the city, the frontier, the mountains, and the Sawād[536] would join us." Ḥayyān answered him, "Your enemy would overtake you before the people would gather to you. By my life, they will not leave you until they gather to you. But I thought I would take you out beside al-Kūfah and the salt marsh, or Zurārah and al-Ḥīrah. Then we would fight them until we reach our Lord. By
[183] God, I knew that, being less than one hundred men, you would not be able to defeat your enemy, nor inflict severe damage on them. But when God knows that you exert yourselves in *jihād* against His enemy and yours, you will have His reward and escape from sin." They replied, "Our view is the same as yours."

At that, ʿItrīs b. ʿUrqūb, Abū Sulaymān al-Shaybānī told them, "I do not share the view of your group. Take into consideration that I do not think you are ignorant of my knowledge of warfare and my experience with affairs." They told him, "You are certainly as you say, so what is your view?" ʿItrīs said, "I don't think that you should go out against the people at the city. You are a few among many. By God, you would not do more than have them surround you, and you would make them happy by killing you. This is not a shrewd policy, if you prefer to go out against your folk. Outwit your enemy with that which is harmful to them." They asked, "So what is your view?" He said, "You should set out for the district in which Muʿādh b. Juwayn b. Ḥuṣayn advised setting up camp—that is Ḥulwān, or you should set out with us to ʿAyn al-Tamr and stay there. Then, when our brothers heard about us, they would come to us from every side." At that, Ḥayyān b. Ẓabyān told him, "By God, if you set out with us, you and all your comrades, in either of these directions, you would not rest there before the cavalry of the people of the city overtook you. Where then will you heal yourselves? By God, there are not

536. The Sawād was the "dark" cultivated alluvial plain of Iraq. See *EI*[1], s.v. Sawād.

enough of you to expect victory in the world against the aggressive oppressors thereby. Rebel beside this city of yours and [184] fight according to the command of God against whoever violates obedience to Him. Don't wait, and don't bide your time. Thus, you will hurry to Paradise and get yourselves out of the discord thereby." They said, "Since that is the case, we have no other choice.[537] We will not oppose you, so rebel wherever you wish."

Ḥayyān waited until it was the end of the first of Ibn Umm al-Ḥakam's two years (as governor). At the beginning of the (second) year, on the first day of the month of Rabīʿ II (January 31, 678), the comrades of Ḥayyān b. Ẓabyān gathered to him, and he addressed them, "O folk, God has assembled you for a good purpose and with good reasons. By God, other than Whom there is no god, I would never take pleasure in anything in the world after I abandoned my pleasure in order to make this revolt of mine against the sinful oppressors. By God, I do not want the world in its entirety for myself nor for God to deprive me of martyrdom in this revolt of mine. I had thought that we should go out until we halted beside the house of Jarīr. Then, when the factions came out against you, you would fight them." At that, ʿItrīs b. ʿUrqūb al-Bakrī said, "However, if we fought them in the center of the city, the men would fight against us while the women and the boys and the slave-girls would ascend [to the rooftops] and throw rocks on us." One of their men then told them, "Halt us, then, beyond the city [at] al-Jisr"—that was the location of Zurārah; however, Zurārah was built afterwards except for some insignificant buildings that were there previously. Muʿādh b. Juwayn b. Ḥuṣayn al-Ṭāʾī advised them, "No, set out with us and halt at Bāniqyā instead. Before long your enemy will come to you, and when that happens we shall confront the folk with our faces and put the houses at our backs. Thus we would fight them from only one direction." When they rebelled, an army was sent against them and they were all killed.

Then the people of al-Kūfah expelled ʿAbd al-Raḥmān b. [185] Umm al-Ḥakam. I was told by Hishām b. Muḥammad: Muʿā-

537. C reads: "we must accept your opinion."

wiyah made Ibn Umm al-Ḥakam governor over al-Kūfah. The latter treated them badly, so they expelled him. He then came to Muʿāwiyah, who was his maternal uncle. The latter told him, "I shall make you governor of Egypt [which is] better than al-Kūfah." Muʿāwiyah did so and sent him there. When the news reached Muʿāwiyah b. Ḥudayj al-Sakūnī, he met Ibn Umm al-Ḥakam two days' journey from Egypt, saying, "Return to your maternal uncle, for, by my life, you shall not treat us the way you treated our Kūfan brothers." He then returned to Muʿāwiyah. When Muʿāwiyah b. Ḥudayj came (to Damascus) as an envoy, the way had been decorated for him—that is, booths of sweet basil were set up for him. He entered Muʿāwiyah's presence while Umm al-Ḥakam was with him. She asked, "Who is this, O Commander of the Faithful?" He answered, "Speak harshly! This is Muʿāwiyah b. Ḥudayj." She remarked, "No welcome to him. It is better to hear about al-Muʿaydī than to see him."[538] At that, Muʿāwiyah b. Ḥudayj said, "Gently, O Umm al-Ḥakam. By God, you married but were not honorable, and you gave birth but were not distinguished. You wanted your sinful son to govern us so he would treat us as he treated our Kūfan brothers. May God not give him that. Should he do so, we would strike him a blow from which he would bend over, even if the [one who is] sitting[539] disliked that." So Muʿāwiyah turned around to her and said, "That's enough."

In this year ʿUbaydallāh b. Ziyād became more violent against the Khārijites. He killed a large group of them he held captive and another group in combat.[540] Among the captives he killed was ʿUrwah b. Udayyah, the brother of Abū Bilāl Mirdās b. Udayyah.

Why ʿUbaydallāh b. Ziyād Killed the Khārijites

[186] I was told by ʿUmar—Zuhayr b. Ḥarb—Wahb b. Jarīr—his father—ʿĪsā b. ʿĀṣim al-Asadī: Ibn Ziyād went out for some wager of his. While he sat waiting for the horses, the people gath-

538. This is ascribed to al-Mundhir b. Māʾ al-Samāʾ. See Maydānī, *Amthāl*, I, 129–31; Freytag, *Proverbia*, I, 223–24.

539. That is, Muʿāwiyah.

540. See Balādhurī, *Ansāb*, IV B, 77–123.

ered, and ʿUrwah b. Udayyah, the brother of Abū Bilāl, was with them. he approached Ibn Ziyād, saying, "There were five [faults] among the peoples before us, and they have come to exist among us—'Do you build a monument on every height, commit folly, and occupy large structures that perhaps you might be immortal, and if you struck you struck as tyrants?' "[541] He mentioned two other faults that Jarīr does not remember. When ʿUrwah said that, Ibn Ziyād supposed that he would only have the audacity to say that while a group of his companions was with him, so he rose, rode off, and left his wager. At that ʿUrwah was asked, "What have you done? You surely know, by God, that he will kill you." When ʿUrwah hid, Ibn Ziyād sought him. He came to al-Kūfah, was seized there, and was sent to Ibn Ziyād, who ordered ʿUrwah's hands and feet to be cut off. Then he summoned him and asked, "What do you think?" ʿUrwah replied, "I think that you ruined this world for me and ruined the other world for yourself." At that, ʿUbaydallāh killed him and sent for his daughter and killed her.

As for Mirdās b. Udayyah, he went out to al-Ahwāz.[542] Ibn Ziyād had imprisoned him previously. This is according to the account I was told by ʿUmar. He said: Khallād b. Yazīd al-Bāhilī related to me: Among others, Ibn Ziyād imprisoned Mirdās b. Udayyah. The jailer used to see his (manner of) worship and his zeal and allowed him to leave at night. When dawn arose, Mirdās would return to him and enter the prison. A friend of Mirdās used to converse with Ibn Ziyād at night, and one night Ibn Ziyād mentioned the Khārijites and decided to kill them in the morning. The friend of Mirdās hurried off to the latter's residence and informed them (of this), saying, "Send [word] to Abū Bilāl in the prison to let him know, for he is a dead man." Mirdās heard that. The warden also learned the news, where- [187]
upon he had a bad night worrying lest Mirdās know the news and not return. When the usual time came for him to return to the prison, all of a sudden there he was. At that, the jailer asked him, "Did you hear what the governor decided to do?" When

541. Qur'ān 26: 128–30.

542. Al-Ahwāz is the province of Khūzistān or its capital city. See *EI²*, s.v. al-Ahwāz, Khūzistān.

Mirdās replied that he had, the jailer said, "Then you came this morning?" He replied, "Yes! You would not be rewarded for your kindness if you were punished because of me." In the morning ʿUbaydallāh came and began to kill the Khārijites. Then he summoned Mirdās, and when the latter was present, the jailer jumped up—he was a milk-brother of ʿUbaydallāh—and seized ʿUbaydallāh's foot, saying, "Grant me this [man]," and he related his story to him. ʿUbaydallāh then granted Mirdās to the jailer who released him.

I was told by ʿUmar—Zuhayr b. Ḥarb—Wahb b. Jarīr—his father—Yūnus b. ʿUbayd: Mirdās Abū Bilāl, who was one of the Banū Rabīʿah b. Ḥanẓalah, went out to al-Ahwāz with forty men. Ibn Ziyād sent an army against them under Ibn Ḥiṣn al-Tamīmī. The Khārijites fought against his men and defeated him. At that, a man of the Banū Taym Allāh b. Thaʿlabah said:

Did you claim two thousand believers are among you,
while forty fight them at Āsik?[543]

You lied. That is not as you claimed,
but the Khārijites are believers.

It is the small group [which] as you have known,
is made victorious against the large group.[544]

[188] ʿUmar said: The last line is not in the account which Khallād b. Yazīd al-Bāhilī recited to me.

It is said that ʿUmayrah b. Yathribī, the judge in al-Baṣrah died in this year and that Hishām b. Hubayrah replaced him there.

ʿAbd al-Raḥmān b. Umm al-Ḥakam was in charge of al-Kūfah in this year. Some of them said that al-Ḍaḥḥāk b. Qays al-Fihrī was in charge there, while ʿUbaydallāh b. Ziyād was in charge of al-Baṣrah and Shurayḥ was in charge of rendering judgment at al-Kūfah.

Al-Walīd b. ʿUtbah led the people in the pilgrimage this year. This is also what Abū Maʿshar and al-Wāqidī said.

---

543. Āsik or Āsak was a district of al-Ahwāz between Arrajān and Rāmhurmuz. See Yāqūt, *Buldān*, I, 61–2.

544. This is probably an allusion to the Battle of Badr.

The Events of the Year 59

(October 23, 678–October 12, 679)

The winter campaign of ʿAmr b. Murrah al-Juhanī by land in Byzantine territory occurred during this year. According to al-Wāqidī, there was no raid by sea that year, although others said that Junādah b. Abī Umayyah raided by sea.

During this year ʿAbd al-Raḥmān b. Umm al-Ḥakam was dismissed from al-Kūfah and al-Nuʿmān b. Bashīr al-Anṣārī was appointed governor there. We have mentioned previously the reason for Ibn Umm al-Ḥakam's dismissal from al-Kūfah.

In this year Muʿāwiyah made ʿAbd al-Raḥmān b. Ziyād b. Sumayyah governor of Khurāsān.

Why Muʿāwiyah Appointed ʿAbd al-Rahmān b. Ziyād as Governor of Khurāsān

I was told by al-Ḥārith b. Muḥammad—ʿAlī b. Muḥammad —Abū ʿAmr—our shaykhs: ʿAbd al-Raḥmān b. Ziyād came to [189] visit Muʿāwiyah, and asked, "O Commander of the Faithful, don't we have a claim [on you]?" Muʿāwiyah replied that he did. ʿAbd al-Raḥmān then asked, "So why don't you make me a governor?" He replied, "Al-Nuʿmān at al-Kūfah is on the right course, and he is one of the Companions of the Prophet. ʿUbaydallāh b. Ziyād is in charge of al-Baṣrah and Khurāsān, and ʿAbbād b. Ziyād is in charge of Sijistān. I don't see a position which is appropriate for you unless I have you share in the position of your brother, ʿUbaydallāh." He said, "Give me a share, for his governorship is so extensive he can stand a partnership." Thereupon, Muʿāwiyah made him governor of Khurāsān.

(According to) ʿAlī—Abū Ḥafṣ—ʿUmar: Qays b. al-Haytham al-Sulamī arrived (in Khurāsān), having been sent by ʿAbd al-Raḥmān b. Ziyād. Qays arrested Aslam b. Zurʿah and imprisoned him. Then ʿAbd al-Raḥmān arrived and fined Aslam b. Zurʿah three hundred thousand dirhams. (According to) ʿAlī—Muṣʿab b. Ḥayyān—his brother Muqātil b. Ḥayyān: ʿAbd al-Raḥmān b. Ziyād reached Khurāsān; thus a generous, greedy, weak man arrived who did not make a single raid, and remained in Khurāsān for two years.

(According to) ʿAlī—ʿAwānah: ʿAbd al-Raḥmān b. Ziyād came to Yazīd b. Muʿāwiyah from Khurāsān after the killing of al-Ḥusayn,[545] while he made Qays b. al-Haytham deputy over Khurāsān. (According to) ʿAlī—Muslim b. Muḥārib and Abū Ḥafṣ: Yazīd asked ʿAbd al-Raḥmān b. Ziyād, "How much wealth did you bring with you from Khurāsān?" he replied, "Twenty million dirhams." Yazīd said, "If you wish, we would ask you for an accounting and collect it from you and return you to your governorship. Or, if you wish, we would allow you [to keep it] and dismiss you, provided that you give ʿAbdallāh b. Jaʿfar [b. Abī Ṭālib] five hundred thousand dirhams." ʿAbd al-Raḥmān answered, "Rather allow me what you just said, and
[190] put someone else in charge there." ʿAbd al-Raḥmān b. Ziyād sent one million dirhams to ʿAbdallāh b. Jaʿfar, saying, "Five hundred thousand are from the Commander of the Faithful and five hundred thousand are from me."

In this year ʿUbaydallāh b. Ziyād went to visit Muʿāwiah accompanied by the Baṣran notables. Muʿāwiyah dismissed

545. Al-Ḥusayn b. ʿAlī was killed on the tenth of Muḥarram 61 (October 10, 680).

ʿUbaydallāh from al-Baṣrah, then he put him in charge of it again and confirmed the governorship for him.

How Muʿāwiyah Dismissed and Re-appointed ʿUbaydallāh as Governor of al-Baṣrah

I was told by ʿUmar—ʿAlī: ʿUbaydallāh b. Ziyād went to visit Muʿāwiyah with the people of Iraq. Muʿāwiyah told him, "I will receive your delegation according to their stations and their dignity." Thus they were permitted to enter; al-Aḥnaf entered with the last of them, since his station was low according to ʿUbaydallāh. When Muʿāwiyah observed him, he welcomed al-Aḥnaf and had him sit with him on his dais. Then he conversed with the folk, and they praised ʿUbaydallāh nicely, while al-Aḥnaf was silent. Muʿāwiyah then asked, "What's the matter with you, O Abū Baḥr? You don't speak." Al-Aḥnaf replied, "If I should converse, I would contradict the folk." At that, Muʿāwiyah announced, "Stand up, for I have dismissed him. Seek a governor whom you approve." Every one of the folk then went to ask one of the Banū Umayyah or one of the Syrian notables. Al-Aḥnaf stayed in his home and did not go to anyone. They spent several days (doing this). Muʿāwiyah then sent for them and assembled them. When they entered his presence, he asked, "Whom did you choose?" They disagreed, and each of their factions named someone (else), while al-Aḥnaf was silent. Muʿāwiyah then asked him, "What's the matter with you, O Abū Baḥr? You don't speak." Al-Aḥnaf replied, "If you make anyone of your family governor over us, we would not consider anyone equal to ʿUbaydallāh, and if you would make anyone else governor, then consider doing so." Muʿāwiyah said, "I have put him back in charge of you." Then he [191]
recommended him to al-Aḥnaf, and rebuked the latter's view because he had caused alienation. When the civil strife broke out, no one fulfilled (his obligation) to ʿUbaydallāh except al-Aḥnaf.

During this year, the affair of Yazīd b. Mufarrigh al-Ḥimyarī and ʿAbbād b. Ziyād occurred, as well as Yazīd's ridiculing the sons of Ziyād.

Why Yazīd b. Mufarrigh Ridiculed the Sons of Ziyād

I reported on the authority of Abū ʿUbaydah Maʿmar b. al-Muthannā that Yazīd b. Rabīʿah b. Mufarrigh al-Ḥimyarī accompanied ʿAbbād b. Ziyād in Sijistān. He was engaged in war against the Turks for ʿAbbād, who was impatient with him. When the army with ʿAbbād was concerned about fodder for their mounts, Ibn Mufarrigh said:[546]

If only the beards would turn into hay,
we would feed it to the horses of the Muslims.

ʿAbbād b. Ziyād had a large beard, so that when Ibn Mufarrigh's poem reached ʿAbbād, the latter was told, "He meant only you." At that, ʿAbbād sought him, but he fled from ʿAbbād and satirized him in many *qaṣīdahs.* Among those verses in which he satirized ʿAbbād were:[547]

If Muʿāwiyah son of Ḥarb should perish,
spread the good news of a crack to the folk of your cauldron.

So testify that your mother was not touched
by Abū Sufyān, taking off the veil,

But it was a matter about which there is uncertainty,
in great fear and alarm,

and:[548]

Tell Muʿāwiyah son of Ḥarb
of a penetration by the Yamānī man.

Are you angry that it be said, "Your father was virtuous"
and pleased that it be said, "Your father was an adulterer"?

So I testify that your relationship with Ziyād
is like the kinship of the elephant with the offspring of a she-ass.

546. See Iṣfahānī, *Aghānī,* XVII, 53.
547. See Iṣfahānī, *Aghānī,* XVII. 57.
548. See Iṣfahānī, *Aghānī,* XVII, 60.

Abū Zayd (said): When Ibn Mufarrigh satirized ʿAbbād he left him and came to al-Baṣrah while ʿUbaydallāh was visiting Muʿāwiyah. ʿAbbād then wrote to ʿUbaydallāh some of the lines in which Ibn Mufarrigh satirized him. When ʿUbaydallāh read the poetry, he entered Muʿāwiyah's presence, recited the lines to him, and asked permission to kill Ibn Mufarrigh. But Muʿāwiyah refused to let ʿUbaydallāh kill him, saying, "Punish him, but don't go so far as to kill him." Ibn Mufarrigh reached al-Baṣrah and sought refuge with al-Aḥnaf b. Qays, who said, "We do not give refuge against Ibn Sumayyah. If you wish, I would protect you from the poets of the Banū Tamīm." Ibn Mufarrigh replied, "That is not what I need to be protected against." He then came to Khālid b. ʿAbdallāh who threatened him, and then to Umayyah and to ʿUmar b. ʿUbaydallāh b. Maʿmar, both of whom threatened him. Finally he came to al-Mundhir b. Jarūd, who protected him and brought him into his house. Since Baḥriyyah bt. al-Mundhir was ʿUbaydallāh's wife, when the latter reached al-Baṣrah, he was informed that Ibn Mufarrigh was staying with al-Mundhir. When al-Mundhir came to greet ʿUbaydallāh, the latter sent the police to the house of al-Mundhir, and they seized Ibn Mufarrigh. Before al-Mundhir even realized it, while he was with ʿUbaydallāh, there was Ibn Mufarrigh standing before him. At that, al-Mundhir stood up before ʿUbaydallāh, saying, "O amīr, I have given him refuge." ʿUbaydallāh replied, "By God, O Mundhir, he praises you and your father while he ridicules me and my father. Then you protect him against me." ʿUbaydallāh ordered for him to be given a laxative to drink. He was to be carried on a donkey with saddle-bags on it.[549] The donkey began to be led about with him on it, while he defecated in his clothing. As he was led through the markets that way, a Persian passed by him, saw him, and asked about him in Persian, "What is this?"[550] Ibn Mufarrigh understood Persian, so he said,[551]

[192] [193]

549. In other accounts a sow and a cat were tied to the donkey. See *EI²*, s.v. Ibn Mufarrigh.

550. In Persian: "*Īn chīst?*"

551. These lines in Persian are also in Iṣfahānī, *Aghānī*, XVII, 51; Jāḥiẓ, *Bayān*, I, 143; and Ibn Qutaybah, *Shiʿr*, 276.

It is water, it is date wine,
It is the juice of raisins,
And it is white-faced[552] Sumayyah.

Then he satirized al-Mundhir b. al-Jārūd:[553]

I renounced being a neighbor of Quraysh,
and was a neighbor of the ʿAbd al-Qays, folk of al-Mushaqqar,[554]

People who protect us, for their protection was
spreading whirlwinds of a fart of Iraq.

So my neighbor from Jadhīmah [555] went to sleep,
and only the hard working [person] protects the protected.

He also said to ʿUbaydallāh:[556]

Water will cleanse what you did, but my declaration
is firmly fixed for you, as long as the bones last.

Then ʿUbaydallāh transported him to ʿAbbād in Sijiistān. At that, the Yamanīs interceded with Muʿāwiyah for him in Syria, so he sent a messenger to ʿAbbād. ʿAbbād then sent Ibn Mufarrigh to Muʿāwiyah. On the way he said:[557]

O ʿAdas! ʿAbbād does not have authority over you.
Escape, while you carry this [one], freed.

By my life, he has saved you from the abyss of ruin,
leader and rope for mankind, strong.

[194] I shall thank you for what good favor you render,
and the likes of me ought to thank benefactors.

---

552. The text reads *rū-yi sepīd*, that is, notorious.
553. See Iṣfahānī, *Aghānī*, XVII, 57.
554. Al-Mushaqqar was a fortress belonging to the ʿAbd al-Qays. It guarded the approach to the town of Hajar in al-Baḥrayn. See Yāqūt, *Muʿjam*, IV, 541.
555. Jadhīmah b. ʿAwf was the branch of the ʿAbd al-Qays to which al-Mundhir b. al-Jārūd belonged. See *EI*², s.v. ʿAbd al-Ḳays.
556. From a long *qaṣīdah* in Iṣfahānī, *Aghānī*, XVII, 57–8.
557. These lines are also in Iṣfahānī, *Aghānī*, XVII, 60; and Ibn Qutaybah, *Shiʿr*, 280, with variants. ʿAdas is either the name of the mule he was riding or the command used to make mules go. See Wright, *Grammar*, I, 295.

When he entered Muʿāwiyah's presence, he wept, saying, "What was done to me would not have been done to any Muslim except for a crime or offense." Muʿāwiyah asked, "Are you not the one who recites the *qaṣīdah* beginning:

> Tell Muʿāwiyah son of Ḥarb,
> about a penetration by the Yamānī man?"

Ibn Mufarrigh replied, "No, by that which magnified truth for the Commander of the Faithful, I did not say that." Muʿāwiyah inquired "Did you not say:

> So testify that your mother was never touched,
> by Abū Sufyān, throwing down the veil,

among much poetry in which you ridiculed Ibn Ziyād? Go, for I have forgiven you for your offense. However, if you should deal with us [again], what has happened would be nothing [compared to what will happen]. So, be off with you, and settle in any land you wish." Ibn Mufarrigh then settled at Mosul. Then he wanted to go to al-Baṣrah. Upon reaching it, he entered the presence of ʿUbaydallāh who gave him a guarantee of safe-conduct.

As for ʿAbū ʿUbaydah, he recounted Ibn Mufarrigh's settling at Mosul, according to what Abū Zayd told me: He related that when Muʿāwiyah asked, "Are you not the one who recites the lines:

> Tell Muʿāwiyah son of Ḥarb,
> about a penetration by the Yamānī man?"

Ibn Mufarrigh swore that he did not say it, but that ʿAbd al-Raḥmān b. al-Ḥakam, the brother of Marwān, said it instead. He also swore that ʿAbd al-Raḥmān imitated him as a means of ridiculing Ziyād, and that he used to reprove ʿAbd al-Raḥmān. At that, Muʿāwiyah was angry with ʿAbd al-Raḥmān b. al-Ḥakam and withheld his stipend until he hurt him. When someone interceded with Muʿāwiyah for ʿAbd al-Raḥmān, he said, "I will not be pleased with him until ʿUbaydallāh is pleased." ʿAbd al-Raḥmān then came to ʿUbaydallāh in Iraq, telling him:

You [and] Ziyād in the family of Ḥarb, [
[are] dearer to me than one of my fingertips.

I regard you as a brother, a maternal uncle, and a cousin,
and I do not know what you think of me privately.

ʿUbaydallāh was pleased with him and replied, "By God, I think you are a poor poet." Muʿāwiyah then asked Ibn Mufarrigh, "Are you not the one who recites the lines:

So testify that your mother was never touched,
by Abū Sufyān, throwing down the veil?

Don't do it again. We forgive you."

Ibn Mufarrigh proceeded until he settled at Mosul and got married. The morning after the night on which the marriage was consummated, he went out to hunt. He met an oil merchant or a perfume dealer on an ass of his. Ibn Mufarrigh inquired, "Where have you come from?" The merchant replied, "From al-Ahwāz." Ibn Mufarrigh asked, "How is the water of Masruqān[558] doing?" He answered, "As usual." Ibn Mufarrigh then left and headed toward al-Baṣah; his family did not know that he had gone. He proceeded until he came to ʿUbaydallāh at al-Baṣrah and entered his presence, and the latter granted him a guaranteed safe-conduct. Ibn Mufarrigh stayed with him until he asked permission to leave for Kirmān[559] ʿUbaydallāh allowed him to do so, and wrote to his official there to take care of and respect him. Ibn Mufarrigh then left for Kirmān, while at that time the official of ʿUbaydallāh in charge there was Sharīk b. al-Aʿwar al-Ḥārithī.[560]

In this year ʿUthmān b. Muḥammad b. Abī Sufyān led the people in the pilgrimage. I was told that by Aḥmad b. Thābit—someone—Isḥāq b. ʿĪsā—Abū Maʿshar. Al-Wāqidī and others said the same.

558. Masruqān was a canal famous for its white water near Shustar in Khūzistān. See Le Strange, *Lands*, 236.

559. Kirmān is a province and region in south-central Iran. See Le Strange, *Lands*, 299–321; *EI*², s.v. Kirmān.

560. According to Balādhurī, *Ansāb*, IV B, 79, Ibn Mufarrigh did not settle in Kirmān until ʿUbaydallāh b. Ziyād had fled from al-Baṣrah to Syria.

The governor in charge of al-Madīnah was al-Walīd b. ʿUtbah b. Abī Sufyān. Al-Nuʿmān b. Bashīr was in charge of al-Kūfah, while Shurayḥ was in charge of rendering judgment there. ʿUbaydallāh b. Ziyād was in charge of al-Baṣrah, while Hishām b. Hubayrah was in charge of rendering judgment there. ʿAbd al-Raḥmān b. Ziyād was in charge of Khurāsān while ʿAbbād b. [196]
Ziyād was in charge of Sijistān and Sharīk b. al-Aʿwar was in charge of Kirmān for ʿUbaydallāh b. Ziyād.

The Events of the Year 60

(October 13, 679–September 30, 680)

According to al-Wāqidī, the raid of Mālik b. ʿAbdallāh against Sawriyah happened in this year, as well as Junādah b. Abī Umayyah's entry into Rūdas and his destruction of its city.

During this year also, Muʿāwiyah imposed the declaration of allegiance to his son, Yazīd, on the delegation that came to him with ʿUbaydallāh b. Ziyād. When Muʿāwiyah became ill this year, he entrusted to his son, Yazīd, what he did concerning the group that had refused to declare allegiance to Yazīd when he had summoned them to do so. Muʿāwiyah's agreement was what Hishām b. Muḥammad related according to Abū Mikhnaf —ʿAbd al-Malik b. Nawfal b. Musāḥiq b. ʿAbdallāh b. Makhramah: When Muʿāwiyah became sick with the illness from which he perished, he summoned his son, Yazīd, saying:

> O my son, I have spared you the effort, made things smooth for you, subdued enemies for you, subjected the necks of the Arabs for you, and created unity for you. I am only afraid that four individuals of Quraysh might challenge you for this matter which was established for you— al-Ḥusayn b. ʿAlī, ʿAbdallāh b. ʿUmar, ʿAbdallāh b. al-Zu-

bayr, and ʿAbd al-Raḥmān b. Abī Bakr. As far as ʿAbdallāh b. ʿUmar is concerned, he is a man whom righteousness has overwhelmed, and if no one else were left, he would acknowledge you. As far as al-Ḥusayn is concerned, the [197]
people of Iraq will not leave him alone until they make him rebel. If he rebels against you, and you should defeat him, then pardon him, because he has close kinship and a great claim. As far as Ibn Abī Bakr is concerned, he is a man, who, if he should see his companions doing something, he would do likewise. He is only interested in women and pleasure. As for the one who crouches for you as a crouching lion and tricks you as a sly fox, and if an opportunity enables [him] he would spring, that is Ibn al-Zubayr. If he does that to you, and you are able to overpower him, then tear him limb from limb.

(According to) Hishām—ʿAwānah: We have heard in another account that when Muʿāwiyah was on the verge of death, which was in this year, Yazīd was absent. Muʿāwiyah summoned al-Ḍaḥḥāk b. Qāys al-Fihrī, who was the head of his police, and Muslim b. ʿUqbah al-Murrī and counseled them saying:

Tell Yazīd my testament: Pay attention to the people of the Ḥijāz for they are your root. Honor whomever of them should come to you, and take care of whomever is absent. Pay attention to the people of Iraq, and if they ask you to dismiss one of their officials every day, do so. For I would rather have a governor be dismissed than for one hundred thousands swords to be unsheathed against you. Pay attention to the people of Syria, for they are your entourage and your leather bag. If something should befall you from your enemy, be victorious with them. When you are successful with them, return the people of Syria to their land. For if they should stay in another land than their own, they would take on other characteristics than their own. I only fear three persons of the Quraysh—Ḥusayn b. ʿAlī, ʿAbdallāh b. ʿUmar, and ʿAbdallāh b. al-Zubayr. As far as Ibn ʿUmar is concerned, he is a man whom religion has overwhelmed, so he would not ask anything from you. As far

as al-Ḥusayn b. ʿAlī is concerned, he is an insignificant man, and I hope that God would protect you from him by means of those who killed his father and deserted his brother. He has close kinship, a great claim, and is a rela-
[198] tive of Muḥammad. I don't think the people of Iraq would leave him alone until they make him rebel. If you should overpower him pardon him, for if I were his master, I would pardon him. As far as Ibn al-Zubayr is concerned, he is a heaving reptile, so if he appears to you, stick to him unless he asks for peace from you. If he does, then accept [it] and spare the blood of your folk as much as you can.

In this year Muʿāwiyah b. Abī Sufyān perished at Damascus. The time of his death was disputed apart from general agreement that his death occurred in the month of Rajab 60 (April 7–May 6, 680) of the *hijrah*.[561] Hishām b. Muḥammad (said): Muʿāwiyah died at the new moon of Rajab 60 (April 7, 680). Al-Wāqidī (said): Muʿāwiyah died on the ides of Rajab (April, 21, 680). ʿAlī b. Muḥammad: Muʿāwiyah died at Damascus on a Thursday, eight days before the end of Rajab 60 (April 29, 680). Al-Ḥārith told me that according to ʿAlī.

The Length of Muʿāwiyah's Reign

I was told by Aḥmad b. Thābit al-Rāzī—someone—Iṣḥāq b. ʿĪsā—Abū Maʿshar: Muʿāwiyah was acknowledged (as caliph) at Adhruh. Al-Ḥasan b. ʿAlī acknowledged him in Jumādāh I 41 (September 2–October 1, 661) and Muʿāwiyah died in Rajab 60 (April 7–May 6, 680). His Caliphate lasted nineteen years and three months.

I was told by al-Ḥārith—Muḥammad b. Saʿd—Muḥammad b. ʿUmar—Yaḥyā b. Saʿīd b. Dīnār al-Saʿdī—his father: Muʿāwiyah died Thursday night on the ides of Rajab 60 (April 21,
[199] 680) and his Caliphate lasted nineteen years, three months and seventeen days.

I was told by ʿUmar—ʿAlī: The Syrians acknowledged Muʿāwiyah as Caliph in Dhū al-Qaʿdah 37 (April 10–May 9, 658),

561. According to Ibn Khayyāt, *Taʾrīkh*, I, 272, Muʿāwiyah died on a Thursday, eight days before the end of Rajab 59 (May 10, 679).

when the two arbiters split. They had previously acknowledged him in order to demand (vengeance) for the blood of ʿUthmān. Then al-Ḥasan b. ʿAlī made peace with him and turned over matters to him in the year 41, five days before the end of the month of Rabīʿ I (July 31, 661). At that, the people as a whole acknowledged Muʿāwiyah, so it was called "the year of the concord." He died at Damascus, in the year 60, Thursday, eight days before the end of Rajab (April 29, 680). His rule lasted nineteen years, three months and twenty-seven days. It is also said that there were nineteen years, ten months and three nights between the death of ʿAlī and the death of Muʿāwiyah. Hishām b. Muḥammad (said): Muʿāwiyah was acknowledged as Caliph in Jumādah I 41 (September 2–October 1, 661). He thus ruled nineteen years and three months except for a few days. Then he died at the new moon of Rajab 60 (April 7, 680).

There is also disagreement about his age and how long he lived. Some said he was seventy-five years old on the day he died.

I was told by ʿUmar—Muhammad b. Yaḥyā—Hishām b. al-Walīd—Ibn Shihāb al-Zuhrī: Al-Walīd asked me about the life span of the Caliphs, so I informed him that Muʿāwiyah was seventy-five years old when he died. At that, he exclaimed, "Bravo! Indeed that is a lifetime." Others said he was seventy-three years old when he died.

I was told by ʿUmar—Aḥmad b. Zuhayr—ʿAlī b. Muḥammad: Muʿāwiyah was seventy-three years old when he died. He [200]
is also said to have been eighty years old, while others said he was seventy-eight years old when he died.

I was told by al-Ḥārith—Muḥammad b. Saʿd—Muḥammad b. ʿUmar—Yaḥyā b. Saʿīd b. Dīnār—his father: Muʿāwiyah died when he was seventy-eight years old. Others said he died when he was eighty-five years old. I was told that by Hishām b. Muḥammad, who reported this according to his father.

Muʿāwiyah's Last Illness

I was told by al-Ḥārith—Muḥammad b. Saʿd—Abū ʿUbaydah—Abū Yaʿqūb al-Thaqafī—ʿAbd al-Malik b. ʿUmayr: When Muʿāwiyah felt heavy, and the people reported that it was death (approaching), he said to his family, "Put antimony all around my eyes, and anoint my head with oil." They did so and made his face shine with oil. Then it was arranged for him to sit. He said, "Prop me up." Then he said, "Allow the people to greet [me] standing, and let no one sit." Men then began to enter and greet (him) standing and to see him treated with kohl and with oil. He was saying, "The people will say that at his end he was the healthiest of people." When they left his presence, Muʿāwiyah said:

By my posing for the gloaters by whom I am seen,
indeed I am not ruined by the uncertainties of time.

[201] And when destiny digs in its claws
You will find that every amulet is useless.

He had discharges, and died that very day.

I was told by Aḥmad b. Zuhayr—ʿAlī b. Muḥammad—Isḥāq b. Ayyūb—ʿAbd al-Malik b. Mīnās al-Kalbī: Muʿāwiyah told his two daughters during his last illness, while they were turning him over, "Turn over[562] [this] shrewd person deftly, [who] accumulated wealth from youth to creeping[563] if he does not enter Hell Fire." Then he quoted:

I have endeavored for you as the runner who is fatigued,
and I have saved you from traveling and departure.

This is said to be from the collection of a reliable person.

I was told by Aḥmad b. Zuhayr—ʿAlī—Sulaymān b. Ayyūb—al-Awazāʿī and ʿAlī b. Mujāhid—al-Aʿlā b. Maymūn—his father: Muʿāwiyah said during his last illness, "Indeed the Messenger of God clothed me with a shirt. One day I held it up while he pared his nails. I then took his parings and put them in a long-necked bottle. So when I die clothe me in that shirt and cut up those parings, grind them up, and sprinkle them in my eyes and in my mouth. Thus God might have mercy on me by their blessing (*barakah*)." Then he quoted the poem of al-

562. See Mubarrad, *Kāmil*, 784.

563. From the proverb: "It fatigued me from youth to creeping," said of someone who accumulates from youth until he walks slowly leaning on a staff. See Maydānī, *Amthāl*, II, 7; Freytag, *Proverbia*, II, 78.

Ashhab b. Rumaylah al-Nahshalī in which he praises al-Qubāʿ:[564]

> When you die, generosity will die and liberality will cease
> among people except for a few, ice cold.[565]
>
> And the hands of beggars will be turned back and held fast
> out of religion and the world by a renewing successor.

At that, one of his daughters or someone else said, "Certainly not, O Commander of the Faithful, may God remove [it] from you instead" He then quoted: [202]

> And when destiny digs in its claws,
> you will find that every amulet is useless.

Then he went blind, but afterwards recovered his sight and told those members of his family who attended him, "Fear God, Almighty and Great, for God, praise Him, protects whoever fears Him, and there is no protector for one who does not fear God." Then he passed away.

I was told by Aḥmad—ʿAlī—Muḥammad b. al-Ḥakam—someone: When Muʿāwiyah was attended by death he ordered for half of his wealth to be returned to the treasury, hoping that the remainder would be good for him, because the Caliph ʿUmar had shared with his officials.

Who Led the Prayer over Muʿāwiyah When He Died

I was told by Aḥmad b. Zuhayr—ʿAlī b. Muḥammad: Al-Ḍaḥḥak b. Qays al-Fihrī led the prayer over Muʿāwiyah, while Yazīd was absent, when Muʿāwiyah died. I was also told by Hishām b. Muḥammad—Abū Mikhnaf—ʿAbd al-Malik b. Nawfal b. Musāḥiq b. ʿAbdallāh b. Makhramah: When Muʿāwiyah died, al-Ḍaḥḥak b. Qays went out and ascended the pulpit, while Muʿāwiyah's shrouds were visible in his hands. After he praised and extolled God, he said, "Indeed Muʿāwiyah was the

564. Al-Qubāʿ was al-Ḥārith b. ʿAbdallāh b. Abī Rabīʿah al-Makhzūmī, the brother of the poet ʿUmar b. ʿAbdallāh b. Abī Rabīʿah al-Makhzūmī. See Mubarrad, *Kāmil*, 624.

565. The text reads: *muṣarrad.* See Ibn Manẓūr, *Lisān*, III, 248.

stick of the Arabs and the blade of the Arabs, by means of whom God, Almighty and Great, cut off strife, whom He made sovereign over mankind, by means of whom he conquered countries, but now he has died and these are his shrouds. We are wrapping him in them and putting him in his grave, and leaving him and his work. Then there will be the interval[566] un-
[203] til the Day of Resurrection. Whoever of you has wanted to see him, be present at dawn worship." He also sent a courier to Yazīd concerning Muʿāwiyah's pain. Yazīd said about that:[567]

The courier has brought a parchment, the rider trots with it,
so the heart was apprehensive of its parchment and alarmed.

We said, "Woe unto you, what is in your letter?"
They said, "The Caliph has certainly felt pain."

So the earth was shaken or was about to be shaken under us,
as if it raised dust from its severed foundations.

One whose person continues to exceed nobility,
the keys of that person are about to drop.

When we arrived, while the door of the house was shut,
and [heard] the voice of Ramlah, the heart was alarmed, so it broke.

I was told by ʿUmar—ʿAlī—Isḥāq b. Khulayd—Khulayd b. ʿAjlān, the mawlā of ʿAbbād: Muʿāwiyah died while Yazīd was at Huwwārīn;[568] they had written to him when Muʿāwiyah had fallen ill. Yazīd arrived after Muʿāwiyah had been buried, so he came to his grave and worshipped over him and prayed for him. Then he came to his residence and recited the lines:

The courier has brought a parchment . . .

---

566. Qur'ān 23:102. The *barzakh* is the interval or barrier between this life and the next, between Hell and Paradise, or between the material and spiritual worlds. See *EI*², s.v. Barzakh.

567. See Iṣfahānī, *Aghānī*, XVI, 33.

568. C reads: Ḥawrān, the mountainous plateau south of Damascus. See *EI*², s.v. Hawrān. Huwwārīn was the location of two villages, two days' journey from Tadmur (Palmyra), where Yazīd b. Muʿāwiyah died in 64(683/4)

Muʿāwiyah's Lineage and His Agnomen

As for Muʿāwiyah's lineage, he was the son of Abū Sufyān. Abū Sufyān's name was Ṣakhr b. Ḥarb b. Umayyah b. ʿAbd Shams b. ʿAbd Manāt b. Quṣayy b. Kilāb. Muʿāwiyah's mother was Hind [204] bt. ʿUtbah b. ʿAbd Shams b. ʿAbd Manāf b. Quṣayy. His patronymic (*kunyah*)[569] was Abū ʿAbd al-Raḥmān.

Muʿāwiyah's Wives and Children

One of his wives was Maysūn bt. Baḥdal b. Unayf b. Waljah b. Qunāfah b. ʿAdī b. Zuhayr b. Ḥārithah b. Janāb al-Kalbī. She bore Yazīd b. Muʿāwiyah for him. ʿAlī said: In addition to Yazīd, Maysūn bore Muʿāwiyah a girl, Rabb al-Masāriq, but she died young, and Hishām did not mention her among the children of Muʿāwiyah. Among his wives was also Fākhitah bt. Qaraẓah b. ʿAbd ʿAmr b. Nawfal b. ʿAbd Manāf. She bore Muʿāwiyah two sons, ʿAbd al-Raḥmān and ʿAbdallāh. ʿAbdallāh was foolish and frail and was nicknamed Abū al-Khayr. I was told by Aḥmad—ʿAlī b. Muḥammad: One day ʿAbdallāh b. Muʿāwiyah passed a miller who had tied his mule to the mill for the flour and put bells on his neck. So he asked the miller, "Why did you put these bells on the neck of your mule?" The miller answered, "I put them on its neck in order to know if it should stop and not turn the mill." ʿAbdallāh then asked, "Have you considered how you would know that he was not turning the mill if he should stop and shake his head?" The miller told him, "This mule, may God make the amīr prosper, does not have intelligence like that of the amīr." As for ʿAbd al-Raḥmān, he died young.

Among his wives was Nā'ilah bt. ʿUmārah al-Kalbī. I was told by Aḥmad—ʿAlī: When Muʿāwiyah married Nā'ilah he told Maysūn, "Go off and observe the daughter of your paternal uncle" After she had observed her, he asked, "How did she [205] look to you?" She answered, "Perfectly beautiful, but I saw a mole beneath her navel where the head of her husband will certainly be put in her lap" At that, Muʿāwiyah divorced her,

569. A *kunyah* is an agnomen, named after a son.

and Ḥabīb b. Maslamah al-Fihrī married her. Then after Ḥabīb, al-Nuʿmān b. Bashīr al-Anṣārī married her. Al-Nuʿmān was killed and his head was put in her lap. Among Muʿāwiyah's wives was Katwah bt. Qaraẓah, the sister of Fākhitah. He raided Cyprus[570] while she was with him, and she died there.

Some of Muʿāwiyah's Affairs and Conduct

I was told by Aḥmad b. Zuhayr—ʿAlī: When allegiance was rendered to Muʿāwiyah as Caliph, he put Qays b. Ḥamzah al-Hamdānī in charge of his police. Then he dismissed him and appointed Zumayl b. ʿAmr al-ʿUdhrī,[571] or al-Saksakī. Muʿāwiyah's secretary and the person in charge of his business was Sarjūn b. Manṣūr al-Rūmī. One of his mawālī called al-Mukhtār was in charge of his guard (*ḥaras*). This is also said to have been a man called Mālik, who was nicknamed Abū al-Mukhāriq, a mawlā of Ḥimyar.[572] Muʿāwiyah was the first to make use of bodyguards. Saʿd,[573] his mawlā, was in charge of his gatekeepers. Faḍālah b. ʿUtbah al-Anṣārī[574] was in charge of rendering judgment. When Faḍālah died, Muʿāwiyah appointed Abū Idrīs ʿĀ'idhallāh b. ʿAbdallāh al-Khawlānī[575] to render judgment. So far this has been the account of Aḥmad according to ʿAlī. Others than ʿAlī said: ʿAbdallāh b. Miḥṣan al-Ḥimyarī was in

---

570. Cyprus was attacked by Muʿāwiyah in 28(648/9) See *EI*², s.v. Ḳubrus.

571. Zumayl b. ʿAmr (or Zamal b. Rabīʿah) b. al-ʿAnaz b. Khashāf b. Khudayj al-ʿUdhrī had been a member of his tribe's delegation to Muḥammad. The latter gave him a standard which he kept until he fought at Ṣiffīn along with Muʿāwiyah, where he was one of the witnesses to the arbitration agreement. He witnessed the rendering of allegiance (*bayʿah*) to Marwān at Jābiyah, and died at the battle of Marj Rāhiṭ in 64(683/4) See Ibn al-Athīr, *Usd*, II, 205; and Ibn Hajar, *Iṣābah*, I, 551, II, 19. For a slightly different account see Ibn Khayyāt, *Ta'rīkh*, I, 276.

572. Ibn Khayyāṭ, *Ta'rīkh*, I, 276, calls him Abū al-Mukhtār.

573. Ibid.: Abū Ayyub.

574. Fadālah b. ʿUtbah (or ʿUbayd) al-Anṣārī (d. 53(673)) was a Companion of Muḥammad at Ḥudaybiyah, participated in the conquest of Egypt, and settled in Syria where Muʿāwiyah put him in charge of rendering judgment at Damascus when he went to Ṣiffīn. He also led sea raids against the Byzantines. See Ibn al-Athīr, *Usd*, IV, 182.

575. Abū Idrīs ʿĀ'idhallāh b. ʿAbdallāh al-Khawlānī (9–ca. 86 [630–ca. 705]) one of the greatest of the Followers, was judge at Damascus from 53(673) until his death. See Ibn al-Athīr, *Usd*, III, 99, V, 134.

charge of the department of the seal. Muʿāwiyah was the first one who used a department of the seal. The reason for that was [206] that Muʿāwiyah ordered one hundred thousand dirhams for ʿAmr b. al-Zubayr to relieve the latter of his debts. Muʿāwiyah wrote about that to Ziyād b. Sumayyah while the latter was in charge of Iraq. ʿAmr then opened the letter and changed the one hundred to two hundred. When Ziyād presented his invoice, Mu'āwiyah disclaimed it, required ʿAmr to return the money, and imprisoned him. His brother, ʿAbdallāh b. al-Zubayr, paid it on his behalf. At that, Muʿāwiyah established the department of the seal, and he tied up letters, which had not been tied (before).[576]

I was told by ʿAbdallāh b. Aḥmad b. Shabbawayh—his father—Sulaymān—ʿAbdallāh b. al-Mubārik—Ibn Abī Dhi'b—Saʿīd al-Maqburī[577]—ʿUmar b. al-Khaṭṭāb: You speak of Kisrā and Qayṣar and their shrewdness while Muʿāwiyah is with you!

I was told by ʿAbdallāh b. Aḥmad—his father—Sulaymān: I read—ʿAbdallāh—Fulayḥ: I was told that when ʿAmr b. al-ʿĀṣ visited Muʿāwiyah with the Egyptians, ʿAmr told them, "Pay attention when you enter the presence of Ibn Hind lest you greet him as Caliph. That will make you great in his eyes. Reduce him as much as you can." When they came to him, Muʿāwiyah told his gate-keepers, "Indeed, as I know Ibn al-Nābighah, he will have reduced my position with the folk, so pay attention when the delegation enters, shake them as strongly as you can, and don't let a single one of them reach me unless he is concerned about his own destruction." The first one who [207] entered his presence was an Egyptian called Ibn al-Khayyāṭ. He entered shaken, saying, "Peace be upon you, O Messenger of God!" The folk did that in succession, and when they left, ʿAmr told them, "God curse you! I forbade you to greet him as amīr, so you greeted him as Prophet."

One day Muʿāwiyah wore his black turban and lined his eyelids with kohl, and he was the most handsome person when he

576. Ibn Khayyāṭ, *Ta'rīkh*, I, 276, adds that ʿUbayd b. Aws al-Ghassānī was Muʿāwiyah's correspondence secretary (*kātib al-rasā'il*).

577. Saʿīd b. Kaysān was called Saʿīd b. Abī Saʿīd al-Maqburī. See Nawawī, *Tahdhīb*, I, 219.

did that. ʿAbdallāh doubted whether he heard that about him or not.

I was told by Aḥmad b. Zuhayr—ʿAlī b. Muḥammad—Abū Muḥammad al-Umawī: ʿUmar b. al-Khaṭṭāb left for Syria and saw Muʿāwiyah come to receive him with a procession; Muʿāwiyah had gone out to ʿUmar with a retinue. At that, ʿUmar told him, "O Muʿāwiyah, you go with a retinue, and you leave in the same way. I heard that you start the day in your residence while petitioners are at your door." Muʿāwiyah replied, "O Commander of the Faithful, our enemy is close to us, and they have scouts and spies, so I wanted, O Commander of the Faithful, for them to see that Islām has power." ʿUmar answered, "This is the ruse of an intelligent man or the deception of a clever man." Muʿāwiyah then said, "O Commander of the Faithful, instruct me with what you want and I shall fullfill it." ʿUmar replied, "Woe unto you! Whenever we discuss something which I disapprove of you doing, you leave me not knowing whether I should order you to do it or forbid you."

I was told by ʿAbdallāh b. Aḥmad—his father—Sulaymān—ʿAbdallāh—Maʿmar—Jaʿfar b. Burqān: Al-Mughīrah wrote to Muʿāwiyah, "Now then, indeed my age has become great, my bones are frail, and the Quraysh detest me, so if you see fit to dismiss me, do so." Muʿāwiyah wrote back to him, "Your letter reached me in which you state that your age became great,
[208] and by my life, no one but you consumed your life. You state that the Quraysh detest you, and by my life, you obtain good only from them. Since you ask me to dismiss you, I have done so. If you were sincere, I have satisfied you; but if you were deceiving, then I have cheated you."

I was told by Aḥmad—ʿAlī b. Muḥammad—ʿAlī b. Mujāhid: Muʿāwiyah said, "If an Umawī were not taking care of his wealth prudently, he would not be like one of them. And if a Hāshimī were not generous and magnanimous, he would not be like one of them. However, you don't hear about the eloquence, generosity and courage of the Hāshimī.

I was told by Aḥmad—ʿAlī—ʿAwānah and Khallād b. ʿUbaydah: Muʿāwiyah had lunch one day while ʿUbaydallāh b. Abī Bakr and his son, Bashīr, were with him—it is also said, someone other than Bashīr—so he ate a lot, and Muʿāwiyah noticed him. 'Ubaydallāh b. Abī Bakr realized it and wanted to signal his son, but he was not able to do so, as his son did not raise his head until he was finished. When they left, he scolded his son for what he did. Then he returned to Mu'āwiyah without his son, So Mu'āwiyah asked, "What did your son, the mouthful, do? "'Ubaydallāh replied "He complained." At that, Mu'āwiyah remarked "I knew that his food would make him sick."

I was told by Aḥmad—'Alī—Juwayriyyah b. Asmā': Abū Mūsā came to Mu'āwiyah and entered his presence in a black burnous, saying "Peace be upon you, O Commander of the Faithful." He replied, "And upon you be peace." When he left, Mu'āwiyah commented, "The shaykh came for me to make him a governor, and, by God, I would not make him one."

I was told by 'Abdallāh b. Aḥmad—his father—Abū Ṣāliḥ Sulaymān b. Ṣāliḥ—'Abdallāh b. al-Mubārik—Sulaymān b. al-Mughīrah—Ḥumayd b. Hilāl—Abū Burdah: I entered Mu'ā- [209]
wiyah's presence when his abcess afflicted him, so he said, "Come over here, O cousin, and look." I looked, and, behold, it had been probed, so I said, "There is no harm to you, O Commander of the Faithful." Yazīd then entered and Mu'āwiyah said, "If you were in charge of anything regarding the people. I would entrust you with this, since his father[578] was my dear friend"—or words to that effect—"except that I thought differently from him about fighting."

I was told by 'Alī—Shihāb b. 'Ubaydallāh—Yazīd b. Suwayd: Mu'āwiyah admitted al-Aḥnaf, and he had begun his turn. Then Muḥammad b. al-Ash'ath entered and sat between Mu'āwiyah and al-Aḥnaf. Mu'āwiyah told (al-Aḥnaf), "We did not admit him before you, and you are ahead of him. You have behaved as someone who felt ashamed of himself. Just as we rule your affairs, we rule your admission. Desire from us what we desire from you, and it will be more lasting for you."

I was told by Aḥmad—'Alī—Suḥaym b. Ḥafṣ: Rabī'ah b. 'Isl al-Yarbū'ī spoke for Mu'āwiyah,[579] so Mu'āwiyah said, "Give

578. Abū Burdah's father, Abū Mūsā al-Ash'arī, had been neutral during the first civil war.

579. That is, he offered to arrange a marriage for Mu'āwiyah.

him *sawīq*[580] to drink." Muʿāwiyah asked him, "O Rabīʿah, how are the people where you are?" He replied, "Disagreeing about such and such a faction." Muʿāwiyah inquired, "So which of them do you belong to?" He answered, "I don't belong to any of them." At that, Muʿāwiyah remarked, "I think there are more of them than you said."[581] Rabīʿah then asked, "O Commander of the Faithful, assist me with twelve thousand tree-trunks to build my house." Muʿāwiyah asked, "Where is your house?" He answered, "In al-Baṣrah, and it is more than two *farsakhs* [twelve km] by two *farsakhs* [square]." Muʿāwiyah inquired, "Is your house in al-Baṣrah or is al-Baṣrah in your house?" Afterwards, one of Rabīʿah's sons entered the presence of Ibn Hubayrah,[582] saying, "May God make the amīr prosper, I am the
[210] son of the chief of his folk. My father spoke for Muʿāwiyah." Ibn Hubayrah asked Salm b. Qutaybah, "Who says this?" Salm said, "This is the son of the most foolish of his folk." Ibn Hubayrah inquired, "Did your father marry off Muʿāwiyah?" When he replied that he had not, Ibn Hubayrah remarked, "Then I don't think your father accomplished anything."

I was told by Aḥmad—ʿAlī—Abū Muḥammad b. Dhakwān al-Qurashī: ʿUtbah and ʿAnbasah, two sons of Abū Sufyān, engaged in a dispute. ʿUtbah's mother was Hind while ʿAnbasah's mother was the daughter of Abū Uzayhir al-Dawsī. Muʿāwiyah was rude to ʿAnbasah, who retorted, "The same to you, O Commander of the Faithful!" When Muʿāwiyah responded, "O ʿAnbasah, ʿUtbah is the son of Hind," ʿAnbasah said:

We were getting along properly, our enmity was straightened out
formerly. Then Hind began to discriminate between us.

And even if Hind did not bear me, indeed I
would be a sword which great men of glory employ.

---

580. *Sawīq* is a broth of barley or wheat to which sugar, honey, dates, oil, or pomegranate syrup may be added. See *EI*[1], s.v. Sawīḳ.

581. That is, Rabīʿah himself constituted one more faction.

582. This is either ʿUmar b. Hubayrah, governor of Iraq from 102(720) until 105(724) or his son Yūsuf b. ʿUmar, governor of Iraq from 129(741) until 132(749) See *EI*[2], s.v. Ibn Hubayra.

Her[583] father a great host in every winter,
and a shelter for weak people which does not collapse from strain.

His pots still exist
for whoever of the two valleys of Tihāmah and Najd might fear.

At that, Muʿāwiyah said, "I shall never felicitate her in your presence."

I was told by ʿAbdallāh b. Aḥmad—his father—Sulaymān—ʿAbdallāh—Ḥarmalah b. ʿImrān: One night Muʿāwiyah heard that the Byzantine Emperor (Qayṣar) was heading for him with an army, that Nātil b. Qays al-Judhāmī took over Filasṭīn and seized its treasury, that the Egyptians whom he had imprisoned had escaped, and that ʿAlī b. Abī Ṭālib was headed for him with an army. At that he told his announcer (*muʾadhdhin*), "Call [to worship] right now"—that was in the middle of the night. ʿAmr b. al-ʿĀṣ then came to him, asking, "Why did you send for me?" Muʿāwiyah replied, "I did not send for you." ʿAmr responded, "The announcer only summoned me just now." Muʿāwiyah explained, "I was shot at by four bows." ʿAmr advised, "As for those who escaped from your prison, [211] they are in the prison of God, Almighty and Great. They are folk who are Sellers; you won't have to go to them. But assign the blood price to whoever brings you one of them or his head, and they will be brought to you. Look to the Emperor [Qayṣar] and be peaceful to him. Offer him wealth and some of the garments of Egypt, and he will accept that from you. Look to Nātil b. Qays. By my life, religion did not motivate him. He only wanted what he got, so write to him, and grant that to him, and congratulate him for it. If you should have power over him, [fine,] and if you don't, then don't be distressed about him. Devote your blade and your iron to this one who has the blood of your cousin upon him." All of the folk had escaped from Muʿāwiyah's prison except Abrahah b. al-Ṣabbāḥ. Muʿāwiyah asked, "What prevented you from escaping with your companions?" Abrahah replied, "I was prevented from that by hatred for ʿAlī,

583. That is, ʿAnbasah's own mother.

not by love for you, and I cannot overcome it." Muʿāwiyah then released him.

I was told by ʿAbdallāh—his father—Sulaymān—ʿAbdallāh b. Masʿadah[584] b. Ḥakamah al-Fazārī from the sons of the family of Badr:[585] Muʿāwiyah moved from one of the districts of Syria to some province of his and settled in a residence in Syria. His camp was spread out for him on the surface of a plain overlooking the road, and he permitted me to stay with him. When the caravans, trains of camels, slave girls, and horses passed by, he said, "O Ibn Masʿadah, may God have mercy on Abū Bakr who did not want this world and this world did not want him.
[212] As for ʿUmar"—or Ibn Ḥantamah—"this world wanted him but he did not want it. As for ʿUthmān, he caused losses to this world and it caused losses for him. As for us, we wallow in it." Then he seemed to repent, saying, "By God, it is the sovereignty which God brought us."

I was told by ʿAḥmad—ʿAlī b. Muḥammad—ʿAlī b. ʿUbaydallāh: ʿAmr b. al-ʿĀṣ wrote to Muʿāwiyah asking him to grant his son ʿAbdallāh b. ʿAmr what Muʿāwiyah had granted the father with regard to Egypt. Muʿāwiyah remarked, "Abū ʿAbdallāh wanted to write, but he babbled. I testify to you that should I outlive him, I would cancel his contract." ʿAmr b. al-ʿĀṣ said, "Whenever I saw Muʿāwiyah reclining on his arm, crossing his legs, blinking his eye, and saying to someone, 'Speak!' I had pity on that man."

I was told by Aḥmad—ʿAlī b. Muḥammad: ʿAmr b. al-ʿĀṣ asked Muʿāwiyah, "O Commander of the Faithful, am I not the most sincere person towards you?" He replied, "Because of that you have gained what you did."

(According to) Aḥmad—ʿAlī—Juwayriyyah b. Asmāʾ: Busr b. Abī Arṭāt spoke against ʿAlī in the presence of Muʿāwiyah while Zayd b. ʿUmar b. al-Khaṭṭāb was sitting (there). At that, Zayd assaulted Busr with a stick and injured him. Muʿāwiyah told Zayd, "You turned on the shaykh of the Quraysh, a chief

---

584. Cairo reads: al-Mubārik.

585. ʿAbdallāh b. Masʿadah (or Masʿūd) b. Ḥakamah b. Mālik al-Fazārī was a Companion who settled at Damascus, fought along with Muʿāwiyah at Ṣiffīn, and led raids against the Byzantines. He lived to acknowledge Marwān at Jābiyah. See Ibn al-Athīr, *Usd*, III, 255–6.

of the Syrians, and you struck him!" Then he turned to Busr, saying, "You revile ʿAlī who is Zayd's grandfather, while Zayd, the son of al-Fārūq,[586] heads the notables. Haven't you considered that he endures that?" Then they were both satisfied. Muʿāwiyah also said, "Indeed I am above letting an offense be more important than my pardon, and foolishness greater than my forbearance, or a flaw which I shall not conceal privately, or a misdeed greater than my beneficence." Muʿāwiyah said, "The beauty of the noble [man] is virtuousness." Muʿāwiyah said, "There is nothing I like better than a bubbling spring in [213] an easy land." ʿAmr b. al-ʿĀṣ then said, "I like nothing better than to spend the night as a bridegroom with the pick of Arab wives." At that, Wardān, the mawlā of ʿAmr b. al-ʿĀṣ said, "I like nothing better than generosity between brothers." Muʿāwiyah said, "I am more entitled to that than you." Wardān replied, "Do what you like."[587]

I was told by Aḥmad—ʿAlī—Muḥammad b. Ibrāhīm—his father: When Muʿāwiyah's official in charge of al-Madīnah wanted to dispatch the courier to Muʿāwiyah, he used to order his herald to announce, "Whoever has a need should write to the Commander of the Faithful." Zirr b. Ḥubaysh or Aymān b. Khuraym wrote a charming letter and cast it among the others. It contained:

> When the men beget their children,[588]
> and their biceps twitch from age,
>
> And their illness becomes chronic,
> they are crops whose harvests approach.

When Muʿāwiyah received the letters and read this one, he remarked, "He has announced my own death to me." Muʿāwiyah also said, "There is nothing sweeter for me than anger which I swallow." Muʿāwiyah told ʿAbd al-Raḥmān b. al-Ḥakam b. Abī al-ʿĀṣ, "O cousin, indeed, you have been very fond of poetry. So beware of flirting with women lest you dishonor honorable ones, and satire lest you dishonor a noble person and provoke

586. The Caliph ʿUmar I was called al-Fārūq.
587. See Masʿūdī, *Murūj*, V, 58–60.
588. That is, they had grandchildren.

someone ignoble. Praise is the bait of the shameless, but be proud of the glorious deeds of your folk, and say those proverbs
[214] that would adorn you and edify others."

I was told by Aḥmad—ʿAlī—Abū al-Ḥasan b. Ḥammād: Muʿāwiyah observed al-Thumā in a woolen cloak, so he slighted him. At that, al-Thumā said "O Commander of the Faithful, the woolen cloak does not speak to you, but the person who is in it does."

I was told by Aḥmad—ʿAlī—Sulaymān: Muʿāwiyah said, "If two men should die, they would not die, while if one man should die, he would die. If I should die, my son would succeed me, and if Saʿīd should die, ʿAmr would succeed him; but if ʿAbdallāh b. ʿĀmir should die, he would die [without a successor]." Marwān heard of it and asked, "Did he mention my son, ʿAbd al-Malik?" When he was told that Muʿāwiyah had not, he remarked, "I would not exchange my son for both of theirs."

I was told by Aḥmad—ʿAlī—ʿAbdallāh b. Ṣāliḥ: Someone asked Muʿāwiyah, "Which person do you like the most?" He replied, "The one who shows the most love to the people for me." Muʿāwiyah also said, "Intelligence and forbearance are the best things granted to mankind. If someone is reminded, he should remember; if someone is granted [something], he should be thankful; if someone is tested, he should be steadfast; if someone is angry, he should suppress [it]; if someone has power [over another], he should forgive; if someone does wrong, he should ask forgiveness; and if someone makes a promise, he should carry it out."

I was told by Aḥmad—ʿAlī b. ʿAbdallāh and Hishām b. Saʿīd—ʿAbd al-Malik b. ʿUmayr: A man was rude to Muʿāwiyah and did it constantly. When Muʿāwiyah was asked, "Are you gentle with this [man]?" He answered, "I do not come between people and their tongues as long as they do not come between us and our rule."

I was told by Aḥmad—ʿAlī—Muḥammad b. ʿĀmir: Muʿāwiyah criticized ʿAbdallāh b. Jaʿfar about singing. One day he entered Muʿāwiyah's presence while Budayḥ was with him, and Muʿāwiyah had his legs crossed. At that, ʿAbdallāh said to Budayḥ, "Well, O Budayḥ, so you sing." When Muʿāwiyah moved his foot,—ʿAbdallāh asked, "What is it, O Commander of the Faithful?" Muʿāwiyah replied, "The noble is joyful." ʿAbdallāh b. Jaʿfar also came to Muʿāwiyah accompanied by Sā'ib Khāthir, a mawlā of the Banū Layth, who was immoral.[589] Muʿāwiyah told him, "Mention what you need" He did, and mentioned a need of Sā'ib Khāthir as well. Muʿāwiyah then inquired, "Who is this?" When he told him, Muʿāwiyah said, "Admit him." When Sā'ib stood at the door of the audience chamber (*majlis*), he sang: [215]

The traces of the settlements are desolate,
the winds play with them and the dripping rain.

And it has been without occupants
for eight or ten years,

And the saffron upon her upper chest,
the throat and the upper chest choking with it.

At that, Muʿāwiyah exclaimed, "Well done!" and took care of his needs.[590]

I was told by ʿAbdallāh b. Aḥmad—his father—Sulaymān—ʿAbdallāh—Maʿmar—Hammām b. Munabbih—Ibn ʿAbbās: "I never saw anyone more suitable for sovereignty than Muʿāwiyah. Indeed people used to find him like the sides of a broad valley. He was not like the narrow, blocked opening," that is, Ibn al-Zubayr.

I was told by ʿAbdallāh—his father—Sulaymān b. ʿUyaynah—Mujālid—al-Shaʿbī—Qabīṣah b. Jābir al-Asadī: I shall certainly inform you about those with whom I associated. I associated with ʿUmar b. al-Khaṭṭāb, and I never saw a man more comprehending with regard to knowledge (*fiqh*), nor better at discussing (things). Then I associated with Ṭalḥah b. ʿUbaydallāh, and I never saw a man who gave more abundantly without being asked than he. Then I associated with Muʿāwiyah, and I never saw a man who liked a friend more than he, or who was

589. Iṣfahānī, *Aghānī*, VII, 188: "a merchant."
590. Ibid., 189.

[216] more the same in private and in public. If al-Mughīrah were put in al-Madīnah, he would not exit from any of its doors[591] unless he did so by treachery.[592]

---

591. The text reads: *abwāb*, which could also mean "gates", but al-Madīnah is not supposed to have been walled in this period.

592. Co reads: "by excuses." C adds: "end of the tenth volume, and, if God wills, what is subsequent will follow it."

BIBLIOGRAPHY

(Works Cited only)

Abbott, Nabia. *Aishah the Beloved of Mohammad.* Chicago: University of Chicago Press, 1942.

'Abd Dixon, A. A. *The Umayyad Caliphate 65–86/684–705 (A Political Study).* London: Luzac & Company, 1971.

Baethgen, Friedrich. *Fragmente syrischer und arabischer Historiker.* Lichtenstein: Kraus Reprint Ltd., 1966.

al-Baghdādī, 'Abd al-Qādir 'Umar. *Al-Khizānat al-Adab.* Cairo: Dār al-Kātib al-'Arabī li-l-Ṭabā'ah wa-l-Nashar, 1967.

al-Bakrī, Abū 'Ubaydallāh b. 'Abd al-Azīz. *Mu'jam mā Ista'jam.* Edited by Saqqā'. Cairo, 1945–51.

al-Balādhurī, Aḥmad b. Yaḥya. *Anṣāb al-Ashrāf.* Vol. 1, edited by M. Hamīdallāh. Cairo, 1959. Vol. 4a, edited by M. Schloessinger and M. Kister. Jerusalem: Hebrew University Press, 1971. Vol. 4b, edited by M. Schloessinger. Jerusalem: Hebrew University Press, 1938. Vol. 5, edited by S. D. Goitein. Jerusalem: Hebrew University Press, 1936.

________. *Kitāb Futūḥ al-Buldān.* Edited by M. J. de Geoje. Leiden: Brill, 1866.

Barthold, W. (V. V. Bartol'd). *Turkestan down to the Mongol Invasion.* 4th edition. London, 1977.

Behrnauer, W. "Mémoire sur les institutions de police chez les arabes, les persans, et les turcs." *Journal Asiatique* 5, no. 15 (1860): 461–508; no. 16 (1860); 114–190, 347–392; no. 17 (1861): 5–76.

Bevan, A. A. *The Naḳā'iḍ of Jarīr and al-Farazdaḳ.* Leiden: Brill, 1905–12.

Bosworth, Clifford. *Sīstān under the Arabs, from the Islamic Conquest to the Rise of the Ṣaffārids (30–250/651–864).* Rome: Istituto Italiano per il medio ed estremo oriente, 1968.

Boucher, R. *Divan de Férazdak*. Paris: Adolphe Labitte, 1870.
al-Buḥturī, al-Walīd b. ʿUbayd. *Al-Hamāsah*. Edited by Louis Cheikho. Beirut: Dār al-Kitāb al-ʿArabī, 1387(1967).
al-Bukhārī, Muḥammad b. Ismāʿīl. *Ṣaḥīḥ al-Bukhārī*. Vols. 1–6. Cairo: Al-Majlis al-Aʿlā li-l-shuʿūn al-Islamiyyah, 1973.
Dennett, D. *Conversion and the Poll Tax in Early Islam*. Cambridge: Harvard University Press, 1950.
al-Dīnawarī, Abū Ḥanīfah Aḥmad b. Da'ūd. *Kitāb al-Akhbār al-Ṭiwāl*. Leiden: Brill, 1912.
Duri, A. A. "Al-Zuhrī, A Study on the beginnings of history writing in Islam." *BSOAS* 19 (1957): 1–12.
EI[1], *Encyclopaedia of Islam*. 1st. edition. Leiden: Brill, 1913–1934.
EI[2], *Encyclopaedia of Islam*. 2nd. edition. Leiden: Brill, 1960–.
El-ʿAlī, S. "Al-Madā'in and its surrounding area in Arabic literary sources." *Mesopotamia* 3–4 (1968–69): 422–25.
El-ʿAlī, S. "Minṭaqat al-Kūfa," *Sumer* 21 (1965): 229–53.
Fariq, K. A. "A Remarkable Early Muslim Governor, Ziyād ibn Abih." *IC* 26 no. 4 (1952): 1–31.
Freytag, G. W. *Arabum Proverbia*. Bonn: A. Marcum, 1838–43.
Frye, R. "The Sasanian System of Walls for Defense." *Studies in Memory of Gaston Wiet*, edited by Miriam Rosen-Ayalon, 7–15. Jerusalem, 1977.
Grohmann, A. *From the World of Arabic Papyri*. Cairo: Al-Maaref Press, 1952.
Gullini, G. "Problems of an excavation in northern Babylonia." *Mesopotamia* 1 (1966): 7–38.
Hinz, Walther. *Islamische Masse und Gewichte*. Leiden: Brill, 1970.
Ibn ʿAbd Rabbihi, Abū Aḥmad b. Muḥammad. *Kitāb al-ʿIqd al-Farīd*. Cairo: Maṭbaʿah Lajnat, 1367–72 (1948–53).
Ibn Abī al-Ḥadīd. *Sharḥ Nahj al-Balāghah*. Cairo: ʿĪsā al-Bābī al-Halabī, 1959–64.
Ibn Aʿtham al-Kūfī, Aḥmad b. ʿUthmān. *Kitāb al-Futūḥ*. Haydarabad, 1391 (1971).
Ibn al-Athīr, ʿIzz ad-Dīn. *Al-Kāmil fi al-Ta'rīkh*. Beirut: Dār Sāder, 1385 (1965)
———. *Usd al-Ghābah fi Maʿrifat al-Ṣahābah*. Cairo, 1285–87 (1868–70).
Ibn Durayd, Abū Bakr Muḥammad b. al-Ḥasan al-Azdī. *Kitāb al-Ishtiqāq*. Edited by F. Wüstenfeld. Göttingen: Dieterische Buchhandlung, 1854.
Ibn al-Faqīh. *Mukhtasar Kitāb al-Buldān*. Leiden: Brill, 1885.

Ibn Hajar al-Asqalānī, Aḥmad b. 'Alī. *Al-Iṣābah fi Tamyīz al-Ṣaḥābah*. Cairo: Maṭba'ah al-Sa'adah, 1328 (1910).
Ibn Hishām. *Kitāb Sīrat Rasūl Allāh, Das Leben Muhammed's*. Edited by F. Wüstenfeld. Göttingen, 1858–60.
Ibn Khayyāṭ, Khalīfah al-'Uṣfurī. *Ta'rīkh*. Edited by A. al-'Umarī. Najaf: Al-Ādab Press, 1386 (1969).
Ibn Manẓūr, Jamāl al-Dīn. *Lisān al-'Arab*. Vols. 1–15. Beirut: Dār Sāder, 1955–56.
Ibn Qutaybah, 'Abdallāh b. Muslim. *Kitāb al-Ma'ārif*. Cairo: Dār al-Ma'ārif, 1969.
_______. *Kitāb al-Shi'r wa-l-Shu'arā'*. Beirut: Dār al-Thaqāfah, 1964.
_______. *'Uyūn al-Akhbār*. Cairo: Al-Mu'assasah al-Miṣriyyah al-'Āmmah li-l-Ta'līf wa-l-Tarjamah wa-l-Tabā'ah wa-l-Nashar, 1964.
Ibn Rustah, Aḥmad b. 'Umar. *Al-A'lāq al-Nafīsah*. Edited by M. de Goeje. Bibliotheca Geographorum Arabicorum, no. 7. Leiden: Brill, 1891.
Ibn Sa'd, Muḥammad. *Kitāb al-Ṭabaqāt*, Vol. 6. Leiden: Brill, 1909. Vol. 7. Leiden: Brill, 1919.
Ibn Ṭabāṭabā, Muḥammad b. 'Alī. *Kitāb al-Fakhrī fī Ādab al-Sulṭāniyyah wa-l-Duwal al-Islāmiyyah*. Paris, 1895; Beirut, 1386 (1966). Translated by C. E. J. Whitting under the title *al-Fakhri: On the Systems of Government and the Moslem Dynasties*. London, 1947.
al-Iṣfahānī, Abū al-Farāj. *Kitāb al-Aghānī*. Bulāq, 1258 (1868–69).
Jafri, S. H. M. *The Origins and Early Development of Shī'a Islam*. London and New York: Longman Group Ltd, 1979. Beirut: Librairie du Liban, 1979.
Jāḥiẓ, 'Amr b. Bahr. *Al-Bayān wa-l-Tabyīn*. Beirut: Dār al-Mashriq, 1388 (1968)
_______. *Al-Ḥayawān*. Cairo: Muṣṭafā al-Bābī al-Ḥalabī, 1364–56 (1938–45).
al-Kharbūṭlī, 'Alī Ḥusnī. *Al-Mukhtār al-Thaqafī, Mir'at al-'Asr al-Umawī*. Cairo: Al-Mu'sasat al-Miṣriyyat al-'Āmmah li-l-Ta'līf wa-l-Tarjamah wa-l-Ṭabā'ah wa-l-Nashar, 1962.
Kohlberg, Etan. "Abū Turāb." *BSOAS* 41 (1978): 347–52.
Lammens, Henri. "Ziad ibn Abihi vice-roi de l'Iraq, lieutenant de Mo'āwia I." *RSO* 4 (1911–12): 1–45, 199–225, 653–93.
Lavoix, H. *Catalogue des monnaies musulmanes de la Bibliothèque nationale: Khalifes orientaux*. Paris: Imprimerie nationale, 1887.

Lichtenstadter, I. "From Particularism to Unity: Race, Nationality and Minorities in the Early Islamic Empire." *IC* 23 (1949): 251–80.

Løkkegaard, F. *Islamic Taxation in the Classic Period with Special Reference to Circumstances in Iraq*. Copenhagen: Branner & Korch, 1950.

al-Marzūqī, Abū 'Alī Aḥmad b. Muḥammad b. al-Ḥasan. *Sharḥ Dīwān al-Hamāsah*. Cairo: Maṭba'ah Lajnat al-Ta'līf, 1371 (1951).

al-Mas'ūdī, Abū al-Ḥasan 'Alī b. al-Ḥusayn. *Murūj al-Dhahab wa-l-Ma'ādin al-Jawhar*. Translated and edited by C. Barbier de Meynard and pavet de Courteille under the title of *Les prairies d'or*. Paris: Imprimerie nationale, 1861–77.

al-Maydānī, Aḥmad b. Muḥammad. *Majma' al-Amthāl*. Cairo: Maṭba'ah al-Sa'ārah bi-Miṣr, 1379 (1959).

Miles, G. *Contributions to Arab Metrology*. I. *Numismatic Notes and Monographs*, no. 141. New York: The American Numismatic Society, 1958.

———, *Early Arabic Glass Weights and Stamps. A Supplement. Numismatic Notes and Monographs*, no. 120. New York: The American Numismatic Society, 1951.

———, *Excavation Coins from the Persepolis Region. Numismatic Notes and Monographs*, no. 143. New York: The American Numismatic Society, 1959.

———, *The Numismatic History of Rayy. Numismatic Studies*, no. 2. New York: The American Numismatic Society, 1938.

Montgomery Watt, W. *The Formative Period of Islamic Thought*. Edinburgh: Edinburgh University Press, 1973.

Morony, M. "Continuity and Change in the Administrative Georgraphy of Late Sasanian and Early Islamic al-'Irāq." *Iran* 20 (1982): 1–49.

al-Mubarrad, Muḥammad b. Yazīd. *Kitāb al-Kāmil*. Leipzig: G. Kreysing, 1864–92.

Musil, Alois. *The Middle Euphrates*. New York: Charles R. Crane, 1927.

Muṣṭafā, Ibrāhīm, et al. *Al-Mu'jam al-Wasīṭ*. Cairo, 1380–81 (1960–61).

Narshakhī, Abū Bakr Muḥammad b. Ja'far. *Tārīkh-ī Bukhārā*. Edited by Razavī. Teheran: Bunyad-i Farhang-i Iran, 1352 (1972) Translated by R. Frye under the title of *The History of Bukhārā*. Cambridge: Mediaeval Academy of America, 1954.

al-Nawawī, Abū Zakariyā Muḥyī ad-Dīn b. Sharaf. *Tahdhīb al-Asmā' wa-l-Lughāt*. Beirut: Dār al-Kutub al-Ilmīyah, 1927.

Nyberg, H. "Die sassanidische Westgrenze und ihre Verteidigung." *Septentrionalia et Orientalia.* 316–26. Stockholm, 1961.
Petersen, E. L. *'Alī and Mu'āwiya in Early Arabic Tradition.* Odense: Odense University Press, 1974.
al-Ṣāwī, 'Abdallāh Isma'īl. *Sharḥ Dīwān al-Farazdaq.* Cairo: Maṭba'ah Muṣṭafā Muḥammad, 1354 (1936).
Sezgin, U. *Abū Miḫnaf. Ein Beitrag zur Historiographie der umaiyadischen Zeit.* Leiden: Brill, 1971.
Shaban, M. A. *The 'Abbāsid Revolution.* Cambridge: At the University Press, 1970.
Sirhān b. 'Umar b. Sa'īd. *Kashf al-Ghummah,* Brit. Mus. ms. Or. 8076.
LeStrange, Guy. *The Lands of the Eatern Caliphate.* Cambridge: At the University Press, 1905.
Suhrāb b. Sarābiyūn. *Kitāb 'Ajā'ib al-Aqālīm al-Sab'ah.* Edited by H. von Mžik. Bibliothek Arabischer Historiker und Geographen, no. 5. Leipzig: Harrassowitz, 1930.
al-Ṭabarī, Abū Ja'far Muḥammad. *Ta'rīkh al-Rusul wa-l-Mulūk.* Leiden: Brill, 1879.
———. *Ta'rīkh al-umam wa-l-mulūk.* Edited by M. A. Ibrahim. Cairo: Maṭba'a al-Istiḳāma, 1357–58 (1939).
Ṭarafah b. al-'Abd al-Bakrī. *Dīwān.* Translated and edited by Max Seligsohn. Paris: E. Bouillon, 1901.
Tārīkh-i Sīstān. Edited by Malik al-Shu'arā Bihār. Teheran, 1314 (1935).
Vollers, K., "Die Geschichte des Mutalammis." *Beiträge zur Assyriologie* 5 (1906): 149–231.
Wensinck, A. J. *A Handbook of Early Muhammadan Tradition.* Leiden: E. J. Brill, 1960.
Wright, William. *A Grammar of the Arabic Language.* Cambridge: At the University Press, 1964.
al-Ya'qūbī, Aḥmad b. Abī Ya'qūb. *Ta'rīkh.* Leiden: Brill, 1883.
Yāqūt b. 'Abdallāh al-Ḥamawī. *Mu'jam al-Buldān.* Leipzig: Brill, 1866.
al-Ziriklī, Khayr al-Dīn. *Al-A'lām.* 4th edition Beirut: Dār al-'Ilm al-Malāyīn, 1979.

Index

A

Abān b. Ṣāliḥ 101.
ʿAbbād b. Ziyād 16, 201, 202, 203, 204, 214.
ʿAbbādān 13.
ʿAbbāsid 19.
ʿAbd al-Mālik b. ʿAbdallāh al-Thaqafī 27.
ʿAbd al-Mālik b. Marwān (Caliph 685–705) 14, 18, 46, 101, 102, 173, 224.
ʿAbd al-Mālik b. Mīnās al-Kalbī 212.
ʿAbd al-Mālik b. Nawfal b. Masāḥiq 153, 208, 213.
ʿAbd al-Mālik b. Qurayb al-Aṣmāʿī 168.
ʿAbd al-Mālik b. ʿUmayr 211, 224.
ʿAbd al-Qādir al-Baghdādī 123, 188.
ʿAbd al-Qays (Banū) 36, 38, 40, 42, 44, 73, 204.
ʿAbd al-Raḥmān, 28.
ʿAbd al-Raḥmān b. Abān al-Qurashī 163.
ʿAbd al-Raḥmān b. ʿAbdallāh b. ʿUthmān al-Thaqafī 137, 192, 193.
ʿAbd al-Raḥmān b. Abī Bakr 91, 186, 187, 209.
ʿAbd al-Raḥmān b. Abī Bakrah 26, 27.
ʿAbd al-Raḥmān b. Abī Sabrah al-Juʿfī 143.
ʿAbd al-Raḥmān b. Ḥabīb 45, 61, 63.
ʿAbd al-Raḥmān b. al-Ḥakam 205, 223.
ʿAbd al-Raḥmān b. Hannād 142.
ʿAbd al-Raḥmān b. al-Ḥārith b. Hishām 153.
ʿAbd al-Raḥmān b. Ḥassān al-ʿAnazī 144, 149, 150, 151.
ʿAbd al-Raḥmān b. Jundab 55, 56, 141, 193.
ʿAbd al-Raḥmān b. Khālid b. al-Walīd 87, 88, 89.
ʿAbd al-Raḥmān b. Masʿūd 183.
ʿAbd al-Raḥmān b. Mikhnaf 132.
ʿAbd al-Raḥmān b. Muʿāwiyah 215.
ʿAbd al-Raḥmān b. Muḥammad b. al-Ashʿath 64.
ʿAbd al-Raḥmān b. Muḥriz al-Ṭumahī 133.
ʿAbd al-Raḥmān b. Muljam al-Murādī, see Ibn Muljam 22.
ʿAbd al-Raḥmān b. Qays al-Asadī 143.
ʿAbd al-Raḥmān b. Ṣāliḥ 74.
ʿAbd al-Raḥmān b. Samurah 85.
ʿAbd al-Raḥmān b. Ṣubḥ 119, 120.
ʿAbd al-Raḥmān b. ʿUbayd, see Abū al-Kanūd 111, 141.

'Abd al-Raḥmān b. 'Umar b. Umm al-Ḥakam al-Thaqafī, see Ibn Umm al-Ḥakam 147, 166, 195, 198, 199.
'Abd al-Raḥmān b. Ziyād 199, 200, 207.
'Abd al-Raḥmān b. al-Walīd 71.
'Abd al-Shams (Banū) 9, 107.
'Abdallāh 9.
'Abdallāh (title) 46.
'Abdallāh b. 'Abbās, see Ibn 'Abbās 3, 9, 14.
'Abdallāh b. Abī 'Aqīl al-Thaqafī 87, 124, 142.
'Abdallāh b. Abī Balta'ah 137.
'Abdallāh b. Abī al-Hurr 13.
'Abdallāh b. Abī Shaykh 72.
'Abdallāh b. Aḥmad b. Mattawayhi al-Marrūdhī, 2, 7.
'Abdallāh b. Aḥmad b. Shabbawayh al-Marwazī 2, 9, 77, 167, 168, 169, 217, 218, 219, 221, 222, 225.
'Abdallāh b. Ahtam 81.
'Abdallāh b. 'Āmir, see Ibn 'Āmir, Ibn Dajājah, and Ibn Umm Ḥakīm 18, 21, 50, 68, 70, 71, 224.
'Abdallāh b. 'Amr b. al-'Āṣ 13, 32, 91, 222.
'Abdallāh b. 'Amr b. Ghaylān 76, 175, 179, 180, 181.
'Abdallāh b. 'Awf b. al-Aḥmar 129.
'Abdallāh b Awfah, see Ibn al-Kawwā' 31, 72.
'Abdallāh b. Aws al-Ṭāḥī 100.
'Abdallāh b. Budayl al-Khuzā'ī 10.
'Abdallāh b. Faḍālah al-Laythī 85.
'Abdallāh b. al-Ḥajjāj al-Taghlibī 143.
'Abdallāh b. Hammam al-Salūlī 98, 131.
'Abdallāh b. al-Ḥārith al-Azdī 50, 57, 60, 134, 136.
'Abdallāh b. al-Ḥārith b. Nawfal 20, 95.
'Abdallāh b. Ḥawīyah al-Sa'dī al-Tamīmī, see Ibn Ḥawīyah 145, 152.
'Abdallāh b. Ḥiṣn 83, 175, 181.
'Abdallāh b. Ja'far b. Abī Ṭālib 11, 200, 224, 225.
'Abdallāh b. Khālid b. Asīd 170, 171, 175, 179, 182.
'Abdallāh b. Khalīfah al-Ṭā'ī 130, 139, 140, 156, 157, 162.
'Abdallāh b. Khāzim b. Ẓabyān 29, 30, 68, 69, 70, 179.
'Abdallāh b. Kurz al-Bajalī 94.
'Abdallāh b. Mas'adah (or Mas'ūd) b. Ḥakamah al-Fazārī 165, 222
'Abdallāh b. Miḥṣan al-Ḥimyarī 216.
'Abdallāh b. Mu'āwiyah, see Abū al-Khayr 215.
'Abdallāh b. al-Mubārik 2, 7, 77, 167, 168, 169, 217, 218, 219, 221, 225.
'Abdallāh b. Qays al-Fazārī 93, 180, 191.

'Abdallāh b. al-Rabī' b. Ziyād al-Ḥārithī 170.
'Abdallāh b. Sabā' 49.
'Abdallāh b. Ṣāliḥ 224.
'Abdallāh b. Shawdhab 167.
'Abdallāh b. 'Umar b. al-Khaṭṭāb, see Ibn 'Umar 167, 208, 209.
'Abdallāh b. 'Uqbah (or 'Utbah) al-Ghanawī, see al-Ghanawī, 45, 55, 56, 61, 63, 65, 193.
'Abdallāh b. Wahb al-Rāsibī 39.
'Abdallāh b. al-Zubayr, see Ibn al-Zubayr 22, 208, 217.
'Abbād b. Ziyād 200.
Abhar 161.
Abrahah b. al-Ṣabbāḥ 221.
Abraham 82.
Abrashahr, see Aparshahr and Nīshāpūr 85, 179.
'Abs (Banū) 138.
Abū 'Abd al-Mālik, see Marwān b. al-Ḥakam 117, 174.
Abū 'Abd al-Raḥmān, see Mu'āwiyah b. Abī Sufyān 215.
Abū 'Abd al-Raḥmān, see Ḥujr b. 'Adī 136.
Abū 'Abd al-Raḥmān al-Iṣfahānī (or al-Iṣbahānī) 29, 72.
Abū 'Abd al-Raḥmān al-Qaynī 91.
Abū 'Abd al-Raḥmān al-Thaqafī 69.
Abū 'Abdallāh, see 'Amr b. al-'Āṣ 222.
Abū 'Abdallāh, see al-Mughīrah b. Shu'bah 77.
Abū 'Abdallāh Muḥammad b. 'Umar al-Wāqidī 11.
Abū al-'Amarraṭah, see 'Umayr b. Yazīd al-Kindī 129, 130, 131.
Abū 'Amr 199.
Abū 'Amr 'Āmir b. Sharāḥīl, see al-Sha'bī 18.
Abū al-A'war al-Sulamī 148.
Abū Ayyūb al-Anṣārī 94.
Abū Baḥr, Ṣakhr b. Qays, see al-Aḥnaf b. Qays 81, 201
Abū Bakr (Caliph 632–634) 46, 222.
Abū Bakr al-Hudhalī 78, 179.
Abū Bakrah, Nufay' b. Masrūḥ 14, 15, 17, 171.
Abū Bilāl, see Mirdās b. Udayyah 81, 100, 196, 197.
Abū Burdah b. Abī Mūsā al-Ash'arī 140, 141, 219.
Abū Ḥafṣ 200.
Abū Ḥardabah 189.
Abū al-Ḥasan al-Madā'inī, see 'Alī b. Muḥammad al-Madā'inī 26, 27, 71, 72, 73, 78, 104, 177, 181, 188.
Abū al-Ḥasan b. Ḥammād 224.
Abū Ḥumrān b. Bujayr al-Hamdānī 52.
Abū Hurayrah 101.
Abū Idrīs 'Ā'idhallāh b. 'Abdallāh 216.
Abū Imāmah 'Ubaydallāh b. Junādah 59.

Abū Isḥāq 74, 136, 137, 154.
Abū Ismāʿīl al-Hamdānī 183.
Abū Jaʿfar, see al-Ṭabarī 33.
Abū Jād 176.
Abū al-Kanūd, see ʿAbd al-Raḥmān b. ʿUbayd 141.
Abū al-Khayr, see ʿAbdallāh b. Muʿāwiyah 215.
Abū Khuṣaylah, see ʿĪsā b. Khuṣaylah 107.
Abū Luʾluʾ al-Ḍabbī 15.
Abū Maʿshar, Najīḥ b. ʿAbd al-Raḥmān, see Maʿshar 19, 31, 165, 171, 179, 182, 183, 191, 192, 198, 206, 210.
Abū Maythāʾ, see Muḥammad b. al-Ashʿath 134.
Abū Mikhnaf 1, 21, 24, 29, 38, 43, 44, 45, 50, 51, 55, 56, 57, 59, 60, 61, 63, 65, 68, 69, 122, 123, 125, 127, 129, 132, 136, 141, 144, 153, 154, 156, 193, 208, 213.
Abū al-Mughīrah, see Ziyād b. Abīhi 28, 31, 77.
Abū al-Muhājir 103.
Abū Muḥammad al-Umawī 218.
Abū Muḥammad b. Dhakwān al-Qurashī 174, 220.
Abū al-Mukhāriq, see Mālik 216.
Abū al-Mukhtār 216.
Abū Mūsā al-Ashʿarī, see al-Ashʿarī 92, 103, 219.
Abū Mūsā al-Faḍl b. Mūsā b. Khuṣaylah 107.
Abū Mushīr 6.
Abū al-Naḍr b. Ṣāliḥ 44.
Abū al-Najm al-Rājiz 111.
Abū al-Raḥmān al-Thaqafī 86.
Abū al-Rawwāgh al-Shākirī 51, 52, 53, 54, 60, 61, 62, 63, 65, 66, 67.
Abū Saʿīd al-Maqburī, See Saʿīd b. Abī Saʿīd 153.
Abū Ṣāliḥ Sulaymān b. Ṣāliḥ 219.
Abū Salimah b. ʿAbd al-Raḥmān b. Awf 95.
Abū Sawwār al-ʿAdawī 99.
Abū Sharīf (or Sharīfah) al-Baddī 148, 149.
Abū al-Shaʿthā 100.
Abū Sufyān, see Ṣakhr b. Ḥarb 73, 74, 153, 202, 206, 215.
Abū Sufyān b. ʿUwaymir 129.
Abū Ṭālib 141.
Abū Turāb, see ʿAlī b. Abī Ṭālib 98, 138, 141.
Abū ʿUbaydah Maʿmar b. al-Muthannā 101, 104, 107, 111, 113, 188, 202, 205, 211.
Abū 04ʾUthmān, see Saʿīd b. al-ʿĀṣ 174, 175.
Abū Uzayhir al-Dawsī 200
Abū Yaʿqūb al-Thaqafī 211.
Abū Zayd al-Anṣārī, Saʿīd b. Aws 18, 19, 104, 203, 205.
Abyssinian 187.
Adam 22.
ʿAdas 204.
ʿAdasah bt. Mālik b. ʿAwf al-Kalbī 34.

Adharbayjān 2.
'Adhrā', see Marj 'Adhrā' 147, 152, 158.
Adhruḥ 8, 10, 92, 210.
'Adī b. Ḥātim 42, 139, 140, 155, 156, 157, 160.
'Adī b. Ḥātim, Mosque of 139.
'Adī (Banū) 155.
Admā' 134.
Aelia Capitolina, see Īliyā and Jerusalem 6.
Afghanistan 18.
al-Afnā' 160.
Aḥmad b. 'Alī 16, 17.
Aḥmad b. Thābit al-Rāzī 19, 31, 164, 179, 182, 183, 191, 192, 206, 210.
Aḥmad b. Zuhayr 15, 74, 211, 212, 213, 215, 216, 218, 219, 220, 222, 223, 224.
Aḥmarī 129.
al-Aḥnaf b. Qays, see Abū Baḥr, Ṣakhr b. Qays Mu'āwiyah al-Tamīmī 81, 105, 163, 201, 203, 219.
al-Ahwāz 19, 90, 197, 198, 206.
'Ā'idh b. Ḥamalah al-Tamīmī 130.
'Ā'ishah bt. Abī Bakr 39, 127, 153.
Ajah, Mt, 157.
'Ajlān b. Rabī'ah 129.
al-A'lā b. Maymūn 212.
Alans 20.
'Alī b. Abī Ṭālib, see Abū Turab 2, 3, 6, 9, 11, 12, 14, 15, 16, 17, 18, 19, 21, 22, 24, 27, 30, 31, 39, 42, 43, 44, 46, 48, 49, 50, 98, 123, 124, 126, 138, 139, 149, 150, 151, 211, 221, 222, 223.
'Alī b. 'Abdallāh 224.
'Alī b. 'Abdallāh b. 'Abbās 19.
'Alī b. Abī Shimr 35, 36.
'Ālī b. Ḥasan 126.
'Alī b. Muḥammad al-Madā'inī, see Abū al-Ḥasan 9, 14, 15, 16, 17, 18, 19, 21, 26, 29, 31, 69, 70, 72, 73, 76, 78, 82, 85, 86, 88, 90, 96, 97, 99, 120, 121, 163, 164, 167, 170, 173, 174, 175, 176, 177, 178, 179, 180, 181, 183, 184, 185, 187, 188, 189, 199, 200, 201, 210, 211, 212, 213, 214, 215, 216, 218, 219, 220, 222, 223, 224.
'Alī b. Mujāhid 176, 183, 212, 218.
'Alī b. 'Ubaydallāh 222.
'Alī b. Zahdam 110.
'Alī (Banū) 100.
amīr 37, 45, 81, 82, 84, 100, 117, 138, 154, 181, 203, 217, 220.
Amīr al-Mu'minīn (Commander of the Faithful) 6.
'Āmir b. Juwayn 24.
'Āmir b. al-Aswad al-'Ijlī 145, 147.
'Āmir b. Shahrān (Banū) 144.
'Āmir b. Mas'ūd b. Umayyah b. Khalaf 142.
'Āmir (Banū) 14.
'Amīrah b. Yathribī al-Ḍabbī 18.

ʿAmr b. ʿAmr 169.
ʿAmr b. al-ʿĀṣ, Abū ʿAbdallāh, see Ibn al-Nābighah 8, 9, 10, 91, 92, 217, 221, 222, 223, 224.
ʿAmr b. Hāshim 74.
ʿAmr b. al-Ḥamiq 31, 98, 99, 129, 130, 137.
ʿAmr b. al-Ḥurayth 98, 99, 126, 140.
ʿAmr b. Muḥriz b. Shihāb al-Saʿdī al-Minqarī 68, 180.
ʿAmr b. Murrah al-Juhanī 199.
ʿAmr b. Yarbūʿ 188.
ʿAmr b. Yathribī al-Ḍabbī 18.
ʿAmr b. Yazīd al-Juhanī 192.
ʿAmr b. al-Zubayr 217.
Amū Daryā 164.
Anas b. Abī Unās b. Zunaym 87, 121, 163.
Anas b. Mālik 85.
ʿAnazah (Banū) 144.
al-ʿAnbar (Banū) 134.
ʿAnbasah b. Abī Sufyān 19, 31, 92, 220, 221.
Anṣār 132.
Anṣārī 155.
Anṭākiyah (Antioch) 93.
Aparshahr, see Abrashahr and Nīshāpūr 179.
Arab 11, 14, 27, 39, 117, 150.
Arabia 157, 163, 189.
Arabic 8, 45.
Arabs 3, 10, 12, 20, 36, 72, 74, 170, 214.
ʿArafat 6, 73.
Arch of al-Jaʿd 83.
Arḥab (Banū) 108–9.
Arḥabiyyah 108, 109.
al-Arqam b. ʿAbdallāh al-Kindī 144, 148, 152.
al-Arqam (Banū) 144.
Arrajān 28, 29, 198.
al-ʿArūḍ 167.
Arwād 172.
ʿArzam 143.
Asad (Banū) 99, 110, 131, 132, 140, 162.
Āsak, see Āsik 198.
al-Aʿshā 184.
al-Ashall 119, 120.
Ashʿarī, see Abū Mūsā 92.
Ashʿath al-Ḥuddānī 99.
al-Ashʿath b. Qays 31.
al-Ashhab b. Rumaylah al-Nahshalī 104, 213.
Ashjaʿ (Banū) 13.
al-Ashtar 134, 136.
Āsik, see Āsak 198.
ʿĀsim b. ʿAwf al-Bajalī 144, 152.
ʿĀsim b. Faḍālah al-Laythī 85.
Aslam b. Zurʿah al-Kilābī 69, 86, 177, 190
Asmāʾ b. Khārijah al-Fazārī 142.
Aʿṣur 131, 132.
al-Aswad b. Qays al-ʿAbdī 38, 43.
ʿAṭāʾ b. Abī Marwan 26.
al-ʿAtīq 112.
Athālah b. Māzin (Banū) 189.
ʿAttāb 57, 58.
ʿAwānah b. al-Ḥakam al-Kalbī 4, 11, 12, 96, 125, 126, 136, 200, 209, 218.
al-Aʿwar Hudbah b. Fiyāḍ 148, 150.

'Awf 99.
'Awfā b. Ḥiṣn 97, 98.
Aws b. Tha'labah al-Taymī 188.
al-Awzā'ī 212.
Āy 78.
A'yān b. Labataḥ b. al-Farazdaq 104, 110, 113.
Aymān b. Khuraym 223.
'Ayn al-Ṣayd 8.
'Ayn Tamr 13.
Azd (Banū) 39, 86, 100, 129, 132, 134.
'Azrah b. 'Azrah al-Aḥmasī 143.

B

al-Ba'īth 104.
Bāb al-Fīl 31.
al-Baddī, see 'Ubaydah b. 'Amr al-Kindī 162.
Bādghīs 85, 163, 164.
Badr, Battle of 33, 198.
Baghdād 9, 19.
al-Baḥrayn 78, 90, 123, 204.
Baḥriyyah bt. al-Mundhir 203.
Bahurasīr (or Behrasīr) 45, 46, 51, 61.
al-Bahzī, see 'Īsā b. Khuṣaylah 109.
Bajīlah (Banū) 132.
Bājumayrā 63, 64, 129.
Bakr b. 'Ubayd 129, 130.
Bakr b. Wā'il (Banū) 111.
Bakrī 112.
Balādhurī 1, 2, 8, 13, 23, 31, 33, 34, 82, 169, 179, 189, 190, 196, 206.
Balkh 163.
Baniqyā 112.
Baradā River 188.
barakah (blessing) 212.
barīd (post system) 118, 163.
Barqah 103.
barzakh (interval or barrier) 214.
Bashīr b. 'Ubaydallāh b. Abī Bakr 218.
al-Baṣrah 1, 9, 13, 14, 15, 18, 19, 21, 22, 26, 29, 39, 56, 69, 70, 71, 72, 73, 74, 76, 77, 78, 80, 81–2, 85, 87, 95, 96, 97, 98, 99, 100, 101, 103, 104, 108, 110, 111, 125, 126, 164, 167, 168, 170, 175, 177, 178, 179, 180, 181, 187, 191, 198, 200, 201, 203, 205, 206, 207, 220.
Baṣran 50, 58, 83, 126, 200.
Baṣrans 56, 72, 87.
al-batrā' (free) 78.
baṭrīq (pl. *baṭāriqah*) (general) 20.
bay'ah (oath of allegience) 2, 141, 218.
Bayhas b. Ṣuhayb al-Jarmī 58, 59.
Baykand, see Paykand 178.
Bazīqiyā 160.
bedouin 188.
Bint Marrār, see Rabī'ah bt. al-Marrār 110.
Bishāpūr, see Sābūr 30.
Book of God 46, 78, 120, 176.
Budayḥ 224.
Buhṭur (Banū) 140, 160.
Bujayr (Banū) 19.
Bukayr b. Ḥumrān al-Aḥmarī 139.

Bukhara 178, 179, 190.
Bukharans 179.
Bukhārī 2.
burnous 137, 219.
Bushanj, see Pūshang 85.
Busr b. Abī Arṭāt al-ʿĀmirī 14, 15, 16, 26, 32, 71, 96, 122, 165, 222, 223.
Busr b. ʿUbaydallāh 16.
Byzantine 71, 88, 91, 94, 96, 122, 165, 166, 169, 172, 180, 183, 191, 192, 199, 216, 221.
Byzantines 20, 32.

C

Caliph 1, 3, 6, 7, 10, 21, 22, 44, 48, 84, 101, 140, 141, 148, 174, 210, 211, 214, 216, 217, 223.
Caliphate 2, 8, 210.
caliphs 20, 46.
Camel, Battle of 8, 30, 39, 42, 44, 85.
Caucasus 20.
Cemetery of Ibn Ḥiṣn 83.
Cemetery of Shaybān, see Shaybān 85.
Central Asia 164, 189.
Christian 110, 189.
Christianity 42.
Christians 118.
Commander of the Faithful 6, 13, 16, 17, 27, 29, 30, 46, 47, 70, 72, 73, 74, 77, 101, 102, 120, 124, 127, 135, 139, 140, 141, 142, 145, 148, 149, 150, 173, 174, 175, 181, 184, 185, 186, 188, 196, 199, 200, 205, 213, 218, 219, 220, 222, 223, 224, 225.
Companion 19, 93, 157, 216.
Companions 85, 154, 200.
Constantinople 32, 172.
Cow, *Sūrah* of the 82.
Ctesiphon 45.
Cyprus 216.

D

Ḍabbah (Banū) 112, 180, 181.
Ḍabbīs 181.
dafr (goat's hair saddle girth) 115.
al-Daḥḥāk b. Qays al-Fihrī 179, 182, 187, 191, 192, 198, 209, 213.
Dajājah bt. Asmāʾ b. al-Ṣalt Sulamī 72.
Damascus 2, 144, 155, 188, 196, 210, 211, 214, 216.
Dār Ḥakīm 131.
Dārim b. Mālik b. Ḥanẓalah, (Banū) 107.
darajah (step) 172.
David 81.
Dāwūd b. Ḥayyān 26.
Day of Resurrection 48, 125, 214.
Daylām 22.
Daylamāyā 62.
Dayr al-Jamājim 64.
Dayr Kaʿb 64.
Deputy of God, see Khalīfat Allāh 84.
Devil 129.
devil 104.
dhirāʿah (or *dhirāʿ*) (cubit) 16, 53.
Dhū al-Ḥijjah 6.

Dhuhayl b.Ṣaʿṣaʿah 105.
Dhul (Banū) 134.
dihqān (landlord) 169.
Dijlah, see Tigris River 110.
Dīnawarī 12, 30, 31, 168.
Ḍirār (Banū) 181.
dīwān (military register) 105.
Diyala River 50.
Ḍubayʿah (Banū) 100.
Duwayyah 109.
Egypt 8, 13, 32, 102, 103, 196, 216, 221, 222.
Egyptian 103.
Egyptians 93, 217, 221.
Euphrates River 11, 62, 77.

F

Fadak 93, 172.
Faḍālah b. ʿUtbah (or ʿUbayd) al-Anṣārī 94, 96, 216.
Fākhitah bt. Qaraẓah b. ʿAbd ʿAmr 215.
Falj 110.
Farāwandah 92.
al-Farazdaq, see Hammām b. Ghālib 103, 104, 105, 106, 107, 108, 110, 112, 113, 114, 118, 119, 168, 169.
Farrūkh 164.
Fars 14, 15, 18, 26, 27, 28, 29, 30, 59, 70.
farsakh (six km.) 56.
farsakhs 62, 65, 178, 220.
Farwah b. Nawfal al-Ashjaʿī 12, 13.
al-Fāryāb 85.
*fay*ʾ (booty) 11, 46, 81.
Fīl (*mawlā* of Ziyād) 166.
Filasṭīn 221.
fiqh (knowledge) 225.
Followers 216.
Fuḍayl b. Khadīj 122.
Fulayḥ 217.
Fuqaym (Banū) 103, 104, 108, 118.
al-Furayyān 110.

G

Gawth b. Ṭayyiʾ 159, 160.
ghādiyah (early-flying birds) 116.
Ghālib 158.
Ghālib b. Faḍālah al-Laythī 93.
Ghālib b. Ṣaʿṣaʿah 104, 105.
Ghālib b. Sulaymān 119, 120.
al-Ghanawī, see ʿAbdallāh b. ʿUqbah 47.
Gharīyūn 144.
al-Ghāriyyān 110.
Ghassān b. Muḍar 100.
Ghaṭafān, Banū 131, 132.
Ghifār b. Mulayk 86.
ghilmān (servants) 51.
ghulām (servant) 35, 85.
Ghiyāth b. ʿImrān b. Murrah b. al-Ḥārith b. Dubb b. Murrah b. Dhūl b. Shaybān 156.
al-Ghūr 92.
Ghūṭah 188.
Ghuwayth 189.
Gīlān 162.
God 8, 10, 11, 12, 13, 15, 16, 17, 22, 23, 24, 25, 28, 30, 35, 37, 38, 39, 40, 41, 43, 44, 45, 46, 47, 48, 49, 50, 51, 52, 53, 54, 55, 57,

God (*continued*)
58, 59, 60, 61, 62, 63, 65, 66, 67, 68, 70, 74, 78, 79, 81, 82, 84, 86, 87, 89, 92, 97, 100, 101, 102, 103, 120, 121, 122, 123, 124, 125, 126, 127, 128, 129, 130, 132, 133, 134, 135, 136, 138, 139, 140, 141, 142, 143, 144, 145, 147, 148, 149, 150, 151, 152, 153, 154, 156, 157, 158, 159, 160, 167, 170, 171, 173, 174, 175, 176, 178, 184, 186, 187, 188, 193, 194, 195, 196, 197, 206, 210, 213, 214, 215, 217, 219, 220, 221, 222, 226.
God's Messenger 4.
Gulf 110.

H

Ḥabbān b. Mūsā 18.
Ḥabīb b. Maslamah al-Fihrī 148, 216.
Ḥabīb b. Shihāb al-Sha'mī 18.
ḥadīth (account about Muḥammad) 2, 126, 154.
Ḥaḍramawt 33, 132, 158.
al-Ḥaḍramī, see Sharīk b. Shaddād 149.
Ḥaḍramīs 160.
Hajar 204.
ḥājib (chamberlain) 74.
ḥajj (pilgrimage), see Pilgrimage 146.
al-Ḥajjāj b. Yūsuf 20, 64, 156.
Ḥajjār b. Abjar al-Ijlī 34, 35, 36, 142.
al-Ḥakam b. Abī al-ʿĀṣ al-Thaqafī 86.
al-Ḥakam b. ʿAmr al-Ghifārī 85, 86, 92, 119, 120, 121, 163, 164.
Ḥakkāk 100.
Hamadhān 161.
Hamām b. Qabīsah al-Namarī 190.
Ḥamdān (Banū) 18, 58, 109, 131, 132, 133, 137, 140.
Ḥamdānīs 143.
Hammām b. Ghālib b. Ṣaʿṣaʿah, see al-Farazdaq 103, 117.
Hammām b. Munabbih 225.
Hammām (Banū) 138.
Ḥamrā' 129, 156.
Ḥamzah (uncle of Muḥammad) 17.
Ḥamzah b. Ṣāliḥ al-Sulamī 21.
Ḥanbal 109.
Hānī b. Abī Hayyah 143.
Ḥanīfah (Banū) 163.
Ḥanẓalah (Banū) 31.
Ḥanẓalah b. ʿAlī al-Aslamī 26.
ḥaras (guard) 128, 216.
Harāt (Herat) 85, 120, 163.
Ḥarb 84, 106, 119, 154, 155, 202, 205, 206.
Ḥarb (Banū) 133, 176, 189, 190.
Ḥārith b. Badr al-Ghudānī 29, 83.
al-Ḥārith b. ʿAbdallāh (or ʿAmr) al-Azdī 72, 76.
al-Ḥārith b. ʿAbdallāh b. Abī Rabīʿah al-Makhzūmī, see al-Qubāʿ 213.

al-Ḥārith b. ʿAyyāf al-ʿAbdī 98.
al-Ḥārith b. al-Azmaʿ 143.
al-Ḥārith b. Ḥusayrah 141.
al-Ḥārith b. Jabalah al-Ghassānī 98.
al-Ḥārith b. Muḥammad 183, 184, 185, 199, 210, 211.
Ḥarmalah b. ʿImrān 221.
Ḥarūrā' 12.
Ḥarūriyyah 12, 31, 53, 100, 171.
al-Ḥasan b. ʿAlī 2, 3, 4, 5, 7, 8, 9, 10, 11, 12, 14, 15, 16, 18, 138, 152, 154, 210, 211.
al-Ḥasan b. Rashīd 178.
Hāshim b. Muḥammad 193.
Hāshimī 218.
Ḥātim 161.
Ḥātim b. al-Nuʿmān al-Bāhilī 87.
Ḥātim b. Qabīsah 119, 120.
Hawāzin (Banū)131, 132.
Ḥawrān 214.
Ḥawshab 156.
al-Haytham b. ʿAdī 78.
al-Haytham b. al-Aswad al-Nakhaʿī 143, 167.
Haytham b. Shaddād, see Shaddād b. al-Haytham al-Hilālī 128.
Ḥayyān b. Ẓabyān al-Sulamī 21, 22, 23, 24, 25, 33, 34, 193, 194, 195.

Hell 214.
Hell Fire 212.
Helmand Valley 18.
Hephthalite 164.
Hephthalites 163.
Ḥidhmir 161.
Ḥijāz 1, 112, 167, 168, 173, 209.
hijrah (emigration of Muhammad from Makka to al-Madīna in 622, beginning of Muslim ėra) 210.
al-Hilālī, see Shaddād b. al-Haytham 129.
Hilālīs 142.
ḥilm (forbearance) 127.
Ḥimyar (Banū) 216.
al-Hind 78, 103.
Hind (Banū) 129, 155, 156.
Hind bt. Muʿāwiyah 73.
Hind bt. ʿUtbah b. ʿAbd Shams b. ʿAbd Manāf b. Quṣayy 17, 220, 215.
Hind bt. Zayd b. Makhramah al-Anṣārī 154.
al-Ḥīrah 34, 36, 155, 194.
Hishām b. Hubayrah 198, 207.
Hishām b. Muḥammad al-Kalbī 1, 21, 33, 38, 122, 125, 126, 127, 136, 195, 208, 209, 210, 211, 213, 215.
Hishām b. Saʿīd 224.
Hishām b. ʿUbayd (or Muḥammad) 96.
Hishām b. ʿUrwah 136.
Hishām b. al-Walīd 211.
Homs 88, 89.
al-Hubāb 162.
Ḥudaybiyah 216.
al-Ḥudayn 142.
al-Hudhalī, see Abū Bakr 78, 179.
Ḥudhām 130.

al-ḥudūd (prescribed punishments) 46.
al-Ḥufayr 109.
al-Hujaym (Banū) 104–5.
Ḥujr b. ʿAdī b. Jabalah al-Kindī, see Ibn Adbar 1, 30, 122, 123, 124, 125, 126, 127, 128, 129, 130, 131, 132, 133, 134, 135, 136, 138, 139, 140, 141, 143, 144, 145, 146, 147, 148, 151, 152, 153, 154, 156, 158, 162, 170.
Ḥujr b. Yazīd al-Kindī 134, 135, 136.
ḥulamāʾ (forebearing people) 37.
Ḥulwān 28, 194.
Ḥumayd b. Hilāl 219.
Humaym (Banū) 144, 158.
Ḥumrah b. Mālik al-Hamdānī 148.
Ḥumrān b. Abān, see Tuwayd 13, 14.
Ḥunayn, Battle of 186.
Ḥusayn b. ʿAbdallāh al-Hamdānī 127.
al-Ḥusayn b. ʿAbdallāh al-Kilābī 148.
al-Ḥusayn b. ʿAlī 5, 11, 138, 186, 200, 208, 209, 210.
al-Ḥusayn b. ʿUqbah al-Marādī 122.
Ḥuṣayrah b. ʿAbdallāh b. al-Ḥārith 50, 55, 57, 60, 65.
Hūt (Banū) 133.
al-Ḥutāt b. Yazīd, Abū Munāzil 105, 106, 108.
al-Ḥuṭayʾah, see Jarwal b. Aws 117.
Ḥuwayy (Banū) 105.
Huwwārīn 214.

I

ʿIbādah b. Qurṣ al-Laythī 19.
Ibn ʿAbbās, see ʿAbdallāh b. ʿAbbās 18, 94, 186, 225.
Ibn ʿAbd Rabbihi 78, 79, 80, 81, 115, 154.
Ibn Abī ʿAmr 85.
Ibn Abī Dhiʾb 217.
Ibn Abī al-Ḥadīd 78, 80, 171.
Ibn Abī Sufyān, see Ziyād b. Abīhi 77.
Ibn Abī Ziyād 168.
Ibn Adbar, see Hujr b. ʿAdī 154.
Ibn ʿĀmir, see ʿAbdallāh b. ʿĀmir 9, 19, 71, 72, 73, 74, 76, 181.
Ibn al-Ashʿath, see Muḥammad b. al-Ashʿath 136, 156.
Ibn Aʾtham al-Kūfī 78, 166, 188.
Ibn al-Athīr 19, 72, 86, 105, 163, 216, 222.
Ibn ʿAwn 186.
Ibn Barṣā al-Ḥitār 131.
Ibn Buzayʿah, see Shaddād b. al-Mundhir b. al-Ḥārith b. Waʿlah al-Dhuhlī 142.
Ibn Dajājah, see ʿAbdallāh b. ʿĀmir 72.
Ibn Durayd 85.
Ibn al-Faqīh 34, 42, 179.
Ibn Hajar 86, 216.
Ibn Ḥantamah, see ʿUmar b. al-Khaṭṭāb 222.

Ibn Ḥawīyah, see ʿAbdallāh b. Ḥawīyah al-Saʿdī 148.
Ibn Hind, see Muʿawiyah b Abī Sufyān 73, 217.
Ibn Hishām 33.
Ibn Ḥiṣn, Cemetery of 83.
Ibn Ḥiṣn al-Tamīmī, see ʿAbdallāh b. Ḥiṣn 100, 198.
Ibn Hubayrah, see ʿUmar b. Hubayrah 220.
Ibn Isḥāq 176.
Ibn Jadhl al-Ṭiʿān al-Kinānī 59.
Ibn Jurmūz 89.
Ibn al-Kawwāʾ, see ʿAbdallāh b. Awfah 31, 72.
Ibn Khayyāṭ 4, 11, 19, 32, 95, 100, 102, 182, 186, 187, 193, 210, 216, 217.
Ibn al-Khayyāṭ (the Egyptian) 217.
Ibn Khāzim, see ʿAbdallāh b. Khāzim 30, 69, 70.
Ibn Khunays 184.
Ibn Manẓūr 114, 116, 118, 140, 160, 162, 169, 177, 213.
Ibn Mufarrigh, see Yazīd b. Rabīʿah b. Mufarrigh al-Ḥimyarī 203, 204, 205, 206.
Ibn Muljam, see ʿAbd al-Raḥmān b. Muljam al-Murādī 22.
Ibn al-Nābighah, see ʿAmr b. al-ʿĀṣ 217.
Ibn Qitrah 117.
Ibn Qutaybah 13, 78, 170, 203, 204.
Ibn Rustah 112.
Ibn Saʿd 13, 21, 107, 113, 126, 179.
Ibn Shihāb al-Zuhrī, see al-Zuhrī 211.
Ibn Sumayyah, see Ziyād b. Abīhī 78, 153, 203.
Ibn Ṭabāṭabā 1.
Ibn Udhaynah al-ʿAbdī 182.
Ibn ʿUmar, see ʿAbdallāh b. ʿUmar b. al-Khaṭṭāb 94, 186, 187.
Ibn Umm al-Ḥakam, see ʿAbd al-Raḥmān b. ʿUmar 195, 196.
Ibn Umm al-Ḥakīm, see ʿAbdallāh b. ʿĀmir 73.
Ibn Uthāl al-Naṣrānī 88, 89.
Ibn Ziyād, see ʿUbaydallāh b. Ziyād 196, 197, 198, 205.
Ibn al-Zubayr, see ʿAbdallāh b. al-Zubayr 94, 186, 209, 210, 225.
Ifrīqiyyah 102, 103.
iḥdāth fī al-dīn (innovation in religion) 46.
Īliyā, see Aelia Capitolina and Jerusalem 6.
ʿilj (lout) 57.
Ilyās of Naṣībīn 11.
imām (religious leader) 70, 84, 125.
Imām 39, 84.
imārah (governorship) 22.
ʿImrān b. al-Ḥusayn al-Khuzāʿī 85.
Iran 6, 12, 14, 22, 163, 206.
Iranian 20, 206.
Iraq 1, 3, 6, 7, 11, 12, 13, 20, 21, 72, 86, 97, 119, 120, 148, 150, 156, 160, 167,

Iraq (*continued*)
194, 201, 204, 205, 209
210, 217, 220.
Iraqi 2.
ʿĪsā b. Khuṣaylah b. Muʿattib, see, Abū Khusaylah and al-Bahzī 107, 108, 110.
ʿĪsā b. ʿAṣim al-Asadī 196.
Iṣbahān (Iṣfahān) 6, 130, 135.
Iṣfahānī 106, 109, 111, 117, 118, 124, 125, 129, 132, 133, 136, 138, 139, 154, 155, 168, 188, 189, 202, 203, 204, 214, 225.
Isḥāq, see Ibn Yaḥyā 77.
Isḥāq b. ʿAbdallāh b. Abī Farwah 101.
Isḥāq b. Ayyūb 212.
Isḥāq b. Idrīs 99.
Isḥāq b. ʿĪsā 19, 31, 164, 179, 182, 183, 206, 210.
Isḥāq b. Khulayd 214.
Isḥāq b. Ṭalḥah b. ʿUbaydallāh 142, 188.
al-Iskandariyyah 91.
Islam 38, 42, 54, 74, 79, 102, 148, 158, 168, 185, 193, 218.
Islamic 171.
Ismāʿīl b. Ibrāhīm 186.
Ismāʿīl b. Nuʿaym al-Namirī 127.
Ismāʿīl b. Rāshid 6.
Ismāʿīl b. Ṭalḥah b. ʿUbaydallāh 142.
isnād (chain of transmitting authorities) 104.
Iṣṭakhr 14, 28, 83.
ʿItrīs b. ʿUrqūb al-Bakrī 194, 195.
Iyād (Banū) 100.
Iyād b. al-Ḥārith 183.

J

Jabal Ṭāʾī 157.
Jabalah (Banū) 132.
Jābir b. ʿAbdallāh 101.
Jābiyah 216.
al-Jaʿd, Arch of 83.
al-Jaʿd b. Qays al-Tamīmī 83, 177, 178.
Jadhīmah b. Awf 204.
Jadīlah 160.
Jaʿfar al-Sadafī 99.
Jaʿfar b. Burqān 218.
Jaʿfar b. Sulaymān al-Ḍubaʿī
Jaʿfar b. Hudhayfa al-Ṭāʾī 33.
Jāhiliyyah 74, 80, 106.
Jāḥiẓ 2, 59, 78, 79, 80, 81.
Jalūlāʾ 30, 160.
Jarabbah 94.
jarībs (units of sixty square cubits) 15.
Jarīr 195, 197.
Jarīr b. ʿAbdallāh 136, 148.
Jarīr b. ʿAbd al-Masīh, see al-Mutalammis 122.
Jarīr b. Ḥāzim 169.
Jarīr b. Mālik b. Zuhayr b. Jadhīmah al-ʿAbsī 21.
Jarīr b. Yazīd 169.
Jāriyah b. Qudāmah 105.
Jarjarāyā 5, 24, 50, 57, 60.
al-Jārūd b. Abī Sabrah 15.
Jarwal b. Aws, see al-Ḥutayʾah 117.
al-Jawn b. Qatādah al-ʿAbshamī 105.
Jayḥūn 164.
Jerusalem, see Īliyā and Aelia Capitolina 6.

Jew 33.
Jewish 42.
Jews 118.
Jibāl 28.
Jibāl Sharwīn 162.
jihād 12, 23, 24, 47, 49, 68, 193, 194.
al-Jisr 195.
Jisr al-ʿAbbāsiyyāt 12.
Jisr al-Baṣrah 19.
Jordan 96.
Jubayr b. al-Ḍaḥḥāk 181.
Jūkhā 50.
Junādah b. Abī Umayyah al-Azdī 166, 172, 183, 192, 199, 208.
Juwayriyyah b. Asmāʾ 173, 219, 222.

K

Kaʿb 172.
Kaʿb b. Juʿayl 117, 118.
Kaʿ b. al-Ashraf 33.
Kaʿb b. Mālik (Banū) 26, 189
Kaʿbah 24, 146, 152.
Kalb (Banū) 34, 188.
Karīm b. ʿAfīf al-Khathʿamī, see al-Khathʿamī 140, 144, 150, 152.
Kaskar 169.
Kathʿam (Banū) 132.
Kathīr b. Shihāb b. Ḥuṣayn al-Hārithī 142, 143.
kātib al-rasāʾil (correspondence secretary) 217.
Katwah bt. Qaraẓah 216.
Khābūr River 77.
Khālid b. ʿAbd al-Raḥmān b. Khālid b. al-Walīd 93.
Khālid b. ʿAbdallāh 163, 203.
Khālid b. al-ʿĀṣ b. Hishām 20, 70.
Khālid b. Maʿdān al-Ṭāʾī 58.
Khālid b. al-Qāsim 101.
Khālid b. ʿUrfuṭah 140.
Khalīfat Allāh, see Deputy of God 84.
Khallād b. ʿUbaydah 218.
Khallād b. Yazīd al-Bāhilī 82, 197, 198.
khandaq (ditch) 112.
Khandaq Sābūr 112.
kharāj (tax, generally on land) 11, 89.
Khārijite 22, 24, 31, 33, 81, 89.
Khārijites 1, 12, 13, 21, 23, 25, 36, 37, 39, 41, 50, 51, 53, 54, 55, 58, 60, 61, 67, 68, 193, 196, 197, 198.
khaṭārah (a kind of camel) 169.
al-Khathʿamī, see Karūn b. ʿAfīf 148.
Khathīr b. Shihāb al-Ḥārithī 143.
Khathīr b. Ziyād 167.
al-Khaṭīm, see Yazīd b. Mālik al-Bāhilī 89, 90.
al-Khawarnaq 155.
Khaybar 33.
Khaybariyyah fever 118.
khulafāʾ (deputies) 29.
Khulayd b. ʿAbdallāh al-Ḥanafī 85, 86, 163, 170, 171.
Khulayd b. ʿAjlān 214.
Khurāsān 1, 2, 18, 68, 69, 70, 72, 78, 83, 85, 86, 87, 92, 93, 119, 121, 163, 164, 170, 171, 175, 178, 179,

Khurāsān (*continued*) 181, 187, 188, 190, 191, 199.
al-Khuraybah 82.
Khusraws, see Kisrā 132, 184.
khuṭbah (sermon or speech) 70, 78.
Khuzāʿah (Banū) 132, 184.
Khuzistān 29, 197, 206.
Kidām b. Ḥayyān al-ʿAnazī 144, 151.
Kinānāh (Banū) 59.
Kindah, Banū 31, 130, 131, 132, 133, 140, 152.
Kindah, Cemetery of 132.
Kindifī 158.
al-Kindiyyah 155.
Kirmān 206, 207.
Kisrā, see Khusraw 168, 169, 217.
kohl (antimony) 212, 217.
kudrah (desert bird) 116.
al-Kūfah 1, 3, 7, 8, 9, 12, 13, 14, 16, 18, 20, 21, 22, 23, 30, 34, 36, 42, 45, 56, 60, 61, 62, 64, 65, 69, 70, 74, 76, 80, 82, 87, 95, 96, 97, 98, 99, 100, 101, 103, 111, 123, 125, 126, 128, 129, 131, 132, 139, 140, 143, 150, 154, 157, 164, 167, 168, 170, 171, 175, 179, 182, 184, 187, 191, 192, 194, 195, 198, 199, 200, 207.
Kūfan 12, 18, 58, 61, 140, 184, 196.
Kūfans 12, 56, 57, 59, 72, 87, 128, 148, 149.
Kunāsah 141.
Kundur 162.
kunyah (agnomen) 215.
Kurayb b. Salmah b. Yazīd al-Juʿfī 143.
Kurds 14, 59.
kursī (chair, throne, or judgment seat) 97.
Kūthā 50, 51, 64.
Kuwayfah, see Little Kūfah 160.

L

Labīd b. ʿUṭārid al-Tamīmī 142.
Laylā 157.
Layth (Banū) 225.
Little Kūfah, see Kuwayfah 160.
Lubābah bt. Awfā al-Jurashī

M

Maʿbad b. Khālid al-Jadalī 77.
al-Madā'in 9, 13, 28, 42, 45, 51, 60, 61, 62, 66, 137.
al-Madā'inī, see ʿAlī b. Muḥammad b. ʿAbdallāh b. Abī Sayf and Abū al-Ḥasan 9, 96.
al-Madhār 50, 51.
Madhhij (Banū) 131, 132, 133, 140.
al-Madīnah 2, 11, 12, 15, 19, 20, 26, 31, 33, 45, 61, 70, 87, 89, 93, 94, 95, 99, 101, 102, 103, 111, 117, 118, 132, 140, 164, 171, 172, 173, 176, 179, 186, 187, 190, 191, 192, 207, 223, 226.
al-Madīnah al-ʿAtīqah 3, 46.
Madinan 19.
Magian 14.

Māh Bahrādhān 28, 30.
Māh Dīnār 28.
al-Mahdī (Caliph 775–85) 46.
al-majālis (assemblies) 23.
majlis (assembly) 225.
Makhlad b. al-Ḥasan 126, 127.
Mālik, see Abū al-Mukhariq 216.
Mālik b. 'Abdallāh al-Khath'amī 180, 192, 208.
Mālik b. Ḥanẓalah b. Mālik b. Zayd Manāt b. Tamīm 108.
Mālik b. Hubayrah al-Sakūnī 88, 91, 93, 94, 148, 152, 153.
Mālik b. 'Ubaydallāh 88.
Mālik b. al-Rayb al-Māzinī 188, 189.
al-Manṣūr (Caliph 754–75) 46.
maqṣūrah (ruler's loge in a mosque) 75, 99.
Marghāb, see Murghāb 179.
Marḥab 33.
Marj 'Adhrā', see 'Adhrā' 144, 145, 146.
Marj Rāhiṭ 216.
al-Marrūdh 2.
al-Marzūqī 59.
Marw 2, 85, 92, 119, 120, 121, 179.
Marw al-Rūdh 2, 85.
Marwān b. al-Ḥakam 20, 32, 70, 75, 87, 93, 94, 95, 117, 172, 173, 174, 179, 182, 187, 191, 192, 205, 216, 224.
Marwān b. al-Haytham 142.
Marwānid 20.
Maskin 3, 11.
masjid (mosque) 11, 15, 22.
Maslamah b. Muḥārib 14, 26, 72, 78, 82, 85, 86, 88, 97, 163, 177, 178, 179, 188, 189.
Maslamah b. Mukhallad 102, 103.
Maṣqalah b. Hubayrah al-Shaybānī 142.
Masruqān 206.
Mas'ūdī 101, 154, 168, 223.
mawālī (clients) 51, 216.
mawlā (client) 13, 14, 19, 45, 103, 164, 166, 216, 223, 225.
Maydānī 97, 106, 126, 130, 196, 212.
Maysān 168.
Maysūn bt. Baḥdal b. Unayf b. Waljah b. Qunāfah b. 'Adī b. Zuhayr b. Ḥārithah b. Janāb al-Kalbī 215.
Maythā' bt. Khalīfah al-Ṭā'ī 139.
Mecca 20, 24, 26, 70, 73, 108, 111, 119, 127, 176, 186.
Messenger of God, see Muḥammad 8, 18, 38, 86, 93, 101, 102, 154, 157, 168, 188, 212, 217.
Mihrān 160.
Miḥṣān b. Tha'labah 142.
mīl (two km.) 53, 56.
minbar (pulpit) 70.
Minjab b. Rāshid al-Ḍabbī 29.
Minqar (Banū) 145.
al-Minqarī 68, 151.
Mirbad 104.

Mirdās b. Udayyah, see Abū Bilāl 197, 198.
Miskīn b. ʿĀmir b. Unayf b. Shurayḥ b. ʿAmr b. ʿUdas 54, 55, 65, 68
Miskīn b. Dārim 168, 169.
Mismaʿ b. ʿAbd al-Mālik 111.
miṣr (garrison city) 11, 22.
mosque 75, 85, 97, 99, 101, 124, 126, 128, 129, 156, 171.
Mosque of ʿAdī b. Ḥātim 139.
Mosque of al-Muʿādil 100.
Mosul 137, 150, 205, 206.
Muʿādh b. Juwayn b. Ḥuṣayn al-Ṭāʾī al-Sinbisī 24, 25, 33, 41, 193, 194, 195.
muʾadhdhin (announcer) 221.
Muʿammar 70.
Muʿawiyah b. Abī Sufyān, see Abū ʿAbd al-Raḥmān and Ibn Hind 1, 2, 3, 6, 7, 8, 9, 10, 11, 12, 14, 15, 16, 17, 20, 23, 26, 27, 28, 29, 30, 39, 69, 70, 71, 72, 73, 74, 75, 76, 77, 78, 83, 89, 91, 93, 94, 95, 97, 98, 101, 102, 103, 105, 106, 107, 122, 123, 124, 125, 126, 127, 136, 137, 141, 145, 147, 148, 149, 150, 151, 152, 153, 154, 163, 166, 167, 170, 171, 172, 173, 174, 175, 176, 177, 180, 181, 182, 183, 184, 185, 186, 187, 188, 190, 191, 192, 195, 196, 199, 201, 202, 203, 204, 205, 206, 208, 209, 210, 211, 212, 213, 214, 215, 216, 217, 218, 219, 220, 221, 222, 223, 224, 225.
Muʿāwiyah b. Ḥudayj al-Sakūnī 91, 102, 103, 196.
al-Muʿaydī 196.
Mubarrad 12, 212, 213.
Muḍar (Banū) 58, 132, 140.
al-Mufaḍḍil b. Faḍālah 103.
al-Mughīrah b. Shuʿbah, Abū ʿAbdallāh 10, 13, 14, 20, 23, 24, 26, 27, 28, 29, 31, 33, 34, 37, 41, 42, 43, 44, 45, 48, 50, 65, 70, 76, 77, 87, 95, 96, 97, 122, 123, 124, 125, 183, 184, 193, 218, 226.
al-Muhājir 103.
Muhājirūn 10.
al-Muhallab b. Abī Ṣufrah al-Azdī 119, 120, 188.
Muḥammad, see Messenger of God 2, 8, 17, 19, 27, 33, 39, 187, 210, 216.
Muḥammad b. Abān al-Qurashī 175.
Muḥammad b. ʿAbdallāh al-Thaqafī 165.
Muḥammad b. ʿAlī 104, 106.
Muḥammad b. ʿĀmir 224.
Muḥammad b. al-Ashʿath, see Ibn al-Ashʿath and Abū Maythāʾ 134, 135, 162, 219.
Muḥammad b. al-Faḍl al-ʿAbsī 21, 170.
Muḥammad b. Ḥafṣ 178, 187.

Muḥammad b. al-Ḥakam 213.
Muḥammad b. Ibrahīm 223.
Muḥammad b. Iṣhāq 166.
Muḥammad b. Mālik 172.
Muḥammad b. Maslamah 32.
Muḥammad b. Mikhnaf 132.
Muḥammad b. Mūsā al-Thaqafī 96.
Muḥammad b. Muslim b. ʿUbaydallāh b. ʿAbdallāh b. Shihāb al-Zuhrī, see al-Zuhrī and Ibn Shihāb 2.
Muḥammad b. Saʿd 104, 210, 211.
Muḥammad b. Sīrīn 126, 127.
Muḥammad b. ʿUmar 96, 101, 102, 103, 166, 172, 173, 210, 211.
Muḥammad b. ʿUmayr b. ʿUṭārid al-Tamīmī 142.
Muḥammad b. Yaḥyā 211.
Muḥammad b. al-Zubayr 166.
al-Muḥill b. Khalīfah 24, 33.
al-muhillūn (violators) 2.
Muḥriz b. Bujayr b. Sufyān 55.
Muḥriz b. Jāriyah b. Rabīʿah b. ʿAbd al-ʿUzzā b. ʿAbd Shams 142.
Muḥriz b. Shihāb b. Bujayr b. Sufyān b. Khālid b. Minqar al-Tamīmī 53, 55, 144–5, 151.
Mujāhid b. Jabr 172.
al-Mujālid b. Saʿīd 18, 136, 137, 225.
al-Mukhtār 216.
al-Mukhtār b. Abī ʿUbayd 4, 143.
Mulqā 109.
al-Mundhir b. Jarūd 203, 204.
al-Mundhir b. Māʾ al-Samāʾ 196.
al-Mundhir b. al-Zubayr 142.
Muqāʿis 112, 113.
Muqātil b. Ḥayyān 68–9, 200.
Murād (Banū) 22.
Murghāb, see Marghāb 2, 179.
Murjiʿite 24.
Murrah (Banū) 156.
Murrah b. Munqidh b. al-Nuʿmān 43.
Muṣʿab b. al-Zubayr 22, 63, 64, 129.
Muṣʿab b. Ḥayyān 200.
Mūsā b. ʿAbd al-Raḥmān al-Masrūqī 3, 6.
Mūsā b. ʿAlī 103.
Mūsā b. Ismāʿīl 99, 171.
Mūsā b. Ṭalḥah 142.
al-Mushaqqar 204.
Muslim 11, 19, 32, 42, 45, 77, 82, 96, 150, 164, 205.
Muslim b. ʿAmr 90.
Muslim al-Jarmī 126.
Muslim b. Muḥārib 200.
Muslim b. ʿUqbah al-Murrī 209.
Muslims 12, 13, 17, 22, 24, 25, 26, 34, 38, 39, 48, 49, 71, 79, 88, 132, 135, 145, 153, 166, 172, 178, 202.
al-Mustawrid b. ʿUllifah 24, 25, 33, 34, 40, 41, 42, 46, 47, 48, 49, 50, 53, 54, 55,

al-Mustawrid (*continued*) 56, 57, 60, 61, 62, 63, 65, 68, 193.
al-Mutalammis, see Jarīr b. 'Abd al-Masīh 122.
Muzāḥimiyyah 65.

N

Nabhān 160.
al-Naḍr b. Ṣāliḥ b. Ḥabīb 21, 22, 24.
Nāfi' b. Khālid al-Ṭāḥī 85, 86, 87.
nāḥiyah (subdistrict) 19.
al-Nahr, Battle of, see Nahrawān 13, 21, 23, 33, 36, 100.
Nahr Sūrā 42.
Nahr al-Malik 61, 61.
Nahrawān, Battle of, see al-Nahr 13, 21, 24, 31, 39, 50, 82.
Nahrawān Canal 24.
Nahshal (Banū) 103, 104, 108.
Nā'ilah bt. 'Umārah al-Kalbi 215.
Najaf 12, 155.
Najd 189, 221.
Nakha' 134.
Nakhlah 196, 187.
Nakhlah al-Yamāniyyah 186.
Nakhlat Muḥmūd 186.
al-Nakrah 110.
Narshakhī 190.
al-Naṣr b. Ṣāliḥ al-'Absī 144.
Nātil b. Qays al-Judhāmī 221.
al-Nawār bt. Khalīfah al-Ṭā'ī 156.
Nawāwī 217.
Nawlah b. Fuqaym (Banū) 110.
al-Nibāj 110.
Nihāwand 28, 160.
Nīshāpur, see Abrashahr 163, 179.
Nīzak Ṭarkhān 164.
Nu'aylah b. Mulayk 86.
Nūḥ b. Qays 99.
al-Nukhaylah 12.
al-Nu'man b. Bashīr al-Anṣāri 147, 199, 200, 207, 216.
al-Nu'mān b. al-Mundhir 98.
Nuṣayḥah 126.

O

Ossets 20.
Oxus River, see Jayḥūn and Amū Daryā 69.

P

Palmyra, see Tadmur 164, 190, 214.
Paradise 68, 195, 203, 214.
patricius, see *baṭrīq* 20.
patrikios, see *baṭrīq* 20.
Paykand, see Baykand 178.
Persepolis 14.
Persian 82, 203.
Persians 12, 112.
pilgrimage, see *ḥajj* 6, 70, 75, 87, 90, 92, 93, 95, 102, 103, 114, 146, 153, 164, 165, 171, 179, 182, 183, 188, 192, 198, 206.
plague 95, 167, 168.
Pleiades 106.
pre-Islamic 2, 80, 123, 155.
Prophet 2, 11, 39, 46, 81, 85, 106, 124, 200, 217.

pulpit 101, 102, 124, 125, 126, 127, 131, 180, 213.
Pūshang, see Bushanj 163.

Q

al-Qaʿqāʿ, Shawr al-Dhuhlī 142.
Qabīṣah b. Dhu'ayb 101, 102.
Qabīṣah b. Ḍubayʿah b. Ḥarmalah al-ʿAbsī 138, 143, 144, 149, 151.
Qabīṣah b. Jābir al-Asadī 225.
Qabīṣah b. al-Dammūn 33, 34, 43, 44.
Qabj Khatun 178.
qāḍī 18, 167.
Qādis 85.
al-Qādisiyyah 12.
al-Qaḥdhamī 72.
qāʾid (general, leader), see *baṭrīq* 20.
al-Qāmighān 42.
qamīs (shirt) 170.
Qarīb 100.
Qārin 179.
Qarqīsīyā 77.
qaṣīdah (ode) 110, 111, 117, 119, 204, 205.
qaṣīdahs 111, 202.
al-Qasīm 189.
qaṣīmah (bridle or patch of sand) 110.
Qaṣīmah Kāẓimah 110.
Qaṣr al-ʿAdasiyyīn 34.
Qaṣr Aws 188.
Qaṣr Ibn Hubayrah 42.
Qaṭan b. ʿAbdallāh al-Ḥārithī 77.
Qaṭan b. ʿAbdallāh b. Ḥuṣayn 142.
al-Qayn (Banū) 14.
Qayrawān 102.
Qays ʿAylān 77.
Qays b. Ḥanzah al-Hamdānī 216.
Qays b. al-Haytham al-Sulamī 18, 21, 68, 69, 70, 73, 85, 200.
Qays b. Qahdān al-Kindī 131.
Qays b. Saʿd 2, 3, 9, 10.
Qays b. Shimr 133.
Qays b. ʿUbād 138, 155, 156.
Qays b. al-Walīd b. ʿAbd Shams b. al-Mughīrah 140, 141.
Qays b. Yazīd 133, 134, 135.
Qayṣar 168, 169, 217, 221.
Qaysiyyah 69, 190.
Qazwīn 162.
qiblah (direction toward the Kaʿbah in Mecca faced by Muslims when they worship) 24, 152, 167.
Qisṭānah, see Qusṭānat al-Rayy 23.
al-Qubāʿ, see al-Ḥārith b. ʿAbdallāh b. Abī Rabīʿah al-Makhzūmī 213.
Qubbayn 65.
Quḍāʿah (Banū) 14, 132.
Quḍāʿī, see Hudbah b. Fiyyād 149.
Qudāmah b. Maẓʿūn 19.
Qudāmah b. al-ʿAjlān al-Azdī 62, 243.
Quḥāfah (Banū) 144, 150.
Quhistān 163.
Qurʾān 31, 34, 48, 78, 82, 99, 176.
Quraysh (Banū) 9, 14, 73,

Quraysh (*continued*)
142, 143, 168, 186, 187, 188, 204, 208, 218, 222.
Quṣayy 108.
Quss al-Nāṭif 151, 152.
Qusṭānat al-Rayy, see Qisṭānah 23.
Qusṭantīniyyah 94.
Qutaybah b. Muslim 164.
Qutaylah 156.

R

Raba'ī 157.
Rabb al-Masāriq bt. Mu'āwiyah 215.
al-Rabī' b. Ziyād al-Ḥārithī 87, 163, 164, 170.
Rabī'ah or al-Rabī' 184.
Rabī'ah (Banū) 50, 58, 140, 142, 151.
Rabī'ah b. Ḥanẓalah (Banū) 198.
Rabī'ah b. Ka'b b. Sa'd (Banū) 105.
Rabī'ah b. 'Isl al-Yarbū'ī 87, 188, 219, 220.
Rabī'ah b. Nājid al-Azdī 134, 135.
Rabī'ah bt. al-Marrār, see Bint Marrār 111.
raḥbah (plaza) 100.
ra'iyyah (flock, subjects) 123.
rajaz (a kind of poetry) 177.
Ramaḍān 32.
Rāmhurmuz 198.
Rāmīthan 178.
Ramlah 214.
Rashīd 130, 135.
Rāsib (Banū) 39, 100.
al-Rawḥā 111.
al-Rayy, see Tehrān 22, 33, 162, 188, 194.
Rhodes 166.
Rib'ī b. Ḥirāsh b. Jahsh al-'Absī 138.
Rifā'at b. Shaddād 137.
Rūdas 208.
rustāq (subdistrict) 137.
rusul (messengers) 38.
Ruwayyah 109.

S

Sabā'iyyah 49, 145.
Sābāṭ 61, 65, 66.
Sābāṭ Bridge 62.
Ṣabrah b. Shaymān b. 'Ukayf 85, 86.
Sābūr, see Bishāpūr 30.
Sa'd 80.
Sa'd (Banū) 68, 85, 142.
Sa'd, *mawlā* of Mu'āwiyah 216.
Sa'd, *mawlā* of Qudamah b. Maẓ'ūn
Sa'd b. Bakr b. Hawazin (Banū) 145, 152.
Sa'd b. Nimrān al-Hamdānī 145, 148, 151, 152.
Sa'd al-Qaraẓ 101.
al-Ṣadif 33.
al-Sadīr 155.
al-Ṣādir 186.
al-Saffāḥ (Caliph 749–54) 46.
Saghāniyān 190.
ṣāḥib (leader) 34.
Sahm b. Ghālib al-Hujaymī 19, 89, 90.
al-Sā'ib b. al-Aqra' al-Thaqafī 142.
Sā'ib Kathīr, *mawlā* of the Banū Layth 225.
Sa'īd 80.
Sa'īd b. 'Abd al-'Azīz 6.

Sa'īd b. Abī Sa'īd al-Maqburī, see Abū Sa'īd al-Maqburī and Sa'īd b. Kaysān 153, 217.
Sa'īd b. al-'Āṣ, see Abū 'Uthmān 30, 94, 95, 103, 117, 118, 164, 165, 171, 172, 173, 174, 175, 184, 224.
Sa'īd b. Kaysān, see Sa'īd b. 'Abī Sa'īd al-Maqburī 217.
Sa'īd b. al-Musayyib 102.
Sa'īd b. 'Uthmān b. 'Affān 187, 189, 190, 191.
Sa'īd b. Zayd 100.
Sā'idiyyin, Cemetery of 132.
al-Sāj 110.
Sajāḥ 31.
Ṣakhr b. Ḥarb, see Abū Sufyān 215.
Ṣakhr b. Qays b. Mu'āwiyah al-Tamīmī al-Sa'dī, al-Aḥnaf 81.
al-Saksakī 216.
al-Sakūn (Banū) 152.
Ṣa'l 109.
Salamah b. Muḥārib 175.
Salamah b. 'Uthmān 17, 29, 97.
Salamah (Banū) 36.
Salāmān b. Sa'd (Banū) 148.
ṣalāṭ (worship) 126, 146.
Sālim b. Rabī'ah al-'Absī (or al'Abdī) 22, 23, 44.
Salm b. Qutaybah 220.
Salmah, Mt. 157.
Salmān b. Rabī'ah al-Bāhilī 76–7.
Samarqand 189.
Samurah b. Jundab al-Fazārī 85, 97, 99, 100, 101, 167, 170, 171, 175.
al-Ṣaq'ab b. Zuhayr 59, 122, 123, 154.
Ṣarāt Canal 42, 45, 46.
al-Sarī b. Abī Waqqāṣ 144.
al-Sarī b. Waqqāṣ al-Ḥārithī 142.
ṣarīmah (bridle or patch of sand) 115, 169.
Sarjūn b. Manṣūr al-Rūmī 216.
Ṣa'ṣa'ah b. Ṣūḥān 38, 40, 43, 107.
Sasanian 45, 169, 179.
Sasania
Sasanians 14.
Sawād 194.
Sāwah 23.
sawīq (broth) 220.
Sawriyah 208.
Sayf b. Wahb Abū Ṭalḥah al-Ma'walī 85, 86, 100.
Ṣayfī b. Fasīl al-Shaybānī 138, 139, 144, 151, 155, 156.
Sellers 41, 68, 221.
Shabath b. Rib'ī al-Riyāḥī 113.
Shabbawayhi, see 'Abdallāh b. Aḥmad al-Marwazī 2.
al-Sha'bī, Abū 'Amr 'Āmir b. Sharāḥīl 18, 82, 97, 123, 136, 137, 183, 225.
Shabīb b. Rib'ī 142.
Shaddād b. al-Azma' 143.
Shadād b. al-Haytham, see al-Hilālī 127, 128, 138, 142.
Shaddād b. al-Mundhir b. al-Ḥārith b. Wa'lah al-Dhuhlī, see Ibn Buzay'ah 142.

shahādah (Muslim statement of faith) 8.
Shahrazūr 12.
Shāmir b. ʿAbdallāh al-Khathʿamī 150, 151.
Shāmir b. Dhī al-Jawshan al-ʿĀmirī 142.
Sharīfah, slave-girl of al-Rabīʿ b. Ziyād al-Ḥārithī 164.
Sharīk b. al-Aʿwar al-Ḥārithī 50, 56, 58, 59, 206, 207.
Sharīk b. Namlah al-Muḥāribī 65.
Sharīk b. Shaddād al-Haḍramī 144, 151.
Shārūn, see Sellers 41.
Sharwīn 162.
Shaṭṭ Hindiyyah 42.
Shaybān (Banū) 155.
Shaybān, Cemetery of Shaybān 85.
Shīʿah 44.
Shihāb b. ʿUbaydallāh 219.
Shīʿite 21, 24, 50, 59.
Shīrāz 14.
Shuʿayb b. ʿAmr al-Umawī 101.
Shuʿbah b. Qilʿim 30.
Shurayḥ b. Ḥāniʾ al-Ḥārithī 143, 144, 145, 146.
Shurayḥ b. al-Ḥārith al-Kindī 20, 70, 87, 143, 164, 167, 168, 198, 207.
shurṭah (police) 15.
Shurṭat al-Khamīs 2–3, 9.
Shustar 206.
Ṣiffīn, Battle of 12, 30, 31, 42, 131, 135, 148, 160, 190, 216.
Sijās 161.
Sijistān, see Sīstān 18, 70, 78, 103, 200, 202, 204, 207.
Simāk b. ʿUbayd al-ʿAbsī 45, 46, 47, 48, 51, 61, 62.
al-Sind 103.
Sirhān b. ʿUmar b. Saʿīd 12.
Sīstān, see Sijistān 18.
Ṣoghdia 189.
Ṣoghdians, see Ṣughd 189.
Sogdiana 189.
sufahāʾ (impudent people) 37.
ṣuffah (porch or portico) 35.
Sufyān b. ʿAwf al-Azdī 96, 165, 180.
Ṣughd, see Ṣogdians 189.
Suḥaym b. Ḥafṣ 219.
Suhrāb 42.
Sulaym b. Maḥdūj 36, 38, 40.
Sulaym b. Yazīd 133.
Sulaymān b. ʿAbd al-Malik (Caliph 715–717) 46, 102.
Sulaymān b. ʿAbī Rāshid 141.
Sulaymān b. Arqam b. Abī Arqam 26, 31.
Sulaymān b. Ayyūb 212.
Sulaymān b. Bilāl 15.
Sulaymān b. al-Faḍl 2, 7, 9, 77, 167, 168, 169, 217, 218, 221.
Sulaymān b. al-Mughīrah 219.
Sulaymān b. Muslim al-ʿIjlī 171.
Sulaymān b. Ṣurad 30.
Sulaymān b. ʿUyaynah 225.
sulṭān (authority) 80.

Sumayyah 74, 142, 154, 168, 199, 204.
sunnah (example) 2, 23, 46, 124.
Sūq al-Ahwāz 29.
Sūrā 42, 45.
sūrah (chapter of the Qur'ān) 82.
Surkhān River 190.
Suwayd b. 'Abd al-'Azīz 101.
Suwayd b. 'Abd al-Raḥmān al-Tamīmī 142.
Syria 1, 6, 14, 28, 69, 75, 80, 88, 96, 101, 107, 145, 177, 204, 206, 209, 216, 218, 222.
Syrian 12, 201.
Syrians 10, 12, 39, 76, 88, 94, 145, 147, 150, 186, 223.

T

al-Ṭabarī, see Abū Ja'far v, viii, 1, 13, 28, 31, 128.
Ṭabaristān 162.
Tabūk 33.
Tadmur, see Palmyra 214.
Ṭāhīs 100.
al-Ṭā'if 10, 14, 20, 46, 176.
Ṭā'īs, see Ṭayyi' (Banū) 156.
Ṭalḥah b. 'Abdallāh b. Khalaf al-Khuzā'ī 188.
Ṭalḥah b. 'Ubaydallāh 39, 225.
al-Ṭāliqān 85.
Tamīm (Banū) 29, 58, 70, 81, 106, 108, 131, 132, 140, 181, 188, 203.
Tarābulus 103.
Taym Allāh b. Tha'labah (Banū) 112, 142, 198.
Taym al-Ribāb (Banū) 24, 35.
al-Taymī 38.
Ṭayyi' (Banū) 42, 100, 139, 140, 156, 159, 160.
Tehrān, see al-Rayy 162.
Tha'lab 113.
Thaqīf (Banū) 14, 16, 20, 27, 33, 72.
al-Thumā 224.
al-Thuwayyah 168.
Tigris River, see Dijlah 11, 24, 45, 47, 50, 61, 62, 110, 168.
Tihāmah 114, 221.
al-Tirmidh 190.
Tubay', son of Ka'b's wife 172.
Ṭufayl b. 'Awf al-Yashkurī 72.
Ṭukharistān 69, 87.
Tulayd b. Zayd b. Rāshid al-Fā'isī 51.
ṭunbūrs (stringed instruments) 154.
Turābī 156.
Turābiyyah 145.
Turks 120, 163, 178, 179, 202.
Tustar 160.
Ṭuwayd, see Ḥumrān b. Abān 13.

U

'Ubadah b. Ḥiṣn 178.
'Ubayd b. al-Abraṣ 98.
'Ubayd b. Aws al-Ghassānī 217.
'Ubayd b. Ka'b al-Numayrī 184, 185.

'Ubayd b. Tha'labah (Banū) 83.
'Ubaydah b. 'Amr (al-Kindī) al-Baddī, see al-Baddī 133, 162.
'Ubaydallāh b. Abī Bakr 218, 219.
'Ubaydallāh b. Aslam b. Sur'ah 181.
'Ubaydallāh b. al-Ḥurr al-Ju'fī 144.
'Ubaydallāh b. Mālik 129.
'Ubaydallāh b. Muslim b. Shu'bah al-Ḥaḍramī 142.
'Ubaydallāh b. Ziyād, see Ibn Ziyād 16, 175, 176, 177, 178, 179, 180, 181, 187, 190, 191, 196, 198, 200, 201, 203, 204, 205, 206, 207, 208.
'Ubaydallāh b. Ziyād b. Ma'mar 178.
Ubayy b. 'Umārah al-'Absī 21.
al-Ubullah 169.
Udhayb 160.
'Uḥud, Battle of 17.
'Umar 200.
'Umar b. 'Abd al-'Azīz (Caliph 717–20) 102.
'Umar b. 'Abdallāh b. Abī Rabī'ah al-Makhzūmī 213.
'Umar b. Bashīr 74.
'Umar b. Hubayrah, see Ibn Hubayrah 220.
'Umar b. al-Khaṭṭāb (Caliph 634–44), see al-Fārūq and Ibn Ḥantamah 21, 32, 46, 213, 217, 218, 222, 225.
'Umar b. Qays Dhū al-Liḥyah 143.
'Umar b. Sa'd b. Abī Waqqāṣ 142.
'Umar b. Shabbah 1, 9, 14, 15, 18, 26, 27, 28, 29, 31, 71, 72, 73, 78, 82, 85, 86, 88, 90, 96, 97, 99, 100, 101, 104, 119, 120, 121, 163, 164, 166, 167, 168, 171, 173, 174, 175, 176, 177, 180, 181, 187, 188, 196, 197, 198, 201, 210, 211, 214.
'Umar b. 'Ubaydallāh b. Ma'mar 203.
'Umārah b. 'Uqbah b. Abī Mu'ayṭ 98, 142.
Umawī 218.
'Umayr 83.
'Umayr b. Abī Ashā'āh al-Azdī 55, 56.
'Umayr b. Aḥmar al-Yashkurī 85, 86, 87.
'Umayr (or 'Umayrah) b. Yathribī 70, 164, 198.
'Umayr b. Yazīd al-Kindī, see Abū al-'Amarraṭah 129, 133, 135.
Umayyah 203.
Umayyah (Banū) 201.
Umm Abān bt. 'Utbah b. Rabī'ah 188.
Umm 'Amr 78.
Umm Ayyūb bt. 'Umārah b. 'Uqbah 31.
Umm al-Ḥakam 192, 193, 196.
umm walad (a slave woman who has borne a child to her master) 33.
'umrah (minor pilgrimage) 146, 153, 183.

'Unāq b. Shuraḥbīl b. Abī Dahm al-Taymī 142–3.
'Uqbah b. 'Āmir al-Juhanī 93.
'Uqbah b. Nāfi' al-Fihrī 94, 102, 103.
'Urwah b. al-Mughīrah b. Shu'bah 143.
'Urwah b. Udayyah 196, 197.
'Urwah b. al-Zubayr 89.
'Utbah b. Abī Sufyān 6, 18, 19, 90, 92, 220.
'Utbah b. al-Akhnas 145, 148, 151, 152.
'Uthmān b. 'Abd al-Raḥmān 6.
'Uthmān b. 'Affān 10, 13, 26, 31, 32, 43, 46, 48, 98, 101, 106, 123, 135, 137, 149, 151, 156, 174, 189, 211, 222.
'Uthmān b. Muḥammad b. Abī Sufyān 206.
'Uthmān b. 'Umayr al-Thaqafī 147.
'Uthmān b. 'Uqbah al-Kindī 125.
'Uthmānī 91.
'Uyaynah b. al-Nahhās al-'Ijlī 77.

V

Veh-Artakhshatr, see Bahurasīr 45.

W

Wādi'īs 143.
Wahb (or Wahīb) b. Jarīr 100, 166, 196, 198.
wa'īd (child condemned to be buried alive) 107.
Wā'il b. Ḥujr al-Ḥaḍramī, Abū Hunaydah 77, 142, 143, 144, 145, 146, 148, 160.
Wakhsh River 190.
walī al-'ahd (heir apparant) 183.
al-Walīd b. 'Abd al-Malik (Caliph 705–15) 14, 102, 164, 211.
al-Walīd b. Hishām 180.
al-Walīd b. 'Utbah b. Abī Sufyān 183, 191, 192, 198, 207.
Walwalān 114.
al-Wāqidī, see Abū 'Abdallāh Muḥammad b. 'Umar 11, 19, 26, 32, 91, 92, 95, 96, 164, 165, 171, 172, 179, 180, 191, 192, 198, 199, 206, 208, 210.
Wardān, *mawlā* of 'Amr b. al-'Āṣ 223.
Warq' b. Sumayy (or Sumayyah, al-Bajalī 144, 152.
Warrād, *mawlā* of al-Mughīrah b. Shu'bah 45.
wazīr (assistant) 84, 155.
White Palace 45.
wilāyah (governorship) 46.
Wuhayb b. Abū Ashā' al-Azdī 66.

Y

Yaḥyā b. Sa'īd b. Dīnār 101, 210, 211.
Yaḥyā b. Sa'īd b. Mikhnaf 132.
Yamāmah 163, 167.
al-Yaman 19, 26, 132, 135, 140, 152.
Yamānī 157, 202, 205.
Yamanīs 204.

Ya'qūb b. Ibrahīm 186.
Ya'qūbī 2, 179.
Yāqūt 12, 23, 28, 34, 42, 61, 64, 65, 86, 109, 111, 112, 144, 155, 160, 162, 168, 179, 186, 198, 204.
Yazīd b. 'Abd al-Malik 46.
Yazīd b. Asad al-Bajalī 71, 145.
Yazīd b. Ḥujayyah b. Rabī'ah al-Taymī 146, 147.
Yazīd b. Mālik al-Bāhilī, see al-Khaṭīm 19, 90.
Yazīd b. Mas'ūd b. Khālid b. Mālik b. Rib'ī b. Salmā b. Jandal b. Nahshal 104.
Yazīd b. Mu'āwiyah 1, 74, 94, 103, 164, 166, 172, 183, 184, 185, 186, 187, 188, 200, 208, 209, 213, 214, 215, 219.
Yazīd b. Rabī'ah b. Mufarrigh al-Ḥimyarī, see Ibn Mufarrigh, 201, 202.
Yazīd b. Ruwaym 99.
Yazīd b. Shājarah al-Rahāwī 94, 183, 192.
Yazīd b. Suwayd 219.
Yazīd b. Ṭarīf 130, 131.
Yūnus b. 'Ubayd 2, 7, 9, 198.
Yūsuf b. 'Umar 220.
Yūsuf b. Yazīd 129.

Z

Zaḥr b. Qays al-Ju'fī 143.
Zā'idah b. Qudāmah al-Thaqafī 193.
Zakariyyā' b. Abī Zā'idah 136, 137, 154.
zakāt (charity) 146, 171.
Ẓamyā' 114, 115.
Zandaward 169.
Zarafshān River 189.
Zayd 131.
Zayd, servant of Nāfi' b. Khālid al-Ṭāḥī 85.
Zayd b. Abī Ḥabīb 103.
Zayd b. Ḥuṣayn al-Ṭā'ī 24.
Zayd b. Jabalah 18.
Zayd b. 'Umar b. al-Khaṭṭāb 222, 223.
Zirr b. Ḥubaysh 223.
Ziyād b. Abī Sufyān, see Ziyād b. Abīhi 145.
Ziyād b. Abīhi, see Abū Mughīrah, Ibn Abī Sufyān, and Ibn Sumayyah 1, 12, 14, 15, 16, 17, 18, 26, 28, 29, 30, 31, 71, 74, 76, 77, 78, 81, 82, 83, 84, 85, 86, 87, 90, 92, 93, 95, 96, 97, 99, 100, 101, 103, 104, 105, 107, 110, 111, 112, 113, 115, 118, 119, 120, 125, 126, 127, 128, 129, 131, 132, 133, 134, 135, 136, 137, 138, 139, 140, 141, 142, 143, 145, 146, 147, 148, 151, 153, 154, 156, 157, 162, 163, 164, 167, 168, 169, 170, 171, 175, 177, 178, 179, 184, 185, 201, 202, 206.
Ziyād al-Bakkā'ī 11.
Ziyād b. Ṣāliḥ 21.
Ziyād b. Sumayyah, see Ziyād b. Abīhi 73, 166, 217.
al-Zubayr b. al-'Awwām 39.
Zuhayr b. Ḥarb 100, 166, 196, 198.
Zuḥḥāf the Kharijite 100.
al-Zuḥḥāf b. Ṣa'ṣa'ah 105.

al-Zuhrī, Muḥammad b. Muslim b. ʿUbaydallāh b. ʿAbdallāh b. Shihāb, see Ibn Shihāb 2, 7, 9.
Zumayl b. ʿAmr al-ʿUdhrī 216.
Zurārah, ancestor of Miskīn b. Dārim 169.
Zurārah, place near al-Kūfa 194, 195.
Zurārah b. Awfā al-Jurashī 85, 182.

www.ingramcontent.com/pod-product-compliance
Lightning Source LLC
Chambersburg PA
CBHW020643230426
43665CB00008B/296
* 9 7 8 0 8 8 7 0 6 3 1 4 5 *